Configuration Management
Principles and Practice

The Agile Software Development Series

Alistair Cockburn and Jim Highsmith, Series Editors
For more information check out http://www.awprofessional.com/

Agile software development centers on four values identified in the Agile Alliance's Manifesto:

- Individuals and interactions over processes and tools

- Working software over comprehensive documentation

- Customer collaboration over contract negotiation

- Responding to change over following a plan

The development of Agile software requires innovation and responsiveness, based on generating and sharing knowledge within a development team and with the customer. Agile software developers draw on the strengths of customers, users, and developers, finding just enough process to balance quality and agility.

The books in **The Agile Software Development Series** focus on sharing the experiences of such Agile developers. Individual books address individual techniques (such as Use Cases), group techniques (such as collaborative decision making), and proven solutions to different problems from a variety of organizational cultures. The result is a core of Agile best practices that will enrich your experience and improve your work.

Titles in the Series:

Alistair Cockburn, *Surviving Object-Oriented Projects*, ISBN 0-201-49834-0

Alistair Cockburn, *Writing Effective Use Cases*, ISBN 0-201-70225-8

Lars Mathiassen, Jan Pries-Heje, and Ojelanki Ngwenyama, *Improving Software Organizations: From Principles to Practice*, ISBN 0-201-75820-2

Alistair Cockburn, *Agile Software Development*, ISBN 0-201-69969-9

Jim Highsmith, *Agile Software Development Ecosystems*, ISBN 0-201-76043-6

Steve Adolph, Paul Bramble, Alistair Cockburn, and Andy Pols, *Patterns for Effective Use Cases*, ISBN 0-201-72184-8

Configuration Management Principles and Practice

Anne Mette Jonassen Hass

✦✦Addison-Wesley

Boston • San Francisco • New York • Toronto • Montreal
London • Munich • Paris • Madrid
Capetown • Sydney • Tokyo • Singapore • Mexico City

Many of the designations used by manufacturers and sellers to distinguish their products are claimed as trademarks. Where those designations appear in this book, and Addison-Wesley was aware of a trademark claim, the designations have been printed with initial capital letters or in all capitals.

The author and publisher have taken care in the preparation of this book, but make no expressed or implied warranty of any kind and assume no responsibility for errors or omissions. No liability is assumed for incidental or consequential damages in connection with or arising out of the use of the information or programs contained herein.

The publisher offers discounts on this book when ordered in quantity for bulk purchases and special sales. For more information, please contact:

U.S. Corporate and Government Sales
(800) 382-3419
corpsales@pearsontechgroup.com

For sales outside of the U.S., please contact:

International Sales
(317) 581-3793
international@pearsontechgroup.com

Visit Addison-Wesley on the Web: www.awprofessional.com

Library of Congress Cataloging-in-Publication Data

Hass, Anne Mette Jonassen.
    Configuration management principles and practice / Anne Mette Jonassen Hass.
        p. cm.
    Includes bibliographical references and index.
    ISBN 0-321-11766-2 (alk. paper)
    1. Software configuration management. I. Title.

QA76.76.C69 H37 2003
005.1—dc21

                                        2002034458

ISBN 0-321-11766-2
Text printed on recycled paper
1 2 3 4 5 6 7 8 9 10—MA—0706050403
First printing, January 2003

Contents

Part II Configuration Management Data 75

Chapter 20   *Managing Configurations under Special Conditions* **239**

List of Figures

List of Tables

Foreword by Kim Caputo

Solving the problems in configuration management can dramatically reduce the cost of rework, not to mention reduce the number of programmer headaches. I was fortunate to work in a company that did very well with configuration management practices on their proprietary systems. However, when they began software development on open systems, it was not so easy. Things that were second nature, that were so internalized that we didn't have to think about them anymore, suddenly became the things we didn't have the foresight to think about on the new systems. We began to have problems again. We had to relearn things that we thought we had learned before, and it was difficult to go back and learn them all over again. The explanations of the concepts, definitions, roles, and responsibilities in this book would have helped us then.

This book will also help those who have never had the appropriate level of discipline in their workplace for configuration management, especially those who have experienced horror stories like these:

- The Lost Software: "I know I wrote it, but I don't know where I put it."
- The Missing Links: "This used to work, but now it points to code that isn't there anymore."
- Stepping on each other's code: Developers doing different fixes in the same code area, overwriting each other.
- You Can't Go Back Again: New fixes are worse, and there's no "undo" button.
- You Can't Put It Together Again: Dropped a document with no page numbers, or dropped two documents, no titles on pages, which was which?

◆ Who's on First? What's on Second? Bug reported by customer, but don't know what version they have, don't know what fix to give them.

◆ "But I Know I Fixed It!"

— Customer calls and says, "It's broken."

— Programmer makes the fix, but forgets to check-in the change.

— Software build is done without the fix (No one audited the baseline).

— Exact same software shipped to the customer.

— Customer calls and says, "It's still broken."

— Programmer says, "But I know I fixed it!"

Configuration management is a cornerstone of software process improvement. (After all, if you can't manage your stuff, how can you tell whether your stuff has improved?) In *CMM Implementation Guide*, I wrote: "In the software industry, many of us have taken steps in software process improvement and made the steps our own, but perhaps many of us have not yet taken the more difficult steps of allowing ourselves to learn from each other and change under cross-cultural influence. It won't happen unless we share our experiences and our techniques. I am sharing my experiences and techniques, not to tell people to do it my way but rather to open the door for us to learn from each other throughout the industry and throughout the world. Perhaps I am not the first to open this door, and I hope that I am not the last. This is an invitation to the dance."

Across the world, nine time zones away, Anne Mette Jonassen Hass has answered the invitation and come through with a wonderful contribution. Here she shares her experiences and techniques for successful configuration management, with several possibilities for solutions that readers can take and make the steps their own. She also includes a wealth of references to reach more information for further learning. I am delighted with this contribution that takes up the call to influence our industry and our world.

—Kim Caputo
Mission Viejo, California

Foreword by Alistair Cockburn

Software configuration management and automated regression testing tools are the two development tools most critical to the success of the agile project. Over the last ten years, the version control and configuration management system was consistently cited to me as the top priority tool to install, both for agility-focused and plan-driven projects. No other tool even came close. (The editor and compiler are so integral that they don't get named.) Teams used to working with a version control and configuration management system refuse to operate without one.

Many teams find that once they have a satisfactory configuration management system in place they can do something more important to their project than merely coordinate their check-ins: They start experimenting with shorter and shorter periods between builds. (This is when the automated regression testing tool becomes important.)

Some teams run fully automated builds every half hour; these also run the suite of unit and system regression tests, post the results on a Web page, and email the owners of any failed code their failing test results! People on these teams report an increase in speed, agility, quality, and personal comfort, knowing they'll learn of unexpected errors within a half-hour of checking in their code.

One company is even experimenting with using such a continuous-build system to synchronize the work between India and the United States. They report that it is helping the two teams stay synchronized with each other across nine time zones.

It is therefore astonishing to see how many teams try to work without a configuration management system. Moreover, it can be frustratingly difficult to find information on the topic.

Anne Mette Hass manages in this book to capture both the heart of the subject and the variations needed in widely varying circumstances—a rare accomplishment. She knows, as you do, that some organizations run with heavy bureaucracy, some with little bureaucracy, some with little formality, some with great formality—and all need configuration management to smooth their collective work. She presents the topic from several angles: the work products, the job roles involved, the organizational issues, the tools, and various levels of formality and bureaucracy. In addition to her insights, Steve Berczuk and Brad Appleton describe, in their appendix, how the terms and practices can be used on the lightest of agile projects.

I have always found this subject daunting, and was pleased to find this text well presented and easy to digest. I could never have written this book; I'm glad that Anne Mette Hass has done it for us.

—Alistair Cockburn
Salt Lake City, Utah

Preface

My Life as a Software Professional

I have two—well, three really—passions in my professional life: test, configuration management, and process improvement.

   I started my career as an all-around developer—a little requirements elicitation, a little analysis, a lot of coding and recoding, and some test—more than 20 years ago. During these first professional years, I always loved testing most—making my work run on the computer and enjoying the satisfaction of being told, in a factual and precise way, that something was wrong. This enabled me to carry out the correction and then finally enjoy the privilege of knowing that at least this error was a secret between me and the computer.

   My experience grew, and my working teams grew. The problems grew. I wasn't always certain I had produced what I was supposed to and that I had tested everything. And sometimes an error would recur!

   I got a job in which I was responsible for system and acceptance test in a company making software for the European Space Agency. For the first time in my then 12-year career, I heard the words *configuration management*. I had no clue as to what it was, but as I spent hours and hours trying to figure it out, discussing it with the person responsible for quality assurance and actually using parts of it in my daily work, I came to understand what a wonderful tool I had.

   For the first time, I was able to trace my test cases to the requirements. I was able to tell, at any point, how many requirements I had covered in my test specification and how many were outstanding. I didn't have to encounter the frustration of having made test cases for requirements that weren't going to be implemented. Where I had forgotten the reason for a turn in the work, I was able to find a previous version of my test specification and see why I had changed it. I loved it!

The last seven years, I've worked as a consultant, spending a good deal of my time on testing assignments of many types in many companies. One of the things I've learned from these assignments is that there is often a difference between what a customer asks for and what he really wants, what he needs (what you want to give him), and what you're able to give him.

Test consultants are often presented with a system to test without the right conditions for performing a professional test. The requirements may be in any state from nonexistent to brilliantly documented, with a pronounced bias toward the former. If requirements are present, they are most often not up to date. This is partly a requirement specification problem and partly a configuration management problem.

Testing requires resources in terms of time and people to perform the test. These resources are often all too scarce. This is a project management problem.

When test consultants plan and perform a test, they need to establish an overview not only of what has to be tested but also how the test is progressing, what errors have been found, and what the state of error correction is. These are configuration management issues.

It's tempting for a consultant to try to deliver what the customer really needs. However, this approach has some limitations and drawbacks. The art is to strike the right balance between what's needed and what's feasible. One of the things to keep in mind as a consultant is to keep up the standards but keep it light. So I try to keep up the configuration management standards as I solve the test assignment—hoping my customer will get an idea of what configuration management is and maybe ask for some assistance in that direction too.

Another part of my time is spent assessing software-producing companies using the BOOTSTRAP maturity model and method. Like the related Capability Maturity Model (CMM), this model includes configuration management. As an assessor in more than 40 assessments, I have time and again seen the blank look in people's eyes when I ask how they perform configuration management. The eyes are rarely less blank if I elaborate and ask about tracing between work products, production of error reports, or other detailed configuration management disciplines.

On the other hand, people are more than willing to talk about problems they've experienced due to lack of control over what is being implemented and tested—and when—and lack of control over what errors have occurred and which ones are being corrected and which are not.

Although configuration management is one of the basic disciplines for sound development (in CMM it is a key process area at level 2), many people go through a considerable part of their careers without any idea of what it is and how it can ease their everyday tasks, just as I did. So I keep emphasizing its importance and very often recommend it as one of the first disciplines a company should work on when embarking on structured process improvement.

Creation of This Book

In 1999, the Danish organization *Datateknisk Forum*, an association of about 70 software-producing companies, asked me to write a book on configuration management. This was the result of a survey among the members as to what topic they needed a book on. Some of the comments and requirements that came back from the survey were

- How do you incorporate configuration management in the development process?
- How do you handle the fact that different kinds of work products, like documents and code, are treated differently?
- How do you obtain integration between different configuration management tools?
- How do you handle multisite development?
- How do you handle configuration management in relation to object-oriented development—component-based development?

I took on the assignment because in my own experience, configuration management has been of great value, not because I felt I knew much about it theoretically. I know much more now, and I hope I've conveyed some of the understanding, knowledge, and appreciation I've gained during my work on this book. If readers try at least some of the detailed disciplines, I hope they will experience the same enthusiasm about its usefulness that I did.

The book is based on literature as well as experience—and also on attitudes and opinions. It contains a lot of examples, advice, and recommendations that are not to be regarded as The Truth but primarily as the sum of a lot of experience—negative as well as positive.

When I learned that the book was to be published in the Agile Series, I knew little about agile development. But as I studied the values and principles, I found that I had practiced it in parts for years. Agile development is a wonderful idea, and one of the cornerstones of its success is configuration management, so it was a pleasure to be able to contribute to the series with one of my favorite disciplines.

The book may seem a bit heavy to some agilists, but I think it's better to discard some formality and detailed activities deliberately, knowing what one hasn't performed, than to just not perform it out of ignorance. So, agilists and others, read and choose!

Purpose of the Book

This book is not supposed to be a primer in configuration management. It does, however, start with an introduction to fundamental principles, to establish a basic understanding of the concepts used. The main part of the book discusses more advanced issues encountered when configuration management has to be implemented. The overall purpose of the book is twofold:

- ◆ To scare those who are engaging in configuration management! The book will give the reader an understanding of the complexity and comprehensiveness of the discipline. *Configuration management is not easy!* If you think it is, you'll be unable to solve its tasks in a professional way.

- ◆ To assuage the fear of those who are engaging in configuration management! The book will provide a fundamental understanding of the principles of the discipline, their interrelations and usage. *Configuration management is not difficult!* All you have to do is do it. If you understand it, it's much easier to specify and plan so it fulfills its purpose and becomes manageable.

It's assumed that the reader has some knowledge of other disciplines within software development, such as planning, design, test, and quality assurance.

Thanks

A lot of people have supported the creation of this book. I have no way of mentioning them all. First, I would like to thank the members and the board of *Datateknisk Forum* and my managers, Mr. Jørn Johansen and Mr. Ole Andersen, for believing in the idea and contributing to the contents.

I would also like to thank my colleagues (especially Ms. Elisabeth Broe Christensen and Mr. Robert Olesen), Mr. Lars Bendix of the University of Lund, Sweden, and not least my husband, Finn, for providing many pieces of good advice and good ideas, and for the interest and patience they have shown during my work on the book. My husband's wry way of looking at things is sometimes annoying but always enlightening—thanks, Finn, for being who you are!

The publisher and my editor, Mr. Ross Venables, deserve lots of thanks for their enthusiasm and encouragement, all the way from my first approach through the development of the manuscript to the complete book.

Last but not least, a big thanks goes to my longtime friend Ms. Pernille Lemvig-Fog and my father, Mr. Birger Jonassen, for their great help with the translation of the text into understandable English.

Introduction

I.1 CONFIGURATION MANAGEMENT IN COMPANY PERSPECTIVE

Every company or organizational unit in a company that develops products should consider configuration management. Configuration management becomes part of the general culture. This means it should be adjusted to the company culture, whether loose, rigorous, or in between. Configuration management may be viewed from different perspectives: people, product, project, cross-organizational, process, and tools. Each is briefly introduced below and discussed at greater length in the book.

People Perspective

Many people affect and are affected by configuration management by fulfilling the roles it involves. These may be categorized as configuration management roles, organizational roles, project-related roles, and external roles.

Product Perspective

Configuration management to be performed for a product depends on the nature of the product. Today, we find more and more complex products composed of different types of subproducts, such as software (applications), hardware (boxes, PCs, peripherals), networks (LAN, Internet), data (system data, parameter values), services (intangible deliveries such as training and maintenance). Any product may have more or less—even no—emphasis on subproducts. A product may, for example, be

- ◆ A pure software product, delivered on a CD-ROM with no hardware, no initial data, no support or any other service, and no network connection
- ◆ A large control system, including
  — Software embedded in some hardware and in the network
  — PC software with a graphical user interface
  — Network connections for remote surveillance and support
  — Initial data and parameters set
  — Training courses and maintenance services included in the delivery

Products may be simple, complex, or somewhere in between. They may be harmless, with no great impact on human lives or other companies, like games or household equipment, or they may be safety-critical, like flight control systems or medical equipment. They may be developed as shrink-wrapped products, like a test tool, or as bespoke software, like a control system for a factory. Any product has a combination of these attributes.

Project Perspective

The work of developing and maintaining a product may be organized in one project or in a number of projects under different management during the product's lifetime. The project perspective is concerned with performing configuration management for a product in the project or projects during its life cycle. A product goes through a number of life cycle activities, for which configuration management should be considered. These may be preparation, requirements specification, design, production (e.g., coding and/or manufacturing), integration, testing, and operation and maintenance, as illustrated in Figure I–1.

The activities mentioned above are just building blocks that are arranged according to the chosen development model. A number of development models exist, such as the waterfall model (similar to Figure I–1), agile development, incremental development, and iterative development. Each subproduct may follow its own development model—for example, the software subproduct may follow an iterative development model, while the hardware subproduct follows a waterfall model.

As Figure I–1 also shows, a number of support functions exist for preparing, developing, operating, and maintaining a product. These functions, which may include

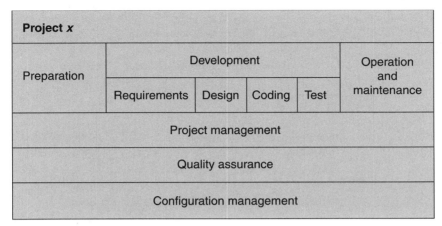

Figure I-1 *Generic Development Model*

project management, quality assurance, and configuration management, should be performed during a product's entire lifetime. Performing these support functions produces objects, which must also be considered for configuration management. The development activities and support functions included in this book are based on the activities and support functions defined in maturity models.

Cross-Organizational Perspective

All companies have cross-organizational objects or assets for which configuration management should be considered: infrastructure, company product assets (such as components for reuse developed using a product-line approach), and company documentation (sales material, plans, quality system, process descriptions, and so on).

Process Perspective

Configuration management may well be the subject for process improvement. In fact, as soon as a company starts to consider configuration management, the process perspective needs to be taken into account. To sustain the work, processes must be understood and implemented and must continuously undergo improvement.

Process improvement and the concept of maturity models to support it, especially in software development, are becoming more and more common in the industry. In the Capability Maturity Model (CMM), configuration management plays a prominent part as a key process area at level 2. Another maturity model, used mostly (and most) in Europe, is the BOOTSTRAP model. As part of a BOOTSTRAP assessment, a company is given a list of its five processes that most require improvement. As of early 2001, more than 50 BOOTSTRAP assessments had been performed in Denmark. Table I–1 shows the three most frequently appearing processes.

Table I–1 *Improvement Recommendations*

Number	Process	Appearances (%)
1.	Project management	75
2.	Configuration management	55
3.	Test	51

More than half the projects had problems in the way they implemented configuration management and needed to improve their practices. This made configuration management the second most frequent process.

Tools Perspective

It is virtually impossible to manage configuration management without one or more tools. Many tools are available, but many companies prefer to develop their own.

I.2 CONFIGURATION MANAGEMENT BETWEEN COMPANIES

Customers

Some companies have other companies as direct customers. In such cases, the customer's demand for configuration management may influence how the discipline is carried out in the delivering company. Typically, delivered products form part of components in other products the customers take care of themselves, or the customer takes over responsibility for the finished product.

A company is a purchaser of products, but it may also act as a supplier—for instance, of a requirement specification or components. The customer's attitude toward configuration management must be clarified where relevant.

Subcontractors

In some cases, subcontractors work for product-producing companies. The way the subcontractors perform configuration management may influence the way it's done in the producing company. Control of the subcontractors is a support function within software development and a discipline or process that ought to be present during a product's whole lifetime. It may be defined for the entire company, if the company has standard procedures for handling subcontractors. (This is not often the case.)

I.3 CONFIGURATION MANAGEMENT IN A BROADER PERSPECTIVE

The World at Large

Universities, research institutes, and companies work with configuration management at several levels. Standards within software development include configuration management as a discipline or a process. During recent years, work in connection with process improvement, including maturity models, has been augmented considerably. Configuration management is included as a process in the best-known maturity models. Furthermore, various institutions and large international projects work with configuration management. These aspects of research into configuration management have been included in the book to provide a larger perspective for what may sometimes seem like an isolated struggle.

A Little Philosophy

Configuration management is the existentialism of software development, because it answers the following questions for individual components or entire products:

◆ Who am I?

◆ Why am I here?

◆ Why am I who I am?

◆ Where do I belong?

Just as in "real life," a certain amount of leisure is necessary for that kind of consideration, but if you have the leisure and use it in a reasonable way, it's possible to increase your quality of life—or, in this case, the quality of your products.

Part I

What Is Configuration Management?

Configuration, "to form from or after," derives from the Latin *com-*, meaning "with" or "together," and *figurare*, "to form." It also means "a relative arrangement of parts or elements." Configuration management therefore refers to managing a relative arrangement of parts or elements. It's as simple as that.

Configuration management, as we know it today, started in the late 1960s. In the 1970s, the American government developed a number of military standards, which included configuration management. Later, especially in the 1990s, many other standards and publications discussing configuration management have emerged.

In the last few years, the growing understanding of software development as a collection of interrelated processes has influenced work on configuration management. This means that configuration management is now also considered from a process point of view.

Chapter 1

Definition of Configuration Management Used in This Book

There are many definitions of configuration management and many opinions on what it really is. This chapter describes the definition on which this book is based. In short:

> Configuration management is unique identification, controlled storage, change control, and status reporting of selected intermediate work products, product components, and products during the life of a system.

Figure 1–1 shows the activity areas included in the definition of configuration management used in this book. It also shows their relations to each other, to common data, and to elements outside the configuration management process area.

When you work professionally with configuration management (as with anything else) it's important to have the fundamental concepts in place. If all else fails, you can go back and seek a solution there.

Definitions of configuration management used in various standards are covered in Chapter 3, and definitions of configuration management used in various maturity models can be found in Chapter 2. The definitions in these standards and maturity models are similar to a large extent. However, they're expressed in slightly different words and with different divisions between the detailed activities that constitute configuration management. It's perfectly okay for a company to use its own definition of configuration management, but it's a good idea to investigate how that definition maps to the definition used in this book and other relevant definitions, to make sure no activity has been left out.

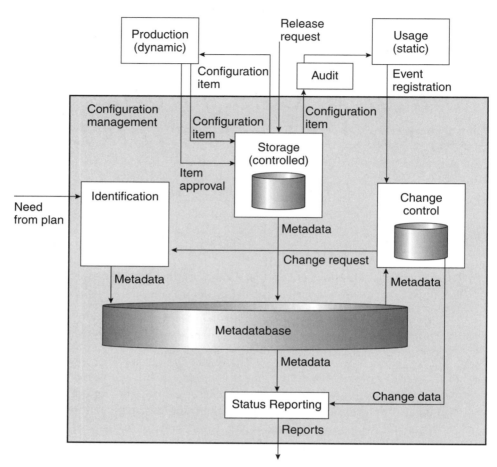

Figure 1–1 *Overview of Configuration Management Activities*

1.1 CONFIGURATION MANAGEMENT ACTIVITIES

The view on configuration management in this book is process oriented. Therefore, the definition includes activity areas, which can be described in terms of process descriptions. The activity areas described in detail in the following paragraphs are identification, storage, change control, and status reporting.

Configuration management has many interactions with other development and support processes. Figure 1–1 illustrates the production and usage activity areas via their respective libraries.

Metadata

All the activity areas in configuration management share metadata for items placed under configuration management. Metadata is a database concept that means data about the data stored in the database. So metadata in this context describes the configuration items. Metadata for a configuration item may include its name, the name of the person who produced the item, the production date, and references to other related configuration items. Figure 1–1 shows a logical separation of metadata, even though this data is often stored physically at the same location (in the same database) as the items in controlled storage.

Change control uses metadata—for example, the trace information for a configuration item for which a change is suggested. Change control does not in itself contribute to metadata, because information produced during change control will be present only if a configuration item is affected by a suggested change. A configuration item can exist without change control information, but it can't exist without metadata.

Configuration Management Is Cyclic—or Is It?

In everyday language, "configuration item" is often used to refer to an item, which is then said to be produced in several versions. This is not strictly correct, but it's acceptable as long as the reference is clearly understood by all involved. In fact, each new version of a configuration item is a new configuration item in its own right.

This can be illustrated by an analogy to an object-oriented approach. The "configuration item" may be seen as a class and the versions as instantiations of the class, as shown in Figure 1–2. Version chains of configuration items—that is, versions 1, 2, 3, and so on—may be formed by indicating which configuration item a given configuration item is derived from or based on.

Configuration management activities may be viewed as cyclic for each item class placed under configuration management. This means that a configuration item class continuously goes "through the mill." The first cycle is initiated by a (planned) need for a configuration item, and later the driving force is a change request (and only this!). This is illustrated in Figure 1–3.

In each cycle, a configuration item will be identified, produced, stored, and released for usage. Event registrations will occur as a consequence of experience gained during usage. These will lead to change control and the creation of change requests, which will lead to identification, and so on, of a new version of the original

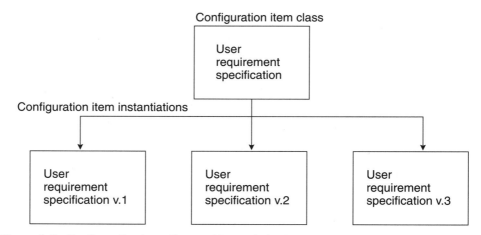

Figure 1–2 *Configuration Item Class and Instantiations*

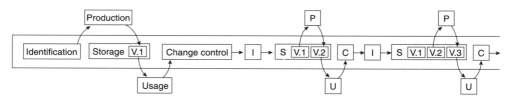

Figure 1–3 *The Life of a Configuration Item Class*

configuration item. Items placed under configuration management must never be changed, but new versions may be created.

Configuration items that are different versions of the same original item are obviously strongly related, but each one is an individual item, which will be identified and may be extracted and used independently. This is one of the main points of configuration management: to be able to revert to an earlier version of an item class.

Quality Assurance Process

Configuration management interacts with quality assurance, as illustrated by the item approval process that accompanies a configuration item from production to storage. The item approval, which may be a written quality record or verbal, is a product of quality assurance. Some see it as a product of configuration management, but it's actually the gateway from production to configuration management, provided by quality assurance.

Auditing

Auditing is included in some definitions of configuration management. An audit ensures that the product—the configuration item released for use—fulfills the requirements and is complete as delivered. This includes configuration management information, so that everything required is delivered in the expected versions and that the history of each item can be thoroughly accounted for. This activity area is not considered part of configuration management in this book. It's viewed as an activity area under general quality assurance, which partly concerns the products and partly the processes, rather than a configuration management activity area.

This may be a controversial point of view, but the idea of audits is a legacy from the Department of Defense origin of configuration management. Today there is a much broader understanding in the software industry of the importance of quality assurance and, therefore, also of configuration management.

Auditing uses configuration information extensively in the form of status reports, but it also uses quality assurance techniques and methods, such as reviewing and test. In practice, people involved in configuration management also carry out the audit. Consequently, the audit will be referred to elsewhere in this book.

1.2 IDENTIFICATION

The purpose of the identification activity area is to determine the metadata for a configuration item—to uniquely identify it and specify its relations to the outside world and other configuration items.

Identification is one of the cornerstones of configuration management, as it's impossible to control something whose identity you don't know. If the tables in a restaurant have no numbers to which orders can be traced, the waiter will have difficulty matching the dishes to the proper guests. Perhaps this will come off all right if you have three or four tables, but definitely not if you have more than 20 and the guests keep coming and going all evening and the waiter who serves the food is not the one who received the order. To be sure everything is under control, the waiters and orders need to be uniquely identified as well. Figure 1–4 shows how identification is influenced by its surroundings.

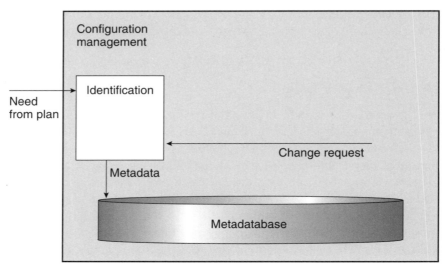

Figure 1–4 *Identification in Context*

Inputs

Two incidents may initiate the identification process:

◆ The first time an item is to be placed under configuration management, identification starts with a need defined in the plans. From the project plan, you know an item has to be produced (for instance, a design or a code module), and from the configuration management plan, you know this item must be placed under configuration management.

◆ When you have to change a configuration item, identification will start with a change request. In this case, Change Control has decided that a new version of the configuration item must be produced, (for example, the requirement specification document must be changed in light of a review), and subsequently this new version must be placed under configuration management.

Outputs

Identification results in the registration of metadata for a configuration item.

Process Descriptions

Methods, conventions, and procedures necessary for the activities in identification may be

- Procedure(s) for registration of metadata, including procedure(s) for tracing
- Procedure(s) for inheritance of metadata
- Convention(s) for unique identification
- Convention(s) for authorization, including restrictions on distribution, if any
- Convention(s) for identification of components in a delivery

Unique Identification

Each organization must define its own conventions for unique identification. One general convention most often is not enough; typically, a number of conventions are necessary for various classes of configuration items, such as documents and code.

These conventions may be difficult to define. You have to consider what purpose the unique identification serves and how to implement it in the easiest way. It will connect the registration and the physical configuration item in such a way that it's always possible to find the configuration item. This should be considered when defining conventions for unique identification. Furthermore, the procedures are tool dependent and often highly predefined in the tools available.

The file name under which the item is saved may constitute the unique identification. It should also be possible to write the unique identification on the configuration item's medium—for instance, on a diskette label. The unique identification also registers the relations between configuration items, such as variations or parts of each other. It may be a good idea to consider making identification a key in a database registration.

It's important to define the conventions for unique identification so that the formation of new configuration items will not make it necessary to change or delete existing configuration items. For instance, the number of digits in a number must be sufficient to cover the total number of configuration items; it's not appropriate to have only two digits if more than a hundred items may be produced.

Examples

Figures 1–5 and 1–6 illustrate unique identification for two types of configuration items.

The document identifier in Figure 1–5 contains

Project and year: SC.91
Document number: 009
Author and affiliation: OA.ect
Activity identifier: T2.3.1
Document type: RP (Report)
Version: 02

Project name	:	SCOPE
Document title	:	SCI Description Format
Document identifier	:	SC.91/009/OA.etc/T2.3.1/RP/02
Distribution	:	Project
		Manager R&D Department
		Manager Technical Support
Date	:	May 2nd, 1991
Author	:	Ole Andersen, Elektronikcentralen
Approved by		
Project Manager	:	_____ Date: _____
QA	:	_____ Date: _____

Figure 1–5 Document Front Page

The test cases in Figure 1–6 are included in a test specification document, and the identification contains (for the first test case)

The current section number in the document: 10.3.1.6
Running unique number: 80
Version of test case: 1.A

| 10.3.1.6 (80) | Test for correct bank identity number | 1.A |
| 10.3.1.7 (93) | Test for correct bank account number | 1.B |

Figure 1–6 *Test Cases*

Authorization

Authorization information may be derived from a quality assurance plan and a development plan. It's an advantage to have general directions for authorization in such plans, such as descriptions of the kinds of people who are responsible for acceptance and production of various types of configuration items.

Perhaps documents placed under configuration management in the form of a draft could be approved by the author himself, while documents placed under configuration management in a version to be used by everybody should be approved by a group consisting of the project manager, the person responsible for quality assurance, and a customer representative.

Roles

Often the person who produces an item is also in charge of its identification. Identification is based partly on conventions for individual data elements and partly on information available from various plans (for instance, general procedures determining who is in charge of the approval of a particular kind of document). It may be necessary to draw on a library tool, for example, if numbers that are part of the unique identification are generated automatically and/or reserved in a storage tool.

Connection with Other Activities

An item cannot be declared as being under full configuration management until it has been placed in controlled storage. It is not sufficient that the item be identified. Identification, production, and placement in storage often overlap or are carried out interchangeably.

Sometimes the identification, or parts of it, is carried out before the item is produced, such as when the decision is made about its production. In other cases, it may be carried out in connection with placing the item in storage (for instance, when a tool increases a counter).

1.3 STORAGE

The purpose of storage is to ensure that a configuration item will not disappear or be damaged, that it can be found at any time and delivered in the condition in which you expect to find it, and that a record is kept to indicate who has been given the item or a copy of it.

Storage is something physical. Items that are stored are physically present at a specific place. In the following discussion, we shall call this place a library, but physically, it may be a directory structure on a workstation, a looseleaf binder, a shelf, or something else. Figure 1–7 shows how storage influences and is influenced by its surroundings.

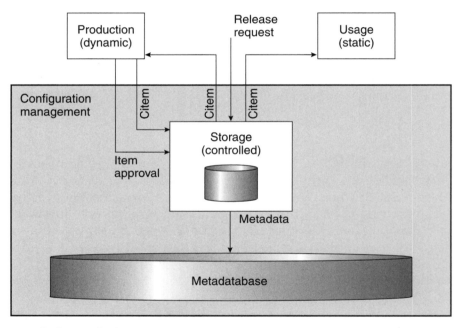

Figure 1–7 *Storage in Context*

Library

Storage takes place in libraries. Traditionally, three types of libraries are mentioned in connection with software development: controlled, dynamic, and static libraries.

The Controlled Library

The controlled or configuration management library is where configuration items are stored. It may be divided into a number of physical libraries, especially where the configuration items are of different types: documents, source code, hardware, and so on. Naturally, hardware cannot be placed in a database on a computer but on a shelf or directly on the site of application.

The Dynamic Library

The dynamic or development library is where items are kept while they are being produced. Typically, this will be in the producer's own area. Therefore, in reality, this library will consist of a considerable number of independent libraries. In this library, it's possible to work with an item without bringing it into contact with other items or exposing it to the influence of other items.

This library is not part of the configuration management system! It's under the responsibility of the development manager, even though many modern configuration management tools also encompass the dynamic library. In some cases the dynamic library and configuration management library may overlap. This should be carefully considered and preferably avoided, unless a deployed tool manages both libraries and the distinction between them is clear.

As an example, many companies use the same tool (such as Visual SourceSafe) during production as well as for configuration management of source code, and practically in the same way. This means that the same library is used as both dynamic and configuration management libraries. During production, a file is often checked in and out several times before it's actually finished. The configuration management library is hence also used as a backup medium for the producers' own intermediate results.

These intermediate results are neither approved nor under change control and consequently not under configuration management, but it may be difficult to distinguish them from versions of the same source code item under configuration management. This is especially true if you're not careful with status codes or if you can't extract configuration items on the basis of different status codes.

Consequently, if libraries are mixed, procedures and conventions should be employed to

- Make clear when the changed version of the source code is approved and actually placed under configuration management and in the configuration management library (by the use of status codes)
- Ensure that if you want to extract an item, you don't just pick up the last version of the item (the one the producer is working with) but a version that has actually been approved and is under configuration management

Another consideration when mixing libraries is space. Space considerations often cause tools to save only the difference between two versions—so-called delta storage. But if the library is used for intermediate results that are later removed, it's not possible for all tools to keep only the differences between configuration-managed versions. The whole new version will have to be kept each time.

The Static Library

The static or user library is where items are used. Usage is all imaginable applications of configuration items, not just by final users. It may be a review, if a document is placed under configuration management in the form of a draft and subsequently has to be reviewed. It may be testing parts of the system, integrating a subcomponent into a larger component, or proper operation or sale of a finished system.

While being used in the static library, items must under no circumstances be changed. The static library may consist of many different physical repositories or storage media—it need not be a library in the classic sense.

When usage involves source code to be included in a module test of another item, the static library may be identical to the dynamic library of the developer. This means that the source code to be used is copied from the controlled library to a read-only copy in the developer's own environment. When usage is review of a document, the static library may be the reviewer's physical workspace, where a copy of the document is placed. When usage is the running in production of a system, the static library may be situated on a production machine or the user's workstation.

This library is not part of the configuration management system! The responsibility for this library may lie in different places, depending on the context of the use—e.g. with the developer, test manager, or customer.

Main Processes

Storage involves three main processes:

◆ Placement in storage from production
◆ Release from storage for usage
◆ Release from storage for production

Placement in Storage from Production

The event initiating placement in storage is that the item reaches a state where it's ready to be placed under configuration management—when it's approved according to its type. It is up to each company to determine when an item can be approved. Approval criteria should be described in a quality assurance plan or the like. A source code item might be considered ready when it compiles, or perhaps when it has passed a module test with certain coverage or with less than a certain number of failures of a given type, such as a given severity. Placing an item in storage should be accompanied by item approval, so it can be documented that the criteria for finishing the item have been fulfilled.

For safety-critical products and/or in very formal configuration management systems, it's sometimes considered useful to deliver the items to a person (for instance, a configuration management librarian) rather than merely enter an item into a tool. This process has a significant positive effect on the quality of the products, as it's too easy to evade quality demands when facing just a tool. However, it's both slower and more expensive to handle placement in storage manually rather than automatically, so the benefits and costs must be considered carefully.

The result of this process is that the item can be reached only through the configuration management library, and metadata for the item is properly up-to-date. Of course, it's necessary to ensure that items already in storage cannot be destroyed— for instance, by being overwritten by new configuration items. An item in version 1.3 must not overwrite version 1.2 of the item having the same name.

Release from Storage for Usage

The event initiating the release of a configuration item from storage for usage is the perception of a need for the item. Release for usage ought to be accompanied by a release request, so it can be documented that the release is permitted and has taken place. To prevent this process from becoming too costly or cumbersome, the release request could be automated, in the form of a permission scheme associated with items under configuration management and automatic control of the permission and logging. Here, too, it may be useful in some cases to have the release take place via a person (a configuration management librarian) rather than via a tool alone.

The result of this process is that the configuration item—or, for documents and software, typically a copy of the configuration item—is delivered to a static library, and an entry in the metadata registers to whom it was delivered and when.

Release from Storage for Production

The event initiating the release of a configuration item from storage for production is the need for production of a new item on the basis of one already produced. This need is typically expressed in the form of a change request. The result is that a copy of the configuration item is delivered to a dynamic library (and always a copy—never the configuration item itself if only one copy exists).

Many configuration management systems and tools can indicate that the configuration item of which they have received a copy is locked or the like. This should be unnecessary if the configuration management library is controlled so that new configuration items cannot destroy existing ones and if planning and implementation of the change request is performed correctly.

If a problem arises from two or more people working with "the same item" at the same time, it reflects a poor configuration management system—lack of control over who is permitted to work with what and lack of proper identification. If several people have to work on the same branch simultaneously, this process must be handled as parallel development.

Process Descriptions

The methods, conventions, and procedures necessary for activities in storage may be

- Procedure(s) for placing items in storage and related updating of metadata
- Procedure(s) for release for usage
- Procedure(s) for release for production
- Template(s) for item approval
- Template(s) for release request

Roles

The librarian in charge of the configuration management library plays a decisive role in establishing and maintaining the configuration management library, so the configuration management library doesn't fall into decay. This is also true for automated configuration management systems. If others establish and maintain the configuration management library, who is responsible for what must be clearly defined.

Connection with Other Activities

Storage may overlap with identification, if, for instance, a tool adds to a counter when an item is placed in storage.

Example

The development environment for a project, especially a large project, is much more than just a developer's directory, an editor, a compiler, and a linker. This example illustrates the controlled library and two dynamic libraries in the form of the directory structure for a project called the Meteorological Archiving and Retrieval Facility (MARF) carried out for the European Meteorological Satellite Organisation (EUMETSAT).

The directory structure, shown in Figure 1–8, includes

- A controlled library, structured according to the architectural design, offering separate subdirectories for data, object code (compiled sources), executables, sources, test scripts, and so on
- Dynamic libraries for all developers, reflecting the structure of the controlled library
- Substructures for version control of sources—where "Ingestion" is one of the architectural modules and "Other-globals" indicate others

The controlled library for the MARF project is /home/MARF/marfdev. Subdirectories under the Sources directory existed according to subsystems, for example:

/home/MARF/marfdev/Sources/Ingestion

/home/MARF/marfdev/Sources/Other-globals

Each subdirectory has a repository, called AtFS (Attributed Files System), where versions of the sources are kept in a controlled manner using a simple configuration management tool. Object files are collected in object libraries, to ease linking and reduce the size of executables. There is one object library for each source subdirectory.

Each developer has a development area (dynamic library) under /home/MARF/ marf/*username*, with a structure identical to the one just described. A link is set up from the AtFS master repository to each user area. Developers use writable copies of

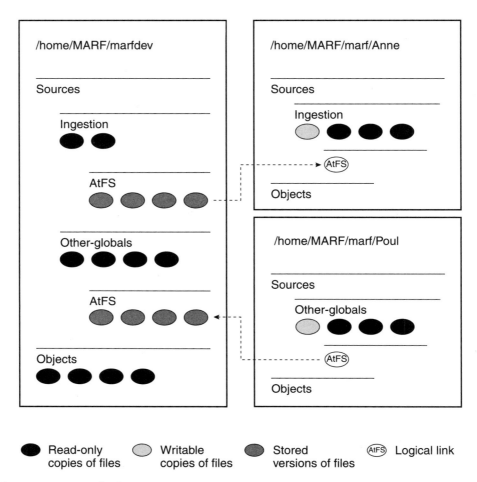

Figure 1–8 *Example Library Structure*

stored files in their own directory structure for development. Read-only copies of dependent files are also placed in the developer's own directory structure, to ease compilation and linking during development and test.

Files are kept in saved versions in the central AtFS areas, and read-only copies are made available there as well. This setup ensures shareability with a minimum of disturbance.

1.4 CHANGE CONTROL

When developing and maintaining a product, changes are inevitable. People make mistakes, customers need changes, and the environment in which the product operates evolves. In addition, people constantly develop their knowledge of the problem and their ability to solve it. In software development, it's generally said that the solution of a problem will create new problems. In other words, we get wiser all the time.

The purpose of change control is to be fully in control of all change requests for a product and of all implemented changes. For any configuration item, it must be possible to identify changes in it relative to its predecessor. Any change should be traceable to the item where the change was implemented. Figure 1–9 shows how change control affects and is affected by its environment.

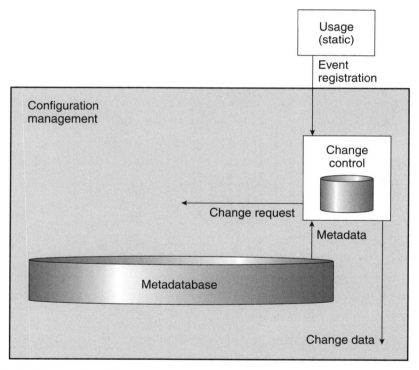

Figure 1–9 *Change Control in Context*

Inputs

Change control is initiated by an event. An event may also be called a wish for modification but need not be expressed as a clearly formulated wish. In this context, an event is any observation of something surprising, unexpected, inconvenient, or directly wrong during usage of the configuration item. It may, for instance, be

- A wrong formulation, caught during the review of a document
- A coding mistake found during a walk-through of a piece of source code
- An enhancement request arising from a new idea from the customer during work on the project
- A mistake found in the integration test
- A wish to expand or enhance the finished product, arising once the product is in operation
- An inquiry to a helpdesk about a problem in connection with usage of a system
- A change required in the code because of an upgrade to a new version of the middleware supporting the system, which may not be backward compatible

An event should be documented in an event registration, which is the input to the change control activity. Some changes, such as those due to a review, can be foreseen and planned, while those due to, for instance, a new customer request cannot.

Outputs

The result of change control is documented events and change requests derived from these events. Both should be securely maintained, as in a database, so that relationships between change requests and configuration items can be reliably maintained. Event registration and change requests may be put under configuration management, but this happens rarely, except where configuration management has to be very formal.

Change Control Activities

A change process is a miniature development project in itself. An event registration should have a written and controlled life cycle, consisting roughly of the phases described in Table 1–1. Each phase should be described in detail, stating the responsibility and specific actions in the company. It may be necessary for a company to describe different kinds of life cycles, depending on the types of events to be handled.

Table 1–1 *Overview of Change Control Phases*

Phase	Description
Creation of the event registration.	The event registration is created, and the event is described.
Analysis of the event registration.	Configuration item(s) affected by possible changes are determined, and the extensiveness of these changes is estimated.
Rejection or acceptance of the event registration.	If the event registration is accepted, a change request is created for each configuration item affected.
The change request initiates a new configuration item.	A new configuration item is identified and created, and the change is implemented. In the course of accepting the new item and placing it in storage, feedback is given to the configuration control board.
Closing of the change request.	The change request can be closed when the change has been implemented and accepted.
Closing of the event registration.	The event registration can be closed when all corresponding change requests are closed.

Quite often the change request is joined with the event registration, so no independent change requests are created. This is not a very good idea, unless it remains possible to extract statistics and status information on individual change requests as well as on the event. This is especially true if an event causes changes in several configuration items, which is often the case.

Usage of Metadata

When performing the change process, metadata is used for analytical purposes. This may be in the form of reports or a direct search in the database or the databases where metadata is maintained. Trace information is often used—for instance, to determine in which configuration item changes are required due to an event. Also information about variants or branches belonging to a configuration item is used to determine if a change has effects in several places.

Finally metadata may be used to determine if a configuration item has other outstanding event registrations, such as whether other changes are in the process of being implemented or are awaiting a decision about implementation.

Consequence Analysis

When analyzing an event, you must consider the cost of implementing changes. This is not always a simple matter. The following checklists, adapted from a list by Karl Wiegers, may help in analyzing the effects of a proposed change. The lists are not exhaustive and are meant only as inspiration.

Identify

- All requirements affected by or in conflict with the proposed change
- The consequences of not introducing the proposed change
- Possible adverse effects and other risks connected with implementation
- How much of what has already been invested in the product will be lost if the proposed change is implemented—or if it is not

Check if the proposed change

- Has an effect on nonfunctional requirements, such as performance requirements (ISO 9126, a standard for quality characteristics, defines six characteristics: functional, performance, availability, usability, maintainability, and portability. The latter five are typically referred to as nonfunctional.)
- May be introduced with known technology and available resources
- Will cause unacceptable resource requirements in development or test
- Will entail a higher unit price
- Will affect marketing, production, services, or support

Follow-on effects may be additions, changes, or removals in

- User interfaces or reports, internal or external interfaces, or data storage
- Designed objects, source code, build scripts, include files
- Test plans and test specifications
- Help texts, user manuals, training material, or other user documentation
- Project plan, quality plan, configuration management plan, and other plans
- Other systems, applications, libraries, or hardware components

Roles

The configuration (or change) control board (CCB) is responsible for change control. A configuration control board may consist of a single person, such as the author or developer when a document or a piece of code is first written, or an agile team working in close contact with users and sponsors, if work can be performed in an informal way without bureaucracy and heaps of paper. It may also—and will typically, for most important configuration items—consist of a number of people, such as the project manager, a customer representative, and the person responsible for quality assurance.

Process Descriptions

The methods, conventions, and procedures necessary for carrying out the activities in change control may be

- Description of the change control process structure
- Procedures in the life cycles of events and changes
- Convention(s) for forming different types of configuration control boards
- Definition of responsibility for each type of configuration control board
- Template(s) for event registration
- Template(s) for change request

Connection with Other Activities

Change control is clearly delimited from other activities in configuration management, though all activities may be implemented in the same tool in an automated system. Whether change control is considered a configuration management activity may differ from company to company. Certainly it is tightly coupled with project management, product management, and quality assurance, and in some cases is considered part of quality assurance or test activities. Still, when defining and distributing responsibilities, it's important to keep the boundaries clear, so change control is part of configuration management and nothing else.

Example

Figure 1–10 shows an example of a process diagram for change control. A number of processes are depicted in the diagram as boxes with input and output sections (e.g., "Evaluation of event registration"). All these processes must be defined and, preferably, described.

1.5 STATUS REPORTING

Status reporting makes available, in a useful and readable way, the information necessary to effectively manage a product's development and maintenance. Other activity areas in configuration management deliver the data foundation for status reporting,

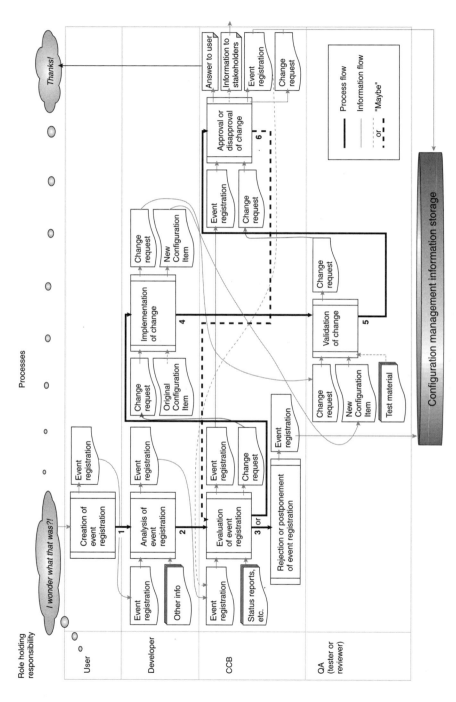

Figure 1–10 *Change Control Process Diagram*

in the form of metadata and change control data. Status reporting entails extraction, arrangement, and formation of these data according to demand. Figure 1–11 shows how status reporting is influenced by its surroundings.

Inputs

Status reporting can take place at any time.

Outputs

The result of status reporting is the generation of status report(s). Each company must define the reports it should be possible to produce. This may be a release note, an item list (by status, history, or composition), or a trace matrix. It should also be possible to extract ad hoc information on the basis of a search in the available data.

Process Descriptions

The methods, conventions, and procedures necessary for the activities in status reporting may be

- Procedure(s) for the production of available status reports
- Procedure(s) for ad hoc extraction of information
- Templates for status reports that the configuration management system should be able to produce

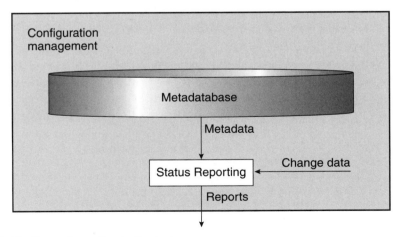

Figure 1–11 *Status Reporting in Context*

Roles

The librarian is responsible for ensuring that data for and information in status reports are correct, even when reporting is fully automated. Users themselves should be able to extract as many status reports as possible. Still, it may be necessary to involve a librarian, especially if metadata and change data are spread over different media.

Connection with Other Activities

Status reporting depends on correct and sufficient data from other activity areas in configuration management. It's important to understand what information should be available in status reports, so it can be specified early on. It may be too late to get information in a status report if the information was requested late in the project and wasn't collected. Status reports from the configuration management system can be used within almost all process areas in a company. They may be an excellent source of metrics for other process areas, such as helping to identify which items have had most changes made to them, so these items can be the target of further testing or redesign.

1.6 FALSE FRIENDS: VERSION CONTROL AND BASELINES

The expression "false friends" is used in the world of languages. When learning a new language, you may falsely think you know the meaning of a specific word, because you know the meaning of a similar word in your own or a third language. For example, the expression *faire exprès* in French means "to do something on purpose," and not, as you might expect, "to do something fast." There are numerous examples of "false friends"—some may cause embarrassment, but most "just" cause confusion.

This section discusses the concepts of "version control" and "baseline." These terms are frequently used when talking about configuration management, but there is no common and universal agreement on their meaning. They may, therefore, easily become "false friends" if people in a company use them with different meanings. The danger is even greater between a company and a subcontractor or customer, where the possibility of cultural differences is greater than within a single company. It is hoped that this section will help reduce misunderstandings.

Version Control

"Version control" can have any of the following meanings:

- Configuration management as such
- Configuration management of individual items, as opposed to configuration management of deliveries
- Control of versions of an item (identification and storage of items) without the associated change control (which is a part of configuration management)
- Storage of intermediate results (backup of work carried out over a period of time for the sole benefit of the producer)

It's common but inadvisable to use the terms "configuration management" and "version control" indiscriminately. A company must make up its mind as to which meaning it will attach to "version control" and define the term relative to the meaning of configuration management. The term "version control" is not used in this book unless its meaning is clear from the context. Nor does the concept exist in IEEE standards referred to in this book, which use "version" in the sense of "edition."

Baseline

"Baseline" can have any of the following meanings:

- An item approved and placed in storage in a controlled library
- A delivery (a collection of items released for usage)
- A configuration item, usually a delivery, connected to a specific milestone in a project

"Configuration item" as used in this book is similar to the first meaning of "baseline" in the previous list. "Delivery" is used in this book in the sense of a collection of configuration items (in itself a configuration item), whether or not such a delivery is associated with a milestone or some other specific event—similar to either the second or third meaning in the list, depending on circumstances.

The term "baseline" is not used in this book at all, since misconceptions could result from the many senses in which it's used. Of course, nothing prevents a company from using the term "baseline," as long as the sense is clear to everyone involved.

Chapter 2

Configuration Management in Maturity Models

A number of maturity models exist for development in general. All include requirements for configuration management, though the requirements vary from model to model. So does the way in which configuration management forms part of the maturity assessment methods. In the following sections, configuration management is discussed in light of the most commonly used and acknowledged maturity models, namely CMM and SPICE (ISO 15504). Sources for each are listed in the bibliography.

Please note that these maturity models use the concept "baseline." This is, of course, kept in quotes. The meaning of "baseline" in these maturity models is similar to the expression "configuration item"—that is, any item placed under configuration management.

2.1 CMM VERSION 1.1

Capability Maturity Model (CMM) version 1.1 is the most widely used maturity model. It was developed and is still supported by the Software Engineering Institute, at Carnegie Mellon University. Version 1.0 was released in 1991, following an initiative from the Department of Defense, which had identified a need for an assessment method of their software suppliers. Version 1.1 was released in 1993. Work has been conducted on version 2.0, but this version seems to have been overtaken by CMMI. Version 2 is therefore not discussed here. CMMI is described later in the chapter.

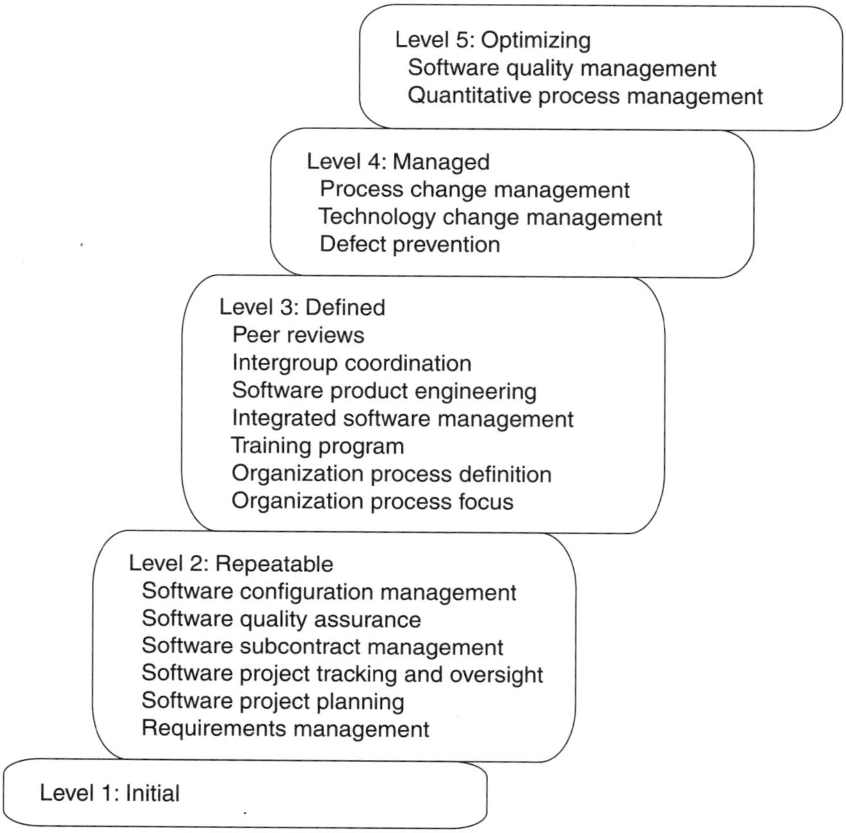

Figure 2-1 *CMM Version 1.1 Maturity Levels*

CMM Maturity Levels

The CMM version 1.1 model is staged—each maturity level has a number of associated key process areas, as shown in Figure 2–1.

Configuration management is a key process area at maturity level 2. To get to maturity level 2, a company has to achieve the goals within all the key process areas at maturity level 2, including configuration management. The goals for configuration management in CMM version 1.1 are

Goal 1: Software configuration management activities are planned.

Goal 2: Selected software work products are identified, controlled, and made available.

Goal 3: Changes to identified software work products are controlled.

Goal 4: Affected groups and individuals are informed of the status and content of software baselines.

Definition

CMM version 1.1 defines configuration management like this:

> The purpose of Software Configuration Management is to establish and maintain the integrity of the products of the software project throughout the project's software life cycle. Software Configuration Management is an integral part of most software engineering and management processes.

Activities

A detailed discussion of the CMM version 1.1 expectations concerning configuration management would be out of scope here. Further details are available in the sources listed in the bibliography. It is, however, instructive to take a look at the activities to be performed, as they provide a good idea of what is expected to achieve the key process area goals. The activities defined by CMM version 1.1 are shown in Table 2–1, along with mapping to this book. (In the list of activities, SCM stands for software configuration management.)

Table 2–1 *Mapping from CMM Version # 1.1 Activities*

CCM Version 1.1 Activity	Mapping to This Book
Activity 1: A SCM plan is prepared for each software project according to a documented procedure.	Chapter 23—Planning Configuration Management—up to Capability Level 2
Activity 2: A documented and approved SCM plan is used as the basis for performing the SCM activities.	Chapter 23—Planning Configuration Management—up to Capability Level 2
Activity 3: A configuration management library system is established as a repository for the software baselines.	Chapter 1—Storage
Activity 4: The software work products to be placed under configuration management are identified.	Chapter 1—Identification Chapter 7—What One Needs to Know about a Configuration Item

(continues)

Table 2–1 *Mapping from CMM Version # 1.1 Activities (continued)*

CCM Version 1.1 Activity	Mapping to This Book
Activity 5: Change requests and problem reports for all configuration items/units are initiated, recorded, reviewed, approved, and tracked according to a documented procedure.	Chapter 1—Change Control Chapter 8—Event Registration Chapter 8—Change Request Chapter 17—Configuration Management
Activity 6: Changes to baselines are controlled according to a documented procedure.	Chapter 1—Change Control Chapter 8—Event Registration Chapter 8—Change Request
Activity 7: Products from the software baseline library are created and their release is controlled according to a documented procedure.	Chapter 1—Storage Chapter 8—Item Approval Chapter 8—Release Request
Activity 8: The status of configuration items/units is recorded according to a documented procedure.	Chapter 1—Identification Chapter 1—Change Control
Activity 9: Standard reports documenting the SCM activities and the contents of the software baseline are developed and made available to affected groups and individuals.	Chapter 1—Status Reporting Chapter 9—What Information Is Available for Configuration Items
Activity 10: Software baseline audits are conducted according to a documented procedure.	Not handled—see Chapter 1, Auditing

CMM version 1.1 also includes expectations concerning verifying implementation, commitment to perform, and the ability to perform for configuration management (and for all other key process areas).

2.2 CMMI

Capability Maturity Model Integration (CMMI) SE/SW/IPPD version 1.02 was published in 2000, and SE/SW/IPPD/SS version 1.1 was published in 2002. CMMI was developed into a single model for organizations pursuing enterprise-wide process improvement, based on

- Capability Maturity Model for Software (SW-CMM) version 2.0, draft C
- Electronic Industries Alliance Interim Standard (EIA/IS) 731, Systems Engineering Capability Model (SECM)
- Integrated Product Development Capability Maturity Model (IPD-CMM) version 0.98

One set of models is characterized as representations, and the representations defined are staged or continuous. The staged representation model is similar to CMM version 1.1 and will therefore not be described further in this section. The continuous representation model is SPICE compatible (see section 2.3) and is the model discussed here. Both are designed to offer essentially equivalent results, and both are in use today.

Another way to look at the CMMI models is from the disciplines and environment angle. Currently the CMMI model includes two disciplines and one development environment: systems engineering (SE) and software engineering (SW) disciplines and the integrated product and process development (IPPD) environment. These are described in Table 2–2.

Table 2–2 *Discipline Description in CMMI*

Discipline/Environment	Description
Systems engineering	The systems engineering discipline covers the development of total systems, which may or may not include software. Systems engineers focus on transforming customer needs, expectations, and constraints into product solutions and supporting those product solutions throughout the product life cycle.
Software engineering	The software engineering discipline covers the development of software systems. Software engineers focus on applying systematic, disciplined, and quantifiable approaches to the development, operation, and maintenance of software.
Integrated product and process development	Integrated Product and Process Development (IPPD) is a systematic approach to product development that achieves a timely collaboration of relevant stakeholders throughout the product life cycle to better satisfy customer needs. The CMMI-SE/SW/IPPD model captures the underlying best practices exhibited by a good IPPD approach. These practices may be used in developing, improving, or appraising the implementation of IPPD.

CMMI is, like CMM version 1.0, developed and supported by the Software Engineering Institute. The material offers guidelines on how to choose between the models and how to tailor the chosen model to specific needs.

CMMI Process Areas

The process areas defined in CMMI are divided into four main groups: process management, project management, engineering, and support. These groups are again divided into process areas, as follows:

Process Management
> Organizational Process Focus
> Organizational Process Definition
> Organizational Training
> Organizational Process Performance
> Organizational Innovation and Deployment

Project Management
> Project Planning
> Project Monitoring and Control
> Supplier Agreement Management
> Integrated Product and Process Development (IPPD) Management
> Risk Management
> Integrated Teaming
> Quantitative Project Management

Engineering
> Requirements Management
> Requirements Development
> Technical Solution
> Product Integration
> Verification
> Validation

Support
> Configuration Management

Process and Product Quality Assurance

Measurement and Analysis

Decision Analysis and Resolution

Organizational Environment for Integration

Causal Analysis and Resolution

Configuration management is, as can be seen, a process area under Support.

Definition

CMMI-SE/SW/IPPD/SS version 1.1 defines configuration management as follows:

> The purpose of Configuration Management is to establish and maintain the integrity of work products using configuration identification, configuration control, configuration status accounting, and configuration audits.

Goals

The goals for configuration management as defined in CMMI are

SG 1 Establish Baselines. Baselines of identified work products are established and maintained.

SG 2 Track and Control Changes. Changes to the work products under configuration management are tracked and controlled.

SG 3 Establish Integrity. Integrity of baselines is established and maintained.

The S in the identification of the goal means that the goal is specific to configuration management—as opposed to generic, or similar across process areas.

Practice-to-Goal Relationships

In CMMI, a number of practices are defined for each goal. The practices for the configuration management goals are

SG 1 Establish Baselines

SP 1.1-1 Identify Configuration Items

SP 1.2-1 Establish a Configuration Management System

SP 1.3-1 Create or Release Baselines

SG 2 Track and Control Changes

    SP 2.1-1 Track Changes

    SP 2.2-1 Control Changes

SG 3 Establish Integrity

    SP 3.1-1 Establish Configuration Management Records

    SP 3.2-1 Perform Configuration Audits

Capability and Maturity Levels

Continuous representation uses capability levels, while staged representation uses maturity levels. The main difference between these two types of levels is the representation to which they belong and how they are applied:

- Capability levels apply to an organization's process-improvement achievement for each process area. There are six capability levels, numbered 0 through 5. Each capability level corresponds to a generic goal and a defined set of generic practices.
- Maturity levels, which belong to a staged representation, apply to an organization's overall process capability and organizational maturity. Each maturity level consists of a predefined set of process areas and generic goals. There are five maturity levels, numbered 1 through 5.

Table 2–3 shows the definitions of capability and maturity levels in CMMI.

Table 2–3 *Definition of Capability and Maturity Levels in CMMI*

Level	Continuous Representation Capability Levels	Staged Representation Maturity Levels
0	Incomplete	N/A
1	Performed	Initial
2	Managed	Managed
3	Defined	Defined
4	Quantitatively managed	Quantitatively managed
5	Optimizing	Optimizing

Achieving Capability Levels

As is the case for specific goals for a given process area, CMMI defines generic goals for each capability level within a process area. The generic goals are the same, no matter what process area you're trying to improve. The goals for the capability levels 1 to 5 are

> **GG 1 Achieve Specific Goals.** The process supports and enables achievement of the specific goals of the process area by transforming identifiable input work products to produce identifiable output work products.
>
> **GG 2 Institutionalize a Managed Process.** The process is institutionalized as a managed process.
>
> **GG 3 Institutionalize a Defined Process.** The process is institutionalized as a defined process.
>
> **GG 4 Institutionalize a Quantitatively Managed Process.** The process is institutionalized as a quantitatively managed process.
>
> **GG 5 Institutionalize an Optimizing Process.** The process is institutionalized as an optimizing process.

Capability levels are determined by reviewing the organization's implementation of the specific and generic practices and its achievement of the associated goals through that capability level. For example, to achieve capability level 2 for a process area, the organization's activities are reviewed against the specific and generic practices and goals through capability level 2.

Level 2 for All Process Areas

Also for the generic goals, CMMI defines a number of generic practices for each goal. The generic practices for the capability level 2 goals are

> GG 2   Institutionalize a Managed Process
>> GP 2.1   Establish an Organizational Policy
>> GP 2.2   Plan the Process
>> GP 2.3   Provide Resources
>> GP 2.4   Assign Responsibility
>> GP 2.5   Train People
>> GP 2.6   Manage Configurations

GP 2.7 Identify and Involve Relevant Stakeholders

GP 2.8 Monitor and Control the Process

GP 2.9 Objectively Evaluate Adherence

GP 2.10 Review Status with Higher-Level Management

Here, configuration management is practice number 6, so it must be performed for any process area in order for the process area to reach capability level 2.

The definition of configuration management as a discipline is as stated above: the integrity of the work products for each process—as identified in the plan for performing the process—must be established and maintained throughout the products' useful life. CMMI further states,

> different levels of configuration management are appropriate for different work products and for different points in time. For some work products, it may be sufficient to maintain version control (i.e., the version of the work product in use at a given time, past or present, is known and changes are incorporated in a controlled manner). Sometimes, it may be critical that work products be placed under formal or "baseline" configuration management. This type of configuration management includes defining and establishing baselines at predetermined points. These baselines are formally reviewed and agreed on, and serve as the basis for further development.
>
> Additional levels of configuration management between version control and formal configuration management are possible. An identified work product may be under various levels of configuration management at different points in time.

Raising the Capability of the Configuration Management Process

In the continuous representations of CMMI, each process area may be performed at a given capability level, and therefore also configuration management. The characteristics of each capability level are described below, from the point of view of configuration management.

To reach capability level 1, the configuration management process is expected to fulfill all the goals for configuration management. Performance may not be stable and may not meet specific objectives such as quality, cost, and schedule, but useful work can be done.

At capability level 2, configuration management is a managed process. A managed process is planned, performed, monitored, and controlled for individual projects, groups, or standalone processes, to achieve a given purpose. Management is concerned with achievement of both the model objectives for the process as well as other objectives, such as cost, schedule, and quality.

At capability level 3, configuration management is a defined process. This is a managed process tailored from the organization's set of standard processes. Deviations beyond those allowed by the tailoring guidelines are documented, justified, reviewed, and approved.

At capability level 4, configuration management is a quantitatively managed process. This is a defined process that is controlled using statistical and other quantitative techniques. Product quality, service quality, process performance, and other business objectives are understood in statistical terms and are controlled throughout the life cycle.

At capability level 5, configuration management is an optimizing process. This is a quantitatively managed process that is improved based on an understanding of the common causes of process variation inherent in the process. An optimizing process focuses on continually improving process performance through both incremental and innovative improvements.

Table 2–4 *Mapping from CMMI Activities*

CMMI Practice	Mapping to This Book
SP 1.1–1: Identify configuration items	Chapter 1—Identification
SP 1.2–1: Establish a configuration management system	Chapter 5—Scoping the Configuration Management Task Part V—Improving Configuration Management
SP 1.3–1: Create or release baselines	Chapter 1—Storage Chapter 1—Change Control Chapter 6—Deliveries for Planned Events Like Milestones
SP 2.1–1: Track changes	Chapter 1—Change Control Chapter 8—Event Registration Chapter 8—Change Request
SP 2.2–1: Control changes	Chapter 1—Change Control
SP 3.1–1: Establish configuration management records	Chapter 8—What One Must Register for a Configuration Item Chapter 1—Status Reporting
SP 3.2–1: Perform configuration audits	Not handled—see Chapter 1, Auditing

2.3 ISO 15504 (SPICE) AND BOOTSTRAP 3.2

SPICE is the coming ISO 15504 standard for software process assessment. BOOT-STRAP 3.2 is a maturity model developed in Europe on the basis of CMM version 1.0, the ESA PSS-05 development model, and ISO 9000. BOOTSTRAP is SPICE compatible—that is, BOOTSTRAP 3.2 is a practical implementation of SPICE. Both models are continuous: the maturity is assessed for all process areas individually in an identical way. Configuration management is a requirement for obtaining level 2 for all process areas. Furthermore configuration management is a process area in its own right.

SPICE Process Model

The process model, including all process areas for SPICE, is shown in Figure 2–2. Configuration management is found as process area SUP.2 under Supporting Life Cycle Processes, Support Processes.

Definition

SPICE (ISO 15504) defines configuration management as follows:

> The purpose of the configuration management process is to establish and maintain the integrity of all the work products of a process or project.

Goals

SPICE does not explicitly set goals but states that as a result of successful implementation of the process,

- A configuration management strategy will be developed.
- All items generated by the process or project will be identified, defined, and baselined.
- Modifications and releases of the items will be controlled.
- The status of the items and modification requests will be recorded and reported.
- The completeness and consistency of the items will be ensured.
- Storage, handling, and delivery of the items will be controlled.

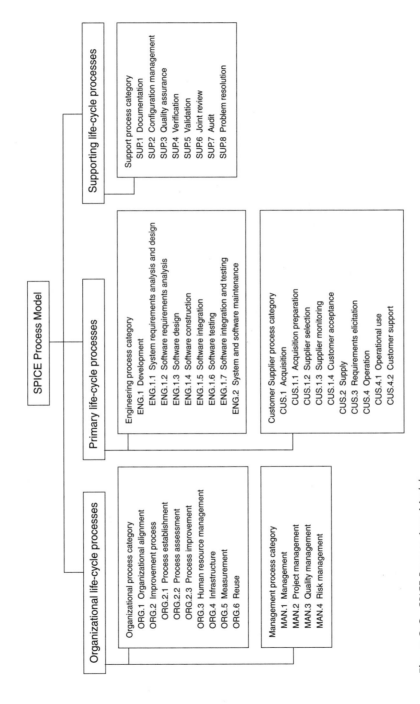

Figure 2-2 *SPICE Process Area Model*

Best Practices

SPICE defines a number of best practices that should lead to a fulfillment of the purpose:

SUP.2.BP1: Develop configuration management strategy. Determine the configuration management strategy, including configuration management activities and schedule for performing these activities.

SUP.2.BP2: Establish configuration management system. Establish a configuration management system including libraries, standards, procedures, and tools.

SUP.2.BP3: Identify configuration items. Identify configuration items, such as software system, modules, components, and related documents by identifying the documentation that establishes the baseline, the version references, and other relevant identification details.

SUP.2.BP4: Maintain configuration item description. Maintain an up-to-date description of each configuration item.

SUP.2.BP5: Manage changes. Record and report on the status of configuration items and modification requests. Changes to any configuration items should be reviewed and authorized.

SUP.2.BP6: Manage product releases. The release and delivery of any configuration items should be reviewed and authorized.

SUP.2.BP7: Maintain configuration item history. Maintain a history of each configuration item in sufficient detail to recover a previously baselined version when required.

SUP.2.BP8: Report configuration status. Regularly report the status of each configuration item and its relationship in the current system integration.

SUP.2.BP9: Manage the release and delivery of configuration items. The storage, handling, release, and delivery of the configuration items should be controlled.

BOOTSTRAP 3.2 has identical goals and activities, although some of them are worded slightly differently.

Maturity Levels

SPICE operates with six maturity levels, defined as shown in Figure 2–3. One of the attributes at level 2 is work product management. This means that for any given process area to obtain level 2, all relevant work products from the performance of the process area must be placed under configuration management. The explicit requirements

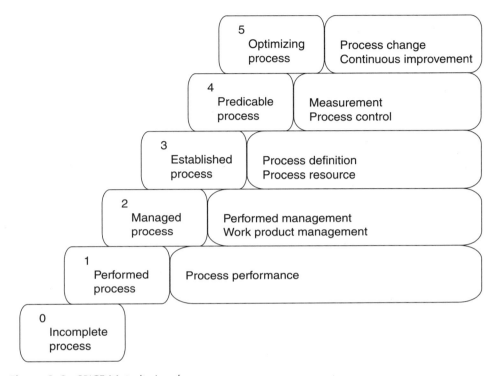

Figure 2–3 *SPICE Maturity Levels*

for this configuration management are as described previously, applied to the process area under assessment.

Maturity of Configuration Management

Since the SPICE model is continuous and configuration management is a process area, configuration management may in itself be performed at the defined maturity levels.

To obtain level 1, configuration management must be performed in such a way that the goals are fulfilled.

Level 2 requires planning of configuration management and follow-up on performance according to the plan. Work products must be controlled with regard to both quality and integrity. This means that relevant work products from configuration management are to be placed under configuration management. This might include the configuration management plan.

To obtain level 3, the configuration management process has to be documented in a standardized way. This must allow for applicable customizations of the process to be introduced and documented and for feedback to be provided to the standard process. The necessary resources for performing configuration management (both human resources and tools and equipment) must be identified and made available.

Level 4 requires that the performance of configuration management and the results from configuration management be controlled though measurements and that the process be adjusted if it gets out of control.

At level 5, the measurements are used to support a continuous improvement of the way configuration management is performed and to measure the effects of this improvement.

Table 2–5 *Mapping from SPICE Best Practices*

SPICE Best Practices	Mapping to This Book
SUP.2.BP1: Develop configuration management strategy	Chapter 5—Scoping the Configuration Management Task
SUP.2.BP2: Establish configuration management system	Chapter 5—Scoping the Configuration Management Task Part V—Improving Configuration Management
SUP.2.BP3: Identify configuration items	Chapter 1—Identification Chapter 7—What One Needs to Know about a Configuration Item
SUP.2.BP4: Maintain configuration item description	Chapter 1—Identification Chapter 7—What One Needs to Know about a Configuration Item
SUP.2.BP5: Manage changes	Chapter 1—Change Control Chapter 8—Event Registration Chapter 8—Change Request
SUP.2.BP6: Manage product releases	Chapter 6—Deliveries for Planned Events Like Milestones
SUP.2.BP7: Maintain configuration item history	Chapter 1—Identification Chapter 1—Change Control
SUP.2.BP8: Report configuration status	Chapter 1—Status Reporting
SUP.2.BP9: Manage the release and delivery of configuration items	Chapter 1—Storage Chapter 8—Release Request

Chapter 3

Configuration Management in International Standards

Numerous international standards and guidelines cover software development and, hence, configuration management. Many standards are related to a specific type of product. Almost all include a safety aspect, as the product types they deal with are classified as safety-critical in one way or another. This may be, for example, products for the medical or aviation industries.

Standards and guidelines reflect the experience of many experts, and using them may serve a number of purposes. It may, for instance, inspire confidence in customers toward the products and provide producers with help and inspiration in the production process.

This chapter provides an overview of standards that (also) deal with configuration management. Standards and guidelines provide, if not a description of "best practice," at least a description of "good practice," and may therefore be useful for inspiration on to how to tackle configuration management. Some of the standards, the ones that seem to be of most interest to software producers, are commented in a little more detail. Sources for each are listed in the bibliography.

The purpose of this chapter is to provide an impression of what is going on internationally with regard to standardization of configuration management.

3.1 OVERVIEW OF RELATED STANDARDS

The overview of standards related to configuration management shown in Table 3–1 is taken from section 4.7 of *Survey of Existing and In-Work Software Engineering Standards and Specifications*. The overview is provided here with the reservation that some of the standards may be out of date or even retired. The book also provides a comprehensive list of the addresses of all the referenced standardization organizations.

Table 3–1 *Standards Overview*

Identification	Title
BS 6488-84	Code of Practice for Configuration Management of Computer-Based Systems. 8 pp.
DOD MIL STD 483A-1985	Configuration Management Practices for Systems, Equipment, Munitions, and Computer Programs. 4 June 1985.
DOD MIL-STD 973	Configuration Management, 1990. 237 pp.
EIA 649	National Consensus Standard for Configuration Management, 1995. 63 pp.
EIA CMB4-1A-84	Configuration Management Definitions for Digital Computer Programs. 46 pp.
EIA CMB4-2-81	Configuration Identification for Digital Computer Programs. 28 pp.
EIA CMB4-3-81	Computer Software Libraries. 23 pp.
EIA CMB4-4-82	Configuration Change Control for Digital Computer Programs. 47 pp.
EIA CMB5-A-86	Configuration Management Requirements for Subcontractors/Vendors. 42 pp.
CMB6-1C-94	Configuration and Data Management References. 21 pp.
EIA CMB6-2-88	Configuration and Data Management In-House Training Plan. 18 pp.
EIA CMB6-5-88	Textbook for Configuration Status Accounting. 69 pp.
EIA CMB6-8-89	Data Management In-House Training Course. 134 pp.
EIA CMB7-1	Electronic Interchange of Configuration Management Data. 11 pp.
EIA CMB7-2	Guideline for Transitioning Configuration Management to an Automated Environment. 17 pp.

(continues)

Table 3–1 *Standards Overview (continued)*

ESA PSS-05-09	*Guide to Software Configuration Management,* issue 1, November 1992
FAA-STD 021	*Software Configuration Management,* FAA-STD-021, Federal Aviation Administration. 116 pp.
FEI-4	*Software Configuration Management,* 1983. 16 pp.
IEEE 828-1990	*Standard for Software Configuration Plans.* 10 pp.
IEEE 1042-1987	*Guide to Software Configuration Management.* 93 pp.
IEEE 1448a-1996	*Supplement to ISO/IEC 12207, Software Life Cycle Processes.*
JTC1 12207-95	*Information Technology—Software Life Cycle Processes.* 55 pp.
KBST V	*Model Software Life Cycle Model (V-Model).* 500+ pp.
MOD DEF-STAN 05-57/2	*Configuration Management Policy and Procedures for Defence Material (Standard)*
NATO STANAG 4159	*Configuration Management*
NATO NAT-PRC-2	*Software Project Configuration Management Procedures*
NIST S.P. 500-161	*Software Configuration Management: An Overview*
RTCA DO/178B-92	*Software Considerations in Airborne Systems and Equipment Certification.* 100 pp.

3.2 BS6488, DOD, IEEE

BS6488

This British standard defines configuration management as

> [t]he discipline of identifying all components and their relationships in a continually evolving system (taking into account relevant system interfaces) for the purpose of maintaining integrity, traceability and control over change throughout the life cycle.

DoD Mil-Std-973

This Department of Defense standard defines configuration management as

> a discipline that applies technical and administrative direction and surveillance over the life cycle of items to
>
> ❖ Identify and document the functional and physical characteristics of configuration items.
> ❖ Control changes to configuration items and their related documentation.
> ❖ Record and report information needed to manage configuration items effectively, including the status of proposed changes and the implementation status of approved changes.
> ❖ Audit configuration items to verify conformance to specifications, drawings, interface control documents, and other contractual requirements.

IEEE-Std-610.12-1990

The IEEE standard includes definitions of "all" terms for software engineering, among which are many related to configuration management. The standard defines configuration management as

> a discipline applying technical and administrative direction and surveillance to: identify and document the functional and physical characteristics of a configuration item, control changes to those characteristics, record and report change processing and implementation status, and verify compliance with specified requirements.

3.3 ESA PSS-05-09

This book of about 80 pages is one of a series of guides for software development produced by the Board for Software Standardisation and Control (BSSC), under the European Space Agency. It contains chapters about configuration management in general, configuration management tools, and preparation of a configuration management plan. The guide is intended for companies producing software for the European space industry. It is, however, easy reading and provides valuable inspiration, even if, in some places, it seems a little old-fashioned.

Introduction from the Guide

The purpose of software configuration management is to plan, organise, control and co-ordinate the identification, storage and change of software through development, integration and transfer. Every project must establish a software configuration management system. All software items, for example documentation, source code, executable code, files, tools, test software and data, must be subjected to software configuration management.

Software configuration management must ensure that

- software components can be identified;
- software is built from a consistent set of components;
- software components are available and accessible;
- software components never get lost (e.g., after media failure or operator error);
- every change to the software is approved and documented;
- changes do not get lost (e.g., through simultaneous updates);
- it is always possible to go back to a previous version;
- a history of changes is kept, so that it is always possible to discover who did what and when.

Project management is responsible for organising software configuration management activities, defining software configuration management roles (e.g., software librarian), and allocating staff to those roles.

3.4 GAMP

The GAMP guide is produced by a number of pharmaceutical companies for suppliers and users of computer systems and automated equipment for the pharmaceutical development industry. It is for companies that have to comply with requirements for validation of systems and equipment established by the U.S. Food and Drug Administration (FDA), although the FDA does not approve the guide as such. The guide discusses many other process areas besides configuration management.

As can be seen in the following paragraph, the guide includes appendices with examples of how to handle various process areas. The guide is straightforward and informative and provides ideas on how to approach configuration management on a smaller, more restrictive scale. The guide is also available on CD.

Description from the Guide

Configuration Management ensures that the automated system remains in a controlled state at all times during the system life-cycle. This will secure quality and consistency in the hardware, software and documentation of the automated system being developed . . . .

The supplier should establish and maintain a formal system for configuration management including document control and change control. In the absence of a configuration management system, that defined in Appendix CC should be followed. The point at which configuration management is applied should be stated in the Quality and Project Plan.

Configuration management includes the disciplines of change control and document management. These may be treated as separate disciplines, for which there are separate procedures but must be incorporated in the overall configuration management plan to ensure traceability.

Document Control is a formal system for the production, review, approval and issue of documents relating to the contract. In the absence of such a system, that defined in Appendix E should be followed . . . .

Change Control is a formal system for the control of all system changes. This procedure should apply to documentation, hardware, software, and network configuration and should cover the following:

- ❖ Documenting changes from one version to the next
- ❖ Approving such changes before they are implemented
- ❖ Identifying all items affected by the change
- ❖ Checking and approving that changes made have been completed correctly

During development any changes to contractual documentation should be agreed with the user. In the absence of a change control system, that defined in Appendix F should be followed . . . .

3.5 ISO 9001:1994, ISO 9000-3, AND ISO 9001:2000

ISO 9001:1994

ISO 9001:1994 is a standard for quality systems with a relatively broad field of application. ISO 9001 is based on the definition of quality as "The degree to which a system, component, or process meets customer or user needs or expectations." The standard covers development, production, and delivery of products and/or services.

ISO 9001 is a general standard, not particularly aimed at software. The words "configuration management" do not appear in the standard, and the concept is therefore not defined. It is, however, possible to find implicit requirements for configuration management. The references in parentheses are to sections in ISO 9001:1994:

- ◆ Design and development changes shall be identified, records maintained, reviewed, and approved (4.4). This implies that the basis for the changes shall be known and controlled.
- ◆ Relevant documents and data (4.5) shall—in practice—be placed under configuration management.
- ◆ Products shall, if it is required, be identified in order to enable traceability (4.8).
- ◆ Records of the review and test status for products shall be maintained (4.12).
- ◆ Nonconforming products shall be controlled (4.13).

The standard also contains requirements concerning the handling of error and change reports for the quality system itself. ISO 9001:1994 is now officially replaced by ISO 9001:2000 (see the section later in this chapter), though many companies still use ISO 9001:1994.

ISO 9000-3

ISO 9000-3 is a guideline for using ISO 9001:1994 for software development. After the release of ISO 9001:2000, ISO 9000-3 is no longer valid but is still of interest to many companies. It contains a description of configuration management in section 6.1.1:

> Configuration management provides a mechanism for identifying, controlling and tracking the versions of each software item. In many cases earlier versions still in use must also be maintained and controlled.
>
> The configuration management system should
>
> a. identify uniquely the versions of each software item;
> b. identify the versions of each software item which together constitute a specific version of a complete product;
> c. identify the build status of software products in development or delivered and installed;
> d. control simultaneous updating of a given software item by more than one person;

e. provide coordination for the updating of multiple products in one or more locations as required;

f. identify and track all actions and changes resulting from a change request, from initiation through release.

Subsequent sections in the guideline contain a description of the contents of a configuration management plan (organizational aspects, activities, tools, methods, and discussion on when objects should be placed under configuration management), along with a description of the basic configuration management activities (identification, traceability, change control, and status reporting).

ISO 9001:2000

ISO 9001:2000 is an updated version of ISO 9001:1994. It does include the words "configuration management" in a note, but no definition of the concept. As in ISO 9001:1994, however, a number of requirements imply performance of configuration management. The references in parentheses are for sections in ISO 9001:2000:

- Relevant documents shall—in practice—be placed under configuration management (4.2.3). The same applies for quality records (4.2.4).

- Design and development changes shall be identified, records maintained, reviewed, and approved (7.3.7), and records of the results of the reviews, and so forth, shall be maintained.

- Products shall, if it is required, be identified in order to enable traceability and status reporting (7.5.3). The note for this section reads: "In some industry sectors, configuration management is a means by which identification and traceability are maintained."

- Nonconforming products shall be controlled (8.3)

The standard also contains requirements concerning the handling of error and change reports for the quality system itself.

Table 3–2 *Mapping from ISO 9001:2000 Sections*

ISO 9001:2000 Section	Mapping to This Book
4.2.3 and 4.2.4	Chapter 5—Scoping the Configuration Management Task Part V—Improving Configuration Management
7.3.7	Chapter 1—Change Control Chapter 8—Event Registration Chapter 8—Change Request
7.5.3	Chapter 1—Identification
8.3	Chapter 1—Change Control

Chapter 4

Organizations Working with Configuration Management

Much has been said and written about configuration management. Hardly because configuration management is a beloved discipline, but rather because it's extensive and complex, difficult to get a grip on, appearing in many contexts in—and even out of—an organization.

This chapter mentions some of the institutions and companies working with configuration management at a professional level, along with some projects that have configuration management as their theme. All have been chosen because they seem to be the most interesting for a wide audience. Those mentioned here are a small sample, but they may serve as an appetizer for those who want to know more. Sources can be found in the bibliography.

4.1 INSTITUTIONS AND COMPANIES

CM Today Yellow Pages

The Yellow Pages for configuration management are the starting point for those who wish to find out what may be found out about configuration management. Links are provided for, among others things, articles, jobs, other Web sites about configuration management, commercial and freeware configuration management systems, and seminars, workshops, and conferences.

Institute of Configuration Management

The Institute of Configuration Management, with headquarters in Arizona, has developed a model they call CMII. It consists of a configuration management process, formed to

- Accommodate changes
- Accommodate the reuse of standards and best practices
- Assure that all requirements remain clear, concise, and valid
- Communicate the above
- Assure conformance

The model furthermore caters to continuous improvement of the included configuration management processes.

Conferences

A number of conferences have configuration management as their subject. The most important are

- **International Workshop on Software Configuration Management.** The proceedings from this conference are printed as Springer Lecture Notes in Computer Science, which are easy to obtain and to learn from.
- **CMII Conference.** The user group for the CMII model holds this conference.

Ovum

Ovum is an international analysis and consultant company that among other things evaluates tools and issues reports about the results of these evaluations. Ovum is known for its evaluations of testing tools, but it also evaluates configuration management tools. Ovum defines configuration management as "a disciplined approach to managing the evolution of software development and maintenance practices and their components as they change over time."

Software Engineering Institute

The Software Engineering Institute is a research and development center partly sponsored by the U. S. Department of Defense. The better location for information on configuration management is the Software Engineering Information Repository at the SEI, known as the SEIR. Their Web site provides good pointers to the subject of configuration management. Registration is required for access, but it's free.

4.2 PROJECTS

ACME

Mr. Brad Appleton, coauthor (with Stephen Berczuk) of *Software Configuration Management Patterns,* has developed a set of Web pages titled the ACME Project—Assembling Configuration Management Environments (for Software Development). The site contains many links to resources and papers as well as recommendations for further reading on software configuration management, including several papers by Appleton and Berczuk that were seminal works on SCM patterns and form the basis for their book. They define software configuration management as

> the process of identifying, organizing, controlling, and tracking both the decomposition and recomposition of: software structure, functionality, evolution, and teamwork. In short, SCM is the "glue" between software artifacts, features, changes, and team members; it forms the ties that bind them all together from concept to delivery and beyond.

The ACME Web site includes a large number of definitions of configuration management collected by Mr. Appleton.

AdCoMs

The AdCoMs, ESPRIT Project No. 22167, was a European research project to define, develop, and implement a generic process model and pilot-demonstrator to manage and control product data shared across an extended company. The model had to be sufficiently flexible to be able to handle continuously changing business needs. The result of the project was an extremely large model for product configuration management aimed at the European industry, primarily the space industry.

DaSC

The Database and Selectors Cel configuration management model is a change-oriented approach that supports concurrent, distributed software development. It is a research project at the Institute for Information Technology in Ottawa, which is part of the National Research Council, Canada.

Chapter 5

Scoping the Configuration Management Task

The need to perform configuration management at all and the level of ambition for the performance of such may stem from a number of sources. It may be formal, external requirements, like those from the customer, from standards (e.g., for safety-critical systems), or for certification, such as ISO 9000. Or it may be more informal requirements originating from the company's strategy and wish for better quality and greater customer satisfaction, such as goals or practices from a maturity model, concrete problems experienced in the company, or time-to-market.

No matter where the need stems from, many considerations determine the scope of the task. Even requirements originating from a standard permit a certain amount of freedom in scope and degree of formalism. When a choice is to be made it's important to include considerations about the profitability of possible initiatives.

5.1 LEVEL OF AMBITION—COST/BENEFIT ANALYSIS

Level of Ambition = Scope + Formalism

The benefits and costs connected with configuration management are linked to the chosen level of ambition, which may be split into two aspects: scope and degree of formalism. Scope is the number of objects placed under configuration management. Degree of formalism is the control—or, if you like, the bureaucracy—with which configuration management is performed.

Configuration management as described in this book may be performed with many degrees of formalism and with many scopes. It's impossible to describe in absolute terms which scope and which formalism are the best; this depends on the requirements and possibilities.

Formalism for a Configuration Item

The degree of formalism of the configuration management for each configuration item may vary during the item's lifetime. Such a course is illustrated in Figure 5–1, where the scale for the degree of formalism is arbitrary and the activities and functions are anonymous.

Objects come into existence at some point during the course of the project. It may be a development-activity-specific object or an object from one of the support functions. At some point, the object is placed under configuration with a certain degree of formalism applied. This is shown in Figure 5–1 to be sometime during

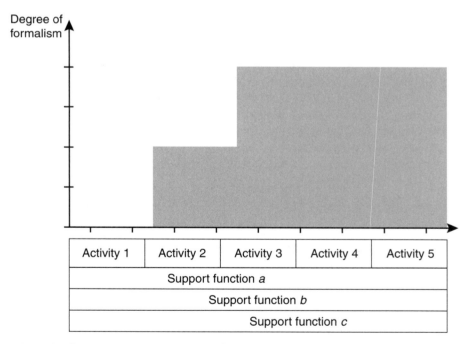

Figure 5–1 *Configuration Management Cost for One Item*

Activity 1, and the degree of formalism at that point is 2. Later, the degree of formalism with which the configuration management of the item is performed is augmented. In Figure 5–1 the new degree is 4. The hatched area is an expression of the costs related to placing and keeping this object under configuration management.

A more specific example could be a source code file, which is placed under configuration management when module test begins—that is, after the developer has worked on the object for a while. When the module has passed the module test and is used in the integration test with other modules, the degree of formalism for the configuration management of the item is augmented.

Degrees of Formalism

Different degrees of formalism may be present within a single project and also within a company as a whole. A high degree of formalism may be required for safety-critical systems, while a lower degree of formalism may be the minimum you can get away with and still meet the company's basic needs.

Standards and maturity models define minimum degrees of formalism. These must be achieved before a company can claim that configuration management is performed at all—for example, to a capability level of 1 in CCMI. This is certainly of interest when considering certification or assessment. However, interest is growing in the way certification and assessments can help process improvement in general.

For "ordinary" projects, it may be an advantage to mix the degrees of formalism, using a lower degree in earlier development activities (during coding for source code and the like) and a higher degree during maintenance for deliveries. Each company must define the degrees of formalism it wants to employ and under which circumstances each degree is to be used.

Earliest and Latest Extremes for Starting Configuration Management

Configuration management for an object is said to be started when the degree of formalism reaches a defined minimum. For example, if identification is performed but controlled storage is not, this is not considered configuration management. The earliest point at which an object can reasonably be placed under configuration management is when the producer decides that the work product is in a state others can use. This may be when a source code module or document is ready for peer review. The latest point at which an object can reasonably be placed under configuration management is when it is part of a delivery to a customer.

Formalism and Tools

A tool often forces a certain degree of formalism upon a configuration management system. Most tools support a lower degree of formalism. Often, a higher degree will have to be sustained by manual procedures. Few tools are flexible enough to provide the possibility of choosing degrees of formalism according to different types of configuration items.

Expansion of Scope—from Candidate to Item

Each project has numerous potential configuration items. In principle, every object produced or procured may be placed under configuration management. This is, however, seldom profitable. The initial cost is the largest expense (e.g., the investment in a tool and/or training courses), but the cost also depends on the number of items, because each item contributes a little bit.

Figure 5–2 presents an expression of the total cost for configuration management in a project. Items contribute to the cost depending on

- When an item is placed under configuration management (the x-axis is time)
- The degree of formalism with which configuration management is performed for an item (the y-axis is an arbitrary scale of formalism)
- Which (how many) items are placed under configuration management (the z-axis depicts the configuration items—one for each interval)

The shaded volume is an expression of the cost of placing the chosen items under configuration management. The decision to place each type of object or individual object under configuration management must be carefully considered in light of a calculation of profitability (discussed later in the chapter).

No Rough Drafts—Please!

Objects being placed under configuration management must constitute a solution to a given assignment. The producer's "rough drafts" do not qualify. This is to say that as long as an object is in production, it must be outside the configuration management system and away from the controlled library.

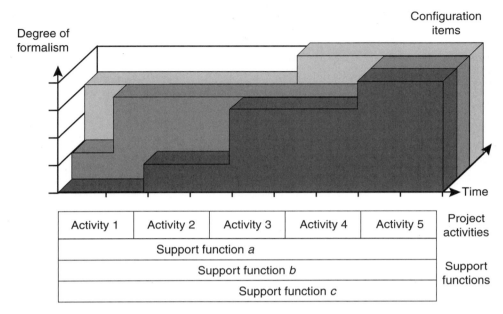

Figure 5–2 *Configuration Management Total Cost*

Expansion from the Middle

It is a widespread practice and position that the least you can get away with in terms of configuration management is to place source code under informal configuration management. If you have started like this and not placed each work product under configuration management as it reaches the appropriate state, you may still continue from that point and place other types of objects under configuration management. The driving force in this process should be the tracing, so that what has already been placed under configuration management is traceable to other configuration items.

Source code modules may be traced backward to design and requirements. If the design and requirements are fairly stable when coding begins, it may be advantageous to place them under configuration management and start the tracing from there. Requirement specifications may be traced forward to system test specifications, which may be the next objects to place under configuration management.

5.2 EXAMPLES

Tables 5–1 and 5–2 are examples of the activities in configuration management systems with low and high degrees of formalism, respectively. The principles are valid for all types of configuration items, such as a document, source code file, or delivery. It is presumed that the tool(s) used will register transactions in the controlled library, creating an automatic log of everything going on. Such logs are often quite limited and are typically suited to a low degree of formalism. A high degree of formalism, which requires logs filled out by people, may seem to promote paper-based configuration management, but this is not necessarily true, as these logs can be kept electronically.

Table 5–1 *Activities with a Low Degree of Formalism*

Activity	Description
Creation	The producer ♦ Identifies a new item ♦ Registers the metadata most needed in the required format and on the required media ♦ Inserts the new item in the controlled library
Usage	The users ♦ Extract copies of the configuration item when they have a need They perform the extraction themselves, directly from the controlled library.
Events	The users ♦ Send e-mails about events to the person responsible for configuration management and to members of the configuration control board
Event evaluation	The person responsible for configuration management makes sure that ♦ Every event registration is evaluated by the original producer (or other experts) ♦ The result of this evaluation is sent by e-mail to the configuration control board
Change decision	The configuration control board ♦ Sends its decision regarding changes to the producer by e-mail

(continues)

Table 5–1 *Activities with a Low Degree of Formalism (continued)*

New items	The producer ◆ Identifies the needed new item ◆ Gets an earlier configuration item as the basis for the production of the new item as appropriate ◆ Registers the most needed metadata in the required format and on the required media ◆ Inserts the new item in the controlled library
And so on . . .	Life goes on like this.

Table 5–2 *Activities with a High Degree of Formalism*

Activity	Description
Creation	The person responsible for configuration management ◆ Identifies a new item ◆ Fills in all metadata in the required format and on the required media for the new item, including full detailed tracing to related items
Approval	The person responsible for quality ◆ Fills in and signs written approval of an item ready to be placed under configuration management
Submission	The producer ◆ Submits a registration of metadata, the item itself, and the item approval to the librarian
Placement in storage	The librarian ◆ Places the item in the controlled library ◆ Takes care of the registration and storage of associated metadata and forms
Release request	The users ◆ Submit written release requests to the librarian, including information on who is going to use the item and for what purpose
Release for usage	The librarian ◆ Releases copies of the configuration item to those who are going to use them, according to the release request ◆ Takes care of registration and storage of related data and forms

(continues)

Table 5–2 *Activities with a High Degree of Formalism (continued)*

Events	Users ◆ Submit written event registration to the person responsible for configuration management
Event evaluation	The person responsible for configuration management ◆ Arranges a written evaluation of each event registration from the original producer of the item and/or other experts
The CCB works	The configuration control board ◆ Meets ◆ Evaluates each event registration ◆ Documents their evaluation on the respective event registrations
Change requests	The configuration control board ◆ Produces the necessary written change requests in accordance with the results of their evaluations
New items	The person responsible for configuration management ◆ Identifies a new item ◆ Releases a configuration item as the basis for the production of a new item, as appropriate
Approval of change	The person responsible for quality ◆ Fills in and signs a written approval of the new item ready to be placed under configuration management
Acceptance of change	The configuration control board ◆ Meets ◆ Evaluates each approval ◆ Documents their evaluation on the respective change requests and event registrations
Submission of change	The producer ◆ Submits metadata registration, the item itself, and an approved change request to the librarian for each new item
Storage	The librarian ◆ Inserts the item in the controlled library ◆ Takes care of the registration and storage of related data and forms

(continues)

Table 5–2 *Activities with a High Degree of Formalism (continued)*

Communication of change	The librarian ♦ Informs all those who have received previous versions of the configuration item that a new, changed version is available This enables stakeholders to decide if they want the new version released for usage.
And so on . . .	Life goes on like this.

5.3 CALCULATION OF PROFITABILITY

Configuration management entails a number of benefits, such as savings and better quality, and a number of costs related to tools, workings hours, and so on. Both will vary from company to company. Configuration management also provides an element of "insurance," by helping, through a relatively small investment, to prevent situations that could cause considerable expense.

To find the right level of ambition for configuration management in a specific context, it's important to calculate profitability based on the potential for savings and the concrete costs. It's also important to measure whether the costs and the benefits are realized as expected.

The following procedure is recommended at the start of every initiative of implementation or improvement of configuration management in a company or a project:

1. Produce a list of the potential savings for the company/project, including related estimates for economic value. Produce estimates for each alternative.

2. Estimate the expenses. Again, produce estimates for each alternative.

3. Prioritize the effort in view of profitability and in coherence with the strategical focus of the company—typical examples on strategical focus areas are customer satisfaction, productivity, quality, and so on.

4. Follow up to ensure that expenses as well as savings are realized as expected, and use the experience to refine your estimating capability before the next improvement effort.

Expenses

Expenses, which must be foreseen, depend on the chosen level of ambition. They may, for example, consist of the following entries:

- Expenses for tools and systems (software and hardware)
- Hours spent by your own staff and possible expenses toward external consultants:
  - For implementation: definitions of processes and systems, training, and so on
  - For various tasks in ongoing configuration management

Savings

Savings may stem from preventing one or more of the following:

- Correcting the same error in several places
- Performing work on the wrong basis (e.g., outdated requirements)
- Having errors corrected once reappear
- Introducing unwanted functionality
- Not knowing which version the customer has received
- Upgrading free due to incompatibility with old equipment
- Performing redundant coding
- Transferring knowledge to new employees goes wrong

Possible savings depend on the problems the company experiences. Table 5–3 shows details of some of these problems, a description of how configuration management may solve them, and a suggestion for estimating the economic value. This table is not a complete checklist but rather a suggestion for some of the more common problems, which may indicate that improvement or introduction of configuration management will be profitable. It may also be used as inspiration to identify other problems that are particularly relevant for the company. For example, the company may find that it is

- Difficult or impossible to reestablish a running product
- Difficult or impossible to make changes in an existing system
- Difficult or impossible to revert to an earlier version that works
- Difficult to establish a stable decision, because decisions are constantly reversed

Table 5–3 *Examples of Possible Savings Using a Configuration Management System*

Problem	Benefits of Configuration Management	Economic Value
The same error is corrected—and then in turn found and corrected by other people in all the other variants of the product.	Immediate recognition of all affected variants and correction of the error at one time in the entire configuration item family.	$(n - 1)$ x (time for diagnosis and correction of error in item in n variants) *and possibly* Savings in travel time and so on by handling all products/customer installations at one time.
A design is produced based on outdated requirements, or a test is performed on the wrong version that contains already found errors.	Registration of status and history for all configuration items.	Time spent working on the wrong basis. *Qualitatively (less measurable):* Employee satisfaction.
Old errors reappear when a new version is delivered to the customer.	Recognition of all versions of configuration items as well as all changes from version to version.	Time spent finding and correcting old errors. *Qualitatively (less measurable):* Greater customer satisfaction due to better quality.
Designers or programmers introduce functionality not covered by requirements.	Only functionality that can be traced to an approved contract and/or requirement specification or change request is included.	Time spent implementing (designing, coding, and so on) the unwanted functionality *and* Time to recognize the "gold plating" *and* Time to consider the problem *and* (Time to remove the "gold plating" *or* Time to follow it through [requirement, test, user guide, and so on.])

(continues)

Table 5–3 *Examples of Possible Savings Using a Configuration Management System (continued)*

Problem	Benefits of Configuration Management	Economic Value
Error at customer is hard to find, since it's unknown which version the customer has.	Immediate knowledge about the customer's version.	Time spent identifying the customer's version *and/or* Saved travel time and expenses (if onsite error correction is needed, for example, because the problem can't be re-created at home) *and/or* Saved rebates at the next sale to the same customer resulting from loss due to the error *and/or* Saved day fines while the customer is waiting (shorter downtime) *and/or (less measurable):* Extra sales due to greater customer satisfaction with regard to service.
Extra sales to a customer. Since it's unclear if existing equipment is in a version that will work (e.g., exchange data) with new equipment, it's decided to upgrade all the old equipment free, to be on the safe side.	Information about which changes have been made in which versions combined with knowledge about which version the customer has bought earlier.	Time and material used for the upgrade of the old equipment. *Qualitatively (less measurable):* ◆ Less disturbance to the customer's business ◆ Shorter installation time
The same functionality is developed over and over in a number of products. You know it, but you drop the idea of finding and isolating the code that is implementing the functionality in one of the other products.	Reusable items are easy to find.	Estimate for new development of items—time to fit the items to new environments.

(continues)

Table 5–3 *Examples of Possible Savings Using a Configuration Management System (continued)*

Problem	Benefits of Configuration Management	Economic Value
A new employee is to enhance the product and sits down to get acquainted with it by reading the documentation. The employee will design the enhancements on the basis of that information. It turns out that the documentation has not been updated and doesn't correspond to the source code—so the employee must start all over and read the source code.	Registration of the relationships between source code and corresponding documents, changes, and date and time for updates.	Time spend on designing on the wrong basis. *Qualitatively (less measurable):* Employee satisfaction.

5.4 PITFALLS IN CONNECTION WITH SCOPING

When calculating profitability, it's necessary to consider at length what to place under configuration management and when this is going to happen in a company or a project. What you need to watch out for during these considerations is that you do not choose to be too demanding, wrong, too coarse or too fine, too embracing or too exclusive, too late or too early.

Too Demanding

Configuration management is basically a bookkeeping function. Even the best configuration management system is not able to solve planning, design, or testing issues. The order in which objects are produced and brought into usage is a planning issue. This planning can be complex, especially if the design is complex. There is no short cut through the configuration management system—at best, the system will only be able to tell the status of configuration items.

The way objects are related to and dependent on each other is a design issue. Again, there is no shortcut through the configuration management system—at best, it will only tell how configuration items are related. This implies that the order in which finished objects may be used as support in the testing of other objects is a test planning issue. It's frequently seen that module testing relies on finished objects instead of drivers and stubs. This is fine, as long as it's understood that this requires extra development and test planning for the necessary information to be accessible—possibly, but not necessarily, through the configuration management system.

A configuration management system may be able to report on an item's state and on how deliveries are composed. It will, however, ease the work if the design is kept as simple as possible.

Wrong

It's almost automatic to think that configuration management is an unwieldy monster ready to swallow all resources and stifle employees' creativity. This may well be the case if needs are not made clear and matched with the basic principles of configuration management. When configuration management is implemented properly and within a suitable scope, it can make everybody's job easier.

Too Coarse or Too Fine

When the decision is to be made about how fine to make the granularity of configuration management, the smallest object to be changed and traced to must be considered and the definition of configuration items tailored accordingly. It's not expedient to define an entire requirement specification document as one configuration item if you have to trace to individual requirements. Nor is it expedient to have an entire subsystem as a configuration item if individual source code modules may be subject to change. Similarly, it's not expedient to define individual chapters or—as is seen occasionally—individual lines in a document as configuration items if the document is always issued in a new version in its entirety and there is no need for a detailed tracing.

Too Embracing or Too Exclusive

Configuration management entails a certain expense, but it provides valuable security and information. Considerations for what to place under configuration management are based on "What do we want to know?" and "What is the need?" At one end of the spectrum, absolutely everything produced and received for a product may be placed under configuration management. At the other, it may be nothing at all. It's a good idea to list all potential configuration items and actively opt out of those you don't want or need. This way, the choice is a conscious one, reducing the risk of overlooking something you're later going to miss.

Also to be considered is that it's rarely necessary to place derived objects, like compiled source code modules, under configuration management. These can be reproduced from the source code using the relevant tool(s). It may, however, be more profitable in the long run to place derived objects under configuration management rather than the tool(s) used for production. But this is an individual consideration from case to case.

Too Late or Too Early

You should not place an object under configuration management before the need outweighs the effort. On the face of it, it's more trouble to have an object under configuration management than not—all events are to be registered, you have to decide on the destiny of all events, and new configuration items are to be identified, created, and placed in storage when a change is implemented. The advantages are of course that the changes are under control and events may be analyzed.

It's worth noticing that the trouble and benefits are often unevenly distributed— that is, those who receive the benefits are often not those who have the trouble. The calculation of the benefit in relation to cost must be done in this larger context.

5.5 HOW TO TREAT WHAT IS KEPT OUTSIDE

In a given project, one will always choose not to place some objects under configuration management— sometimes a few; other times, many more. These objects are not necessarily less important, and they must be taken seriously. Handling these objects is not, however, the responsibility of the configuration manager but usually of the project manager, development manager, or, in some cases, the person who produced the object. These objects must of course also be identified and stored securely. They may well be related to configuration items.

Objects to Keep Outside

Objects not normally placed under configuration management may include

- Those that have no significance for the delivery of the complete product (e.g., letters and other administrative material)
- Those that don't change once they have been produced (e.g., minutes of meetings and status reports)
- Those that may otherwise be reproduced (e.g., compiled versions of source code or executable files)

In the third case, it must be considered whether it's more expedient to place the tools used to produce the objects or derived objects themselves under configuration management—that is, whether to place, for example, the source code and compiler or the source code and the compiled module under configuration management.

Identification

It can be an advantage to define conventions for unique identification even for objects not placed under configuration management. To give an example, documents, such as status reports, may be covered by a naming convention for documents in general, whether a document is placed under configuration management or not.

It may also be an advantage to note comprehensive information about tools, to make it possible to reference these from the configuration items, even if the tools themselves are not under configuration management. In this case you can always hope it will be possible to get hold of a specific tool if you need it later.

Storage

Even objects not under configuration management will have to be kept somewhere. That is to say, you need a library that is not the controlled configuration management library but that is still under some form of control. This may be solved in various ways, but the best solution is a controlled (that is, defined and controlled) library, independent of the configuration management library. Objects not under configuration management should never be stored in a way that might raise doubt about whether they are under configuration management or not (that is, other than in the configuration management library).

Part II

Configuration Management Data

Configuration management is about communication: communication between those who want items, those who produce them, and those who use them.

Items are placed under configuration management—that is one configuration management activity. Information is attached to the items, and maintaining this information is also a configuration management activity. Facilitating usage of the information about the items is yet another activity.

Chapter 6

What Can Be Placed under Configuration Management

Many objects are produced or maybe purchased in the course of producing products. In principle, everything may be placed under configuration management. An object placed under configuration management is called a *configuration item*. A configuration item is any possible part of the development or delivery of a system or product that it's necessary to identify, produce, store, use, and change individually.

Configuration items may vary considerably in complexity. A configuration item may be an individual item or a collection of other items, so-called deliveries, which can be placed under configuration management in their own right.

6.1 PHYSICAL OR ELECTRONIC OBJECTS

Source code is far from the only type of objects that might be placed under configuration management, though this is traditionally the most common type. If you look at a product's entire life cycle, objects may belong to the product itself or may support its development and maintenance.

Configuration Item Class Hierarchy

No matter how and where objects are produced, they fall into distinct classes: physical and electronic. These are illustrated in Figure 6–1, which shows an extract of the class hierarchy that can be drawn for configuration items. The last row shows instantiation of the configuration item classes just above. Some differences between the two classes need to be understood in terms of configuration management.

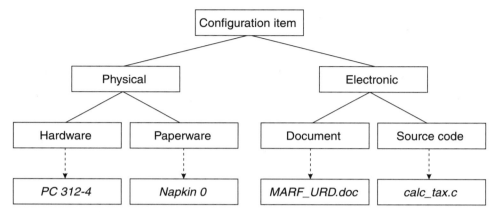

Figure 6–1 *Configuration Item Class Hierarchy*

Physical Objects

The characteristics of a physical object in configuration management perspective are

- ◆ It exists in a limited number of copies—sometimes only one.
- ◆ When a copy of the object is delivered, the number of available copies is reduced.
- ◆ It cannot be stored on a computer but must be stored in a physical place.
- ◆ Writing metadata on the object may or may not be possible.
- ◆ Most traditional configuration management tools cannot handle a physical object without a proxy-object in electronic form.
- ◆ Only the most advanced stock handling systems are able to extract a physical object from storage based on the metadata.

A few examples of physical objects are

- ◆ The paper napkin on which the original idea was sketched
- ◆ Workstations to be delivered as parts of the system
- ◆ Workstations used for development
- ◆ Cables
- ◆ The box that the hardware parts with the embedded software are to be placed in
- ◆ Boards

Electronic Objects

The characteristics of an electronic object in configuration management perspective are

- An unlimited number of copies may be easily produced.
- Delivery of a copy does not reduce the available number of copies.
- Copies may be produced/extracted/delivered without anybody noticing.
- Copies may be in either electronic or physical form.
- It must be stored electronically.
- Metadata for the object may be contained in the object itself and/or in the computer (as part of the operating system and/or a tool).
- Metadata can be a direct pointer to the object and can be used to extract the object from storage.

A few examples of electronic objects are the user requirement document written in Word, a software module written in C, a database system (middleware), and an operating system.

6.2 TYPES OF OBJECTS IN PRODUCT PERSPECTIVE

Products may be composed of different types of subproducts, such as software, hardware, network, data, and services. For each type of subproduct, individual objects of many types may be placed under configuration management. An object for a subproduct could also be a subcomponent, component, or product itself.

In the following, some examples of objects to place under configuration management for the actual product are given for each type of subproduct. The lists are by no means exhaustive but may serve as inspiration when considering objects to place under configuration management.

Note that it may sometimes be difficult to draw a firm line between types of subproducts. Each company must establish its own definition of individual subproducts—the one used here is just an example.

Software

For software-related objects, the types to place under configuration management may, for example, be header files, include files, source code files, system libraries, object files, and executable files. The last two types are derived types of the others. It may be expedient to place such objects under configuration management along with (or possibly instead of) the types of objects used for their production. The considerations may include speed of delivery and space for storage.

Hardware

Hardware in this context is the hardware to be delivered as part of the product. This may be cables, machinery (mainframe, personal computer, workstation), print cards, storage (ROM/EPROM/EEROM), a programmable logical device (PLD), or peripherals (CD burner, plotter, printer, scanner).

It's important to keep different environments apart, such as the development environment, test environment, production environment, and so on. The same objects may be part of more than one environment—for example, if the test environment is used for production after the test activities. In such instances, it's necessary to attach a time factor to the objects, to keep them from being part of more environments at the same time, as this may cause severe problems.

Network

The network subproduct of a product may be complicated, and it may well be that some of it, such as the Internet, is outside the control of the company delivering the product. Objects to place under configuration management for the network subproduct may be firewalls (both software and hardware firewalls exist), a physical network (LAN/WAN), ports or cards, protocol interfaces, servers, and switches. These objects may be either electronic or physical and must be treated accordingly.

Data

Data to be delivered for a product may be parameter values or basic system data, like allowed currencies. Data will often be delivered as files, either flat files or database files. This means that data is electronic and must be treated as such.

Services

Services to be delivered for a system are intangible and cannot be placed under configuration management. Tangible objects may sustain them, however, and these may be placed under configuration management. This could be procedure descriptions, service agreements or contracts, training material (computer-assisted training material, teacher's manual, slides) or user manuals. These objects may be electronic or physical and must be treated accordingly.

Tools

Tools used for the production of the abovementioned objects may be placed under configuration management. Tools may be word processor(s), drawing tools, editor(s), compiler(s), database tools, and many others.

6.3 TYPES OF OBJECTS IN PROJECT PERSPECTIVE

A project is usually divided into a number of life cycle activities. These may be preparation, requirements specification, design, production, integration, test, and operation and maintenance. During the entire lifetime of the product, and therefore during the entire lifetime of each project, support functions that should be performed include project management, quality assurance, and configuration management. In each of the life cycle activities and for each of the support functions, a number of types of objects are produced, and these may be placed under configuration management.

Below are some examples of objects to place under configuration management for life cycle activities and support functions. The objects may or may not be delivered to the customer, but they are in any case not part of the actual product the end user deploys. Again, the lists are by no means exhaustive but may serve as inspiration.

Life Cycle Activities

Project documentation produced in the life cycle activities may, for example, be preparation (contract, statement of work, user requirements), requirements specification (software requirements, other subproduct requirements, prototypes, scenarios), design (architectural design specification, detailed design specification, drawings, diagrams, technical notes), production (no nonproduct objects are produced here), integration (no new objects are produced here), testing (drivers, stubs, test data[base], test specifications and procedures, test reports), and operation and maintenance (reproduction procedures, installation procedures, implementation procedures).

Support Functions

Objects produced during performance of support functions may be project management (project plans, schedule, minutes of meetings, reports), quality assurance (plans, quality records), and configuration management (plans, release requests, event registrations, change requests, status reports).

Tools

See Tools in the previous section.

6.4 TYPES OF OBJECTS IN CROSS-ORGANIZATIONAL PERSPECTIVE

Cross-Organizational Perspective

All companies have some cross-organizational objects or assets for which configuration management should be considered. This may be administrative documents, company product assets, infrastructure, or a quality system. Again, some examples are given for each of the abovementioned types, to serve as inspiration.

Administrative Documents

Administrative documents to place under configuration management may for example be correspondence (letters, e-mail, faxes), sales material (brochures, prototypes, presentations), order-related material (proposals, tender material, contracts), and plans (company vision, strategic plans, organizational plans, personnel plans). Some of these types may be project specific; others may be for an entire company or a smaller administrative unit within a company.

These types of objects are not often placed under configuration management, but it may be worth considering doing so, at least for some of the more important ones. What is important is, however, a company decision.

Company Product Assets

The development of products using a product-line approach is usually under cross-organizational responsibility. The company product assets may also be known as components for reuse. Such assets may be anything from the smallest piece of source code to entire subsystems. Inspiration for what to place under configuration management may be found in the two previous sections, as assets may be seen from both a product and a project perspective, and in the following section, as assets may well be deliveries. It is especially important to keep company product assets under strict configuration management, as much work depends on them; it's important that they remain assets and do not become liabilities.

Infrastructure

The infrastructure in a company provides the environments in which the employees work, such as development, test, production, and administration. For all types, the objects to place under configuration management may include development tools (compilers, linkers), hardware (personal computers, printers, workstations), operating systems, networks, and tools (word processors, drawing programs, and technical tools such as design and test tools).

Quality System

The "quality system" is the formal term for what may also be known as the company's process descriptions or documentation that describes how the company conducts its business. These may include process descriptions, templates, and standards. These may seem like a few simple object types, but it may be a huge task to keep them under configuration management. It's important for a company that wants to do well to have a good configuration management system for these types of objects.

6.5 DELIVERIES UNDER CONFIGURATION MANAGEMENT

Individual configuration items may be assembled in deliveries, which may and should be configuration items in their own right. Deliveries are hierarchies of configuration items and may be constructed of other deliveries in a ramified hierarchy. The individual configuration items in a delivery may be of all types in any required mixture.

The need for a delivery may arise when it is expedient to handle the entire assembly of configuration items as one unit. This often happens when some larger part of a system, maybe even the entire system, is to be delivered for use. The use may be the basis for a new activity in development, an external test (such as onsite acceptance), or the start of production for the customer. Therefore, the concept of deliveries is important from a configuration management point of view, even though a delivery should, in principle, be treated like any other configuration item.

Examples

A requirement specification may be treated as a delivery, assembled from individual requirements each of which is under configuration management. This is illustrated in Figure 6–2. From the hardware-related world, a delivery may be assembled as illustrated in Figure 6–3.

Project Relationships

The relationships between configuration items in deliveries are purely for the purpose of release for use and configuration management. These relationships must not be confused with relationships established through planning or design, for example. The two kinds of relationships may in many instances be identical, and generic lists may be useful for both configuration management and other disciplines.

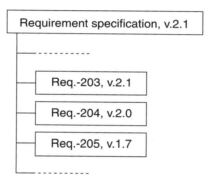

Figure 6–2 *Requirement Specification Delivery*

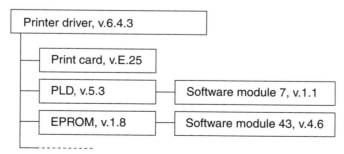

Figure 6–3 *Hardware-Related Delivery*

However, it's worth remembering—especially for a busy configuration manager—that the definition and communication of planning or design relationships are the responsibility of the project manager or the development manager respectively, not of the configuration manager.

6.6 DELIVERIES FOR PLANNED EVENTS LIKE MILESTONES

Development Model

A development model is a breakdown of the work for development, production, and maintenance of a product into smaller, limited activities. These activities follow each other in a predefined course. The classical waterfall model is an example of how a development model may be constructed. Another example is the iterative development model, where some of the activities are shorter but are repeated a number of times during the project life cycle.

No matter which development model one chooses for a given project, each activity should end with a milestone—a specific point with a specified outcome. One of the outcomes for a milestone should be a specific delivery: a milestone delivery. Other points during a project's life cycle may be planned and defined with an associated delivery.

Milestones

The number, names, and content of milestone deliveries depend on the project and the chosen development model. An example of milestones with associated milestone deliveries in a project following a waterfall model is

- Conclusion of preparations
- Conclusion of user requirements specification
- Conclusion of specification of software requirements
- Conclusion of architectural design
- Conclusion of detailed design
- Conclusion of coding and module test
- Conclusion of integration test
- Conclusion of system test
- Conclusion of acceptance test
- Final delivery

These deliveries will typically grow larger as the project progresses and new versions of earlier configuration items replace old ones, with changes rippling through to all affected items. Table 6–1 shows an example of milestone deliveries and their contents and development over time. The numbers shown for the configuration items are their respective version numbers.

The milestones in Table 6–1 are not identical to the activities already mentioned, partly for space reasons, partly to show that milestones may vary from project to project. Some of the configuration items in the deliveries are deliveries in their own right. For example, a subsystem may be a delivery consisting of several source code files and header files. For the sake of clarity, only the top deliveries are included in Table 6–1.

Table 6–1 Contents of Milestone Deliveries

Included Configuration Items	Milestone					
	Closing of Requirements	Closing of Architectural Design	Closing of Detailed Design	Closing of Module Test	Closing of System Test	Final Acceptance of System Test
Project plan	1.0	2.0	3.0	4.0	4.1	4.1
Configuration management plan	1.0	2.0	3.0	4.0	4.0	4.0
Test plan and test specification	1.0	2.0	3.0	4.5	5.2	6.3
Requirement specification	1.0	1.2	1.3	1.4	1.6	1.6
Architectural design	—	1.0	1.2	1.3	1.3	1.3
Detailed design	—	—	1.0	1.1	1.2	1.3
User manual	—	—	—	1.0	1.1	1.1
Subsystem 1	—	—	—	1.0	1.1	1.2
Subsystem 2	—	—	—	1.0	1.1	1.2
Compiler	—	—	—	4.3	4.3	4.3
Linker	—	—	—	7.2.5	7.2.5	7.2.6
Complete system	—	—	—	—	1.0	1.1
Release note	—	—	—	—	—	1.0

A dash indicates that the configuration item is not part of the delivery.

Chapter 7

What One Needs to Know about a Configuration Item

Each configuration item will have a certain amount of information attached to it that must be kept up during the item's lifetime. As the data involved in this are data for items under configuration management, we shall accordingly use the term *metadata* for the present purpose.

7.1 OVERVIEW OF METADATA FOR A CONFIGURATION ITEM

Data Elements

Figure 7–1 gives an overview of which data elements may form part of metadata for a configuration item—that is, the data that describe the configuration item. Data elements can be divided into these general groups:

- ◆ Unique identification
  - — The relation "belongs to" and
  - — All data pertaining only to the configuration item itself, as shown inside the "Configuration item" box in Figure 7–1
- ◆ Authorization
  - — The relations "produced by," "under responsibility of," and "approval by"

◆ Relations to other configuration items
  — The relations "traces to," "produced with," "derived from," and "consists of"
◆ Distribution
  — The relations "may be distributed to" and "has been distributed to"

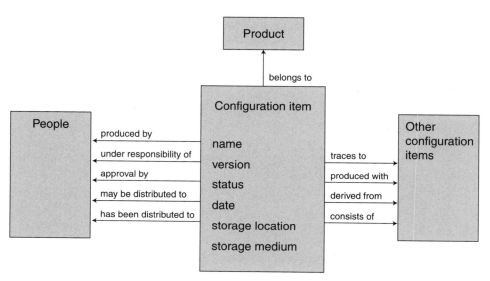

Figure 7–1 *Overview of Metadata*

The data elements in each of these groups are treated in detail in the following sections.

Metadatabase Medium

The registration of metadata may be carried out in different ways and in different media. Metadata for a configuration item may also spread over several media. Earlier, it was common to perform the registration on paper. This means that a form was filled in, stored, and kept up-to-date for each configuration item. This is not so common today, where databases are widely used for registration.

Part of the registration may take place in the configuration item itself. As an example, the author's name is often written on the front page of documents or in the header in code files. Part of the registration may also take place in the tool used for storage of the configuration item. But tools do not always make it possible to register all necessary metadata.

The most important thing is to consider which types of information should be registered and in which ways, as well as how the information can be procured for status reporting. It might be a good idea to use databases or the like instead of stating information directly in files, although it may seem a bit more burdensome. As a rule, it's easier to generate a report from a database than by reading through a (possibly) large number of files with statements in free text.

Other Data Elements

A configuration item may have relevant data elements to register other than those shown above. This may be full name, if a more descriptive name is needed than the one required for unique identification, or it may be a description, if more information is needed. Special information may be needed, in connection with variants or the like. This is treated in Part IV, where it's relevant. The data elements mentioned above are those that are strictly necessary from the point of view of configuration management.

7.2 METADATA FOR UNIQUE IDENTIFICATION

Every configuration item must have a unique identification, which may be made up of one or more of the data elements shown in Figure 7–2.

Belongs To

"Belongs to" is an indication of the overall affiliation of the configuration item. A configuration item will typically belong to a product. In some cases, configuration items may belong to several products jointly, such as in component development. In these cases, the affiliation must indicate that the configuration item belongs to a component assortment.

Name

The name of a configuration item may be built up in many ways. Typically, it will be some combination of text, type, and running number, written together or separated according to given conventions. Table 7–1 describes each of these parts.

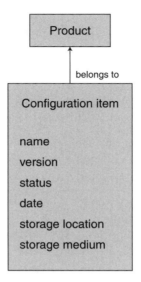

Figure 7–2 *Metadata for Unique Identification*

Table 7–1 *Configuration Item Name Parts and Their Functions*

Part	Function
Text	The text may be a mnemonic or an acronym describing where the configuration item belongs and its function. For code objects, the text will typically function as part of the unique identification, consisting of the general component with a short indication of the purpose of the code object (e.g., CUS_ADD for a code object involved in handling customers' addresses).
Type	The type indicates the product type of the configuration item. Type descriptions may be set at a general level such as DOC for documents or COD for code objects. Type descriptions may also refer to a more detailed level, such as PMP for "Project Management Plan" or PSC for code objects written in Pascal. It's particularly important to specify the type if this is the only difference between configuration items. This will be the case if, for example, two otherwise identical documents are written in Word and WordPerfect.
Running number	The running number distinguishes between configuration items of the same type. This is not the version number for a configuration item but individual numbers. Technical notes might, for example, be identified as TN_nnnn, where TN_ is the type description and nnnn is the running number.

Version

The version expresses the historical development of a configuration item. Version information might be the only way to distinguish between two configuration items, because each version is regarded as a separate configuration item. When a new configuration item is developed on the basis of an item already in existence, all other parts of the unique identification will often be inherited.

Information on version may contain several strata, depending on the degree of detail one wishes to maintain. Moreover, there are many ways to designate and express information on the strata.

To give an everyday example: for books, one would normally mention edition and issue. Presently, I am reading a book with the specification "1st edition, 5th issue." In this case, the information on version is a description in two strata, separated by a comma. For the tool used in writing the present book, the information on version is expressed as version 2.30.07.DK. This is a description in four strata, separated by periods: the first stratum consists of one number, the next two consist of two two-digit numbers, and the last is a two-letter designation (or so it appears).

Status

Status expresses the present state of the configuration item. It might be necessary to make status part of the item's identification if items are brought under configuration management before everybody can rely on them or if identification is undertaken before the item is brought under configuration management.

Status may enter into the version designation—for example, "dA" for draft A of a document, corresponding to the status "under quality assurance." Similarly, with other types of configuration items, one might use version numbers with decimals for those only the producer can use (typically a piece of source code), while version numbers without decimals may designate items everybody can use.

It's the decision of the individual organization when an item should be identified and when it should be brought under configuration management, and, accordingly, how status conventions are to be defined. Examples of status codes can be seen in Table 7–2.

Date

Date means version date. This expresses when the configuration item has been created. In most cases, registration of the version date cannot be undertaken until the configuration item is placed in storage.

Storage Location

Storage location tells where the configuration item is to be found physically. This will make it easier to find the item. Storage location may be implicitly specified somewhere else, such as a general directory structure on a server described in the configuration management plan for all items of a certain type. Storage location will then be expressed in the complete path and file name of electronic configuration items in which the unique identification may—to some extent or wholly—form part.

Storage location can also be indirectly specified, as part of the name. This may have the form of a classification, as is the case with public library books. Storage place may also be of a physical nature: a shelf in a cupboard in a room in a . . . , and so on.

Storage Medium

The same considerations apply as described for storage location.

Example of States for a Document

Some examples of typical states for a document:

- ◆ **Under preparation:** identification has been undertaken, but the item is not yet under configuration management—it cannot be used by anybody else but the producer, and events are not registered (version control).
- ◆ **Under quality assurance:** the item is under configuration management but can be used only for quality assurance activities (e.g., review). Events are registered.
- ◆ **Approved:** the item has been approved via relevant quality assurance activities and may be used by everybody. Events are registered.

Example of States for a Source Code Unit, Including in Build

Table 7–2 shows an example of states for a source code unit during its development. The status codes are described in the following paragraphs. Table 7–2 also includes a description of who is responsible for the unit at any given time—the authority needed to progress a unit or a build though the life cycle.

Table 7–2 *Source Code Unit State Examples*

Activity/State	Unit Status	Responsible
Development, ongoing	Busy	Developer
Development, pausing	Saved	Developer
Unit CI in "useful" state	Proposed	Developer
Unit undergoing formal unit test	Proposed	Approver signature
Formal unit test ready for approval	Proposed	Developer
Formal unit test is approved	Proposed	Approver signature
Formal unit release established	Published	Configuration management
Build undergoing formal integration	Proposed	Integrator
Formal integration test is ready for approval	Proposed	Integrator
Formal integration test is approved	Proposed	Test manager signature
Formal build release established	Published	Configuration management

The statuses a unit may have are

Busy. Ensures version control, so no one else inadvertently starts to modify the same source file.

Saved. Shows that the version is private to the developer.

Proposed. Shows that the version is in a state useful to other developers. Only versions with status "proposed" (or higher) may be used in official unit tests.

Published. Shows that the version has been unit-tested and that the unit test has been formally approved.

Accessed. Shows that the version has taken part in an officially approved integration test.

Frozen. Shows that the version has been part of an official release.

7.3 METADATA FOR AUTHORIZATION

Authorization expresses who can do what and who has done what to a configuration item. Authorization may consist of the data elements shown in Figure 7–3.

Typically, a software project will have three types of authorization, expressed by the relations "produced by," "under the responsibility of," and "approval by." In some cases, there may be more. The names of the people authorized must be registered, and signatures and dates may be registered as a formal documentation that the tasks in question have been solved.

It's up to each organization to define conventions for authorization. Often a contract may, to some extent at least, express how authorization is defined. A contract may demand that the customer have a representative in the group responsible for approval of requirement specification documents as well as for the whole system.

Producer

The producer or producers are responsible for producing the item and placing it under configuration management. The producer may also be the person(s) producing new versions on the basis of change requests. For source code, the producer will typically be the programmer. For documents, it will typically be the author or authors—designers in the case of a design document or the project manager in the case of a project plan.

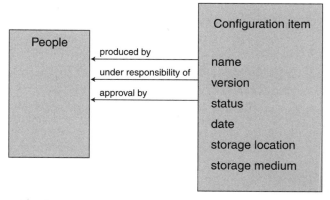

Figure 7–3 *Metadata for Authorization*

The Person Holding Overall Responsibility

The person holding overall responsibility has final responsibility for the correct production and delivery of the configuration item in the project in which the item is produced. It may be the project manager or the product manager, or it may be a group leader under a project manager or the person responsible for test.

The Person Responsible for Approval

The person responsible for approval may be the producer in the informal or early activities of configuration management; it may be the person responsible for quality in configuration management with a higher level of formalism; or it may be a group of stakeholders when configuration management is carried out with a high level of formalism. The person responsible for approval may be identical to a configuration control board, which is responsible for the approval of any changes to a configuration item and in some cases also for determining that an item is ready for configuration management.

Ownership

In some contexts, the concept of ownership of a configuration management item is employed. This is often an expression of who may extract an item for production—that is, who can make changes to it. Ownership may be given to the producer or the person responsible, but under all circumstances it should be the configuration control board that decides who can make changes to an item (produce a new version) when it has been placed under configuration management.

7.4 METADATA FOR RELATIONS TO OTHER CONFIGURATION ITEMS

Practically all configuration items have one or more relations to other items. These relations will typically be described by the data elements shown in Figure 7–4. There may also be relations to items that are not configuration items. In these cases, registration may become more difficult, especially if these items do not have a unique identification. This must be taken into account when considering which items to place under configuration management and how items not placed under configuration management should be treated.

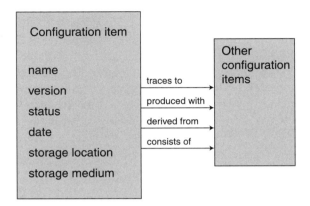

Figure 7–4 *Metadata for Relations to Other Configuration Items*

Traces To (and From!)

Information carried in the traces to a configuration item provides the reason for the item's being the item it is, such as its wording, shape, or design. Tracing refers to items from preceding activities in the development, on which the configuration item is based. Often, the project plan will indicate which configuration items must be traced to each other. Tracing may, for example, be carried out in accordance with the V-model:

◆ Software requirements are traced to user requirements.

◆ Acceptance test specifications are traced to user requirements.

◆ Architectural design is traced to software requirements.

◆ System test specifications are traced to software requirements.

◆ Detailed design is traced to architectural design and software requirements.

   and so on . . .

This is only a minor extract of all the tracing possibilities a product may hold. In principle, it must be possible to trace all configuration items to preceding configuration items. However, the first configuration item produced cannot be traced to anything. Figure 7–5 illustrates the tracing between a requirement specification document and a system test specification.

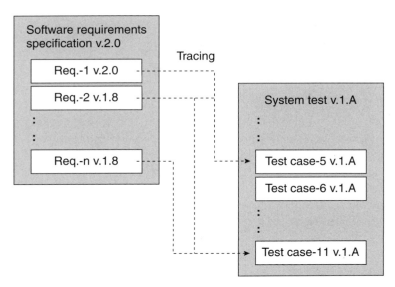

Figure 7–5 *Example of Tracing*

Tracing Registration

Tracing is often a many-to-many relation. The prerequisite for being able to trace is that configuration items have a unique identification that does not change, is easy to reference (short and simple), and is accessible (visible and easy to copy for the person producing the tracing information).

Tracing must be registered in a way that makes it possible to report tracing in both directions. This means that it should be possible to find out which test cases a specific software requirement is traced to and which software requirements a specific test case is traced to. It should also be possible to find out which software requirements do not have traces to at least one test case, and vice versa.

A new version of a configuration item will typically inherit the traces of the previous version. This tracing should be controlled, so that the tracing is maintained and remains correct for all versions.

Importance of Tracing

Tracing is a part of registration that is often neglected, because it's regarded as a big and almost impossible task. This might be the case, and it may be especially difficult to introduce tracing in the middle of a project. However, it is often possible to undertake some kind of reverse engineering to procure trace information for already completed configuration items.

Tracing is immensely important for the people who produce configuration items and especially for those who change them. The quality will improve when people understand the relations between the items within a system—the purpose and historical background of a given configuration item.

Moreover, tracing may reveal if something has been forgotten, or if gold plating has been done (something incorporated without anything to substantiate it). This is a way to keep costs in check. If nothing else, requirements should at least be traced to implementation and test-related configuration items.

Tracing may also be used to double-check the design. If one requirement traces to a large number of design items, it may be a sign of a design that is too complex and needs going over again.

Produced With

"Produced with" is a statement of which tool has been used in the production of the configuration item, so that the same tool may be used for future changes. It's not always considered necessary to place tools under configuration management or to register which tool a given configuration item is produced with. For delivery configuration items, it may be convenient to express what has been used (e.g., a make-file) to assemble the configuration item for release to usage. In this way, the "made with" information may be combined with the "consists of" information.

Derived From

"Derived from" expresses the history of the configuration item. As a rule, the history is seen partly in the inheritance of parts of the unique identification and partly in the change of version designation according to given conventions. "Derived from" must be expressed only if the name has been changed from one version to the next.

Consists Of

Only composite configuration items (deliveries) consist of other configuration items. A code module does not consist of other configuration items, but a software requirement release may consist of a project plan, user requirement specification, software requirement specification, and system test plan.

The most practical thing is to express which configuration items a given item consists of rather than which ones it belongs to. This will normally make it easier to assemble a composite configuration item for release to usage. The items a delivery configuration item consists of should be expressed precisely, so status can be taken into consideration when assembling the item, rather than just assembling it with the latest available version.

Information under "Consists of" will often be inherited from another version of a configuration item, and here it's important to note that the composition may change from one version to another. Items may have been eliminated from one delivery version to the next. Consequently, these items must also be eliminated from the information under "Consists of."

7.5 METADATA FOR DISTRIBUTION

Information on distribution may consist of the data elements shown in Figure 7–6.

May Be Distributed To

"May be distributed to" may be necessary for classified configuration items. It may be expressed explicitly (as a list of names) or implicitly (as in "for internal use only").

Has Been Distributed To

"Has been distributed to" will be registered following a release request. Obviously, this can not happen until the configuration item is being released from storage to usage. This information may include a registration of why release has taken place—for

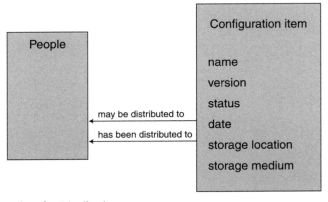

Figure 7–6 *Metadata for Distribution*

example, whether the purpose was review, integration test, or the release of an entire system to a customer. This information is especially important for products related to food and drugs (control software for production of drugs or medical equipment).

This information may be registered only after a certain point in the life cycle of a configuration item: after it has reached a state where it may be used externally. It may also be that this information is registered only for certain types of delivery configuration items, such as entire systems, and not for individual items or smaller deliveries for internal use.

Chapter 8

What One Must Register for a Configuration Item

This chapter describes administrative work concerning configuration items. It's not necessarily paperwork in the sense of filling in and storing heaps of forms, but the process must be accompanied by documentation.

8.1 ITEM APPROVAL

Item approval is evidence that items satisfy the criteria for placing under configuration management. This is not necessarily final approval of the object as being ready for release to, say, a customer, but rather the approval needed before the object is placed under configuration management. Another purpose may be to communicate metadata to the person who is to register metadata for the configuration item, such as the librarian, if these metadata are not communicated otherwise.

Quality Approval

Item approval forms an interface between configuration management and quality assurance. Item approval is (or should be) a result of quality assurance activities for an item, intended for use by the person responsible for configuration management or the librarian in connection with placing the item under configuration management. The relationship is shown in Figure 8–1.

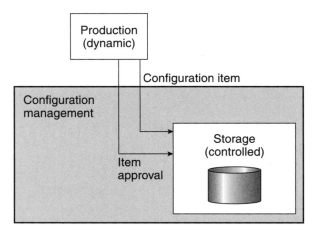

Figure 8–1 *Item Approval in Context*

Medium

An item approval will typically be a form; either paper based or electronic. An electronic item approval may be communicated as e-mail. In some cases, however, it may be a paper-based original of the configuration item, signed by the people involved and kept in a controlled physical library.

Content

An item approval should contain these data elements:

- ◆ Configuration item concerned
- ◆ Dated signatures (electronic or other) by the producer, the person responsible, and the approver
- ◆ Condition(s) for approval
- ◆ Related metadata

Configuration Item

The configuration item to which the approval applies must be indicated by full unique identification. In some cases, this identification, or parts of it, may be generated only in connection with placement in storage. If so, this must be apparent from the item approval.

Signatures

Those involved in production and approval of the item should sign the item approval. Signatures may be regarded as too formal, but some means of registration of authorization of approval should be considered. Electronic approvals and signatures may be desirable, but if this possibility doesn't exist, item approval must be paper based.

Condition(s) for Approval

Conditions of item approval depend totally on circumstances. Factors influencing the conditions are the type of configuration item, the quality assurance activities needed, and the item's status. To give some examples: the conditions for approving a draft document may be that the nearest superiors of the author have reviewed it and handed in a review report to quality assurance, and, moreover, that the author has revised the document in accordance with the review report. The conditions of approving source code may be that a documented and reported module test has been carried through with an achieved minimum coverage and that the code does not contain any known errors.

Metadata

Each company must consider how metadata not registered under identification can be communicated by the producer in connection with placement in storage. Such data elements may with advantage be registered on an item approval. This may be information on what the configuration item has been produced with or exactly which parts a delivery consists of.

Examples

This section contains two examples of item approvals: one for a configuration management system with a low degree of formalism and one for a high degree of formalism. In systems of the lowest formality, a simple library tool (for version control or the like) may provide item approval automatically in a transaction log, as a record of insertion in the controlled library.

Low Degree of Formalism

Figure 8–2 shows e-mail used as approval registration. The recipient is a central account associated with the system (here System1). All project members may access the account, and e-mails may be sorted by sender, date, or subject to produce various overviews of the information. Entering additional information in the text field may be required, as appropriate.

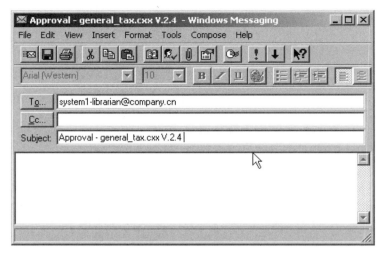

Figure 8–2 *Mail Message Used as Approval Registration*

High Degree of Formalism

Figure 8–3 shows a unit approval form that follows each unit during its life cycle in a large, high-formality project. It may be used for signatures to document a unit's progress through its life cycle. At the same time, it may serve as a checklist for various approvals in the life cycle.

8.2 RELEASE REQUEST

The purpose of a release request is to document what is released from the configuration management library, and to whom. A release request forms the interface between the controlled library (the configuration management library) and the surrounding world. The person responsible for configuration management or the librarian should use it as the basis for releasing configuration items for usage. The relationship is shown in Figure 8–4.

Medium

A release request may be a form, either paper based or electronic. An electronic release request may be communicated as e-mail. Release requests are, however, often communicated by word of mouth. This is acceptable if the metadata registers to whom the item has been released (for items where such registration is necessary).

Unit Approval Form		
Unit Name		
Version (n.m)		
Developer		
Approver		
Unit Approval Cycle		
Unit ready for Test Readiness Review		
Conditions	All code statements covered by unit test:	
	If No – state coverage and reason:	
	Dry run has been performed after new build:	
Remarks		
Developer's Signature		Date
Unit ready for Unit Test		
Conditions	The guidelines in the Test Plan are followed:	
	A dry run of the test has been performed after new build:	
	Files necessary for performing the unit test are available and under CM (all dependencies + others):	
	Valid reason for coverage of less than 100 %:	
	(i.e., the benefit of the test is not comparable to the costs related to creating it)	
	Statements not covered by the test have been verified by inspection:	
Remarks		
Approver's Signature		Date
Unit Test Approved, Unit Ready for Storage		
Conditions	The test script, test report, and other files are available and ready to place under CM:	
	The test results are as expected:	
	The dependency files are marked according to the performed test:	
	Change Requests, if any, are closed; see attached list:	
Remarks		
Librarian's Signature		Date

Figure 8–3 *Unit Approval Form—High Degree of Formalism*

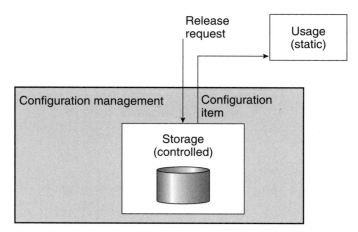

Figure 8–4 *Release Request in Context*

Content

A release request should contain these data elements:

- Configuration item concerned
- Dated signature(s) by requester or requesters
- If desired, dated signature by the person responsible
- Reason for release request
- Delivery medium and/or destination

The first three items are the same as for the approved item described above.

Reason

It might in some cases, but far from all, be useful to register why release has taken place. Often, the use made of the item will be implied in who the requester is.

Delivery Medium and/or Destination

This indicates the way a given configuration item is to be delivered (a paper copy, burned on a CD, or copied onto a specific area on a specific computer).

Stock Control

For physical configuration items—as opposed to electronic ones, which can be copied endlessly without damaging the original—configuration management may overlap with stock control. Stock control implies, among other things, controlling the number of copies delivered and at one's disposal. In such cases, the interfaces must be agreed on. This means that one must decide whether release should take place via stock control—which is then reported to configuration management—or vice versa.

Examples

This section contains two examples of release requests—one for a configuration management system with a low degree of formalism and one for a high degree of formalism. As with item approvals, a simple library tool may serve this function for systems of the lowest formality.

Low Degree of Formalism

Figure 8–5 shows an e-mail used as registration of a release request. The recipient is a central account associated with the system (here System1). All project members may access the account, and e-mails may be sorted by sender, date, or subject to produce various overviews of the information. Entering additional information in the text field may be required, as appropriate.

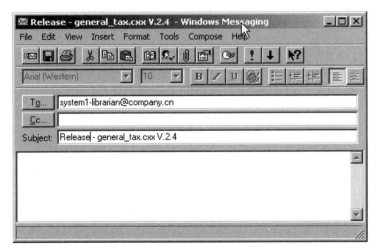

Figure 8–5 *Mail Message Used as Release Registration*

High Degree of Formalism

Figure 8–6 shows a Release Request Form. It may be used for registering to whom a configuration item has been released, and why, how, and when.

Release Request Form		
Configuration Item Name		
Version		
Type	Single / Delivery	
Delivery Medium or Destination		
Requester		
Name(s) of Requester(s)		
Remarks		
Main Requester's Signature		Date
Release Information		
Release	Release approved:	
	If No – state reason:	
	Release Note created:	
Delivery	Components list created:	
	Complete delivery controlled:	
Remarks		
Librarian's Signature		Date

Figure 8–6 *Release Request Form—High Degree of Formalism*

8.3 EVENT REGISTRATION

There are various types of events:

- A review observation for a document
- A waiver (a statement that a customer waives a given requirement)
- An error report from a test run
- An inquiry to a helpdesk concerning a finished product already in operation

Some events may be planned (the first on a list), while others cannot (the last on a list). Event registrations are input to change control.

Life Cycle and Responsibility

An event must go through a defined life cycle. Typical event phases may be

- Created
- For evaluation by the producer of the affected configuration item
- Under decision by the configuration control board
- Under change in accordance with change request(s) attached to the event
- Closed

The general responsibility for driving an event through its life cycle lies with the configuration control board. It may hand over the responsibility, for example, to the person responsible for development, the author, or the tester. This general responsibility is not included in the event registration, as it's a management decision on a higher level.

No matter which phases are defined for an event, phase information must be registered successively as the event runs through each phase. It may be practical to save the registration history for an event registration—information on the phases the event has gone through and the time of those phases—and not just overwrite the earlier phase, date, and time when a new phase is started.

It may also be practical to keep the possibility open for an iterative course, so that phases may be run through several times. For instance, the configuration control board may send an event back to evaluation by the producer. The phases mentioned above must be regarded as the minimum course.

Content

There are numerous ways to frame an event registration. No matter which way is chosen, it should contain the following data elements:

- ◆ Configuration item concerned
- ◆ Information about the event: identification, event type, and short title
- ◆ Phase information for the event: phase, date and time, name of person responsible, name(s) of other people involved, description, and classification

Configuration Item

The configuration item in which the event is found must be indicated as precisely as possible—preferably with the unique identification. If the item is a delivery, the delivery should be identified, if the person who has observed the event cannot immediately identify the precise single item to which the event is attached.

Identification

Each event registration must have a unique identification. This will typically be a number in a specified series—one series per product, project, or event type (or some combination).

Event Type

A company may choose to carry out event registrations in different ways and with different content, according to the type of event, such as paper-based review observations and error reports from tests in one database and communications with helpdesk in another. It is also possible to make type information part of the content. Event types may be review or inspection, test (which may be separated into module test, integration test, and accept test), internal use, and customers' use (production).

Title

An event registration must be given a short, informative title. This will give an easy general overview, such as in lists, over outstanding or corrected errors.

Phase Indication

A phase indication or equivalent status code will show where in the life cycle a given event registration is or was at a given time. The phases or status codes that have been defined and that must be used should be expressed as unambiguously as possible. This may be as a section heading on a form or as an entry on a selection list in a database.

Date and Time

The meaning of this data element is the same for all phases: the point at which a phase is started or a certain status has been attained. This must be expressed as precisely as possible—in any case, at least as a date. It may be appropriate, for the sake of metrics concerning elapsed time, to express the status time with greater accuracy.

Created

In this phase, the rest of the data elements may have the meanings shown in Table 8–1.

Table 8–1 *Data Elements for Event Registration in the Creation Phase*

Data Element	Meaning
Name of the responsible person	The name of the person who has created the event registration. It may be the observer, but it may also be a person at a helpdesk.
Name of observer	The name of the person who has observed the error, such as a customer or a test consultant.
Description	The description must contain a comprehensive description of the event itself and its circumstances, so the event can be reproduced or immediately understood. Reference to other information should be possible, such as screen dumps or the precise time of the event. The description may also contain a data element for a suggested solution.
Classification	Classification will be provisional, based on the data supplier's view of the situation.

For Evaluation

In this phase, the rest of the data elements may have the meanings shown in Table 8–2. As for the estimated time required to solve any problems, a checklist for assessing the effects of any changes may be found in Chapter 1.

Under Decision

In this phase, the rest of the data elements may have the meanings shown in Table 8–3.

Table 8–2 *Data Elements for Event Registration in the Evaluation Phase*

Data Element	Meaning
Name of the responsible person	The name of the person who must take care that evaluation is carried out. This will typically be the project manager, group manager, or the like.
Name of information supplier	This will typically be the producer or some other person with equivalent expert knowledge of the affected configuration item.
Description	This may be divided into these data elements: ◆ Suggested solution ◆ Workaround for the problem, if any ◆ Affected configuration items ◆ Other affected objects ◆ Estimated time for effecting the solution
Classification	Classification will be provisional, based on the information supplier's view of the situation.

Table 8–3 *Data Elements for Event Registration in the Decision Phase*

Data Element	Meaning
Name of the responsible person	The name of the person who must take care that a decision is reached. This will typically be the person who is responsible for configuration management or the project manager.
Name of information supplier	This must be the configuration control board for the item in question.
Description	A short argument for the decision that has been reached. The decision will be shown in the subsequent phases, which may be ◆ To be changed ◆ To be closed as a duplication of . . . ◆ Rejected ◆ Postponed to . . .
Classification	This will be the final classification made on the basis of a closer assessment of the event.

Under Change

In this phase, the event is transferred to the change request(s) the configuration control board has created to make changes. The person responsible for this phase will typically be the project manager or a group manager. The rest of the data elements have no relevance for this phase.

Closed

In this phase, the event is closed. This may happen as a consequence of approval of all attached change requests or of rejection of the event. The configuration control board will be responsible. Further data elements have no relevance for this phase, unless one wishes to give a reason for the closing of the event here. It may, moreover, be appropriate to indicate when information has been given back to the person or people who once observed the event.

Classification

Events may be classified according to these classes: omission, gold plating, fault (which may be divided into several categories or types as required), inappropriateness, enhancement request, not reproducible, and information (not a fault). Many examples of classification and taxonomy of errors are given in the literature.

Examples

This section contains two examples of event registration forms—one for a configuration management system with a low degree of formalism and one for a high degree of formalism. In systems of the lowest formality, e-mail may be used to communicate events.

Low Degree of Formalism

Figure 8–7 shows an Excel workbook used to register and follow events. All project members may access the workbook, and event entries may be sorted by any of the columns to produce various overviews of the information. The file e1.doc may contain a further explanation of the event, possibly including screen dumps.

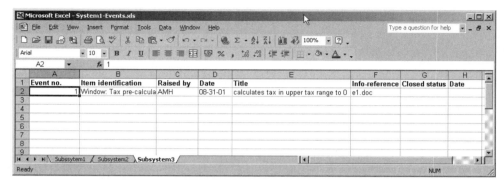

Figure 8–7 *Excel Workbook Used for Event Registrations—Low Degree of Formalism*

High Degree of Formalism

Figure 8–8 shows an event registration form. It may be used to follow each event during its life cycle and for signatures for documentation of progress. Since the life cycle of events can be complicated, a procedure describing the life cycle and how to register information is useful.

Event registration today will seldom be on paper. Many good tools, some even freeware, will handle event registration, and it's also fairly easy to make one's own system with modern office tools, such as Access. In some cases, such as with remote users, it may be necessary to first create event registration on paper and later transfer the information to a system. Figure 8–8 gives an idea of the information to collect for an event and may also serve as inspiration for the layout of a full event report.

8.4 CHANGE REQUEST

Change requests derive from event registrations. An event registration always gives rise to a change request for each of the configuration items to be changed—even though the same change will be implemented two different places. An event registration must not be closed until all change requests have been approved. It may look as illustrated in Figure 8–9.

Event registration and change requests are frequently combined, so that information belonging to the change request is registered directly in the event registration. Although this may seem more efficient, it really isn't, because it makes it more difficult to track changes. It's a good idea to always make both an event registration and a change request, even if they have a one-to-one relationship, because it's then

Event Registration Form	
Event Number	
Short Title	
Configuration Item Name	
Version	
Type	Single / Delivery

Event Life Cycle			
Status = Created			
Registration created by		Date & time	
Event observed by		Date & time	
Comprehensive observation description	Include references to attachments, if any.		
Event observed during	Requirement review / Design / Design review / Coding / Code review / Module test / Integration test / System test / Alpha test / Beta test / Production / Other:		
User's classification	Fatal / Serious / Annoying / Negligible / Other:		
Status = For evaluation			
Event forwarded for evaluation by		Date & time	
Event evaluated by		Date & time	
Evaluator's classification	Error / Omission / Misunderstanding / Enhancement / Not reproducible / Duplication of: / Other:		
Comprehensive solution description, if applicable	Include references to attachments, if any.		
Other affected configuration items — state effect			
Estimated correction effort			

Figure 8–8 *Full Event Life Cycle Registration Form—High Degree of Formalism (continues)*

Estimated retest and regression test effort			
Fault created during	Requirement specification / Design / Coding / Other:		
Workaround description, if any	Include references to attachments, if any.		
Status = Under decision			
Event forwarded for decision by		Date & time	
CCB decided		Date & time	
CCB's decision	To be corrected / Rejected / Postponed		
Change priority	Immediate change / High / Medium / Low / Lowest		
Rejection reason			
Postponed until			
Event observer informed by		Date	
Status = Under Change			
Change request(s) opened by		Date & time	
All change requests accepted/closed by		Date & time	
Total actual change effort			
Total actual test effort			
CCB's decision	To be closed / To be reevaluated / To be recorrected		
Status = Closed			
Conditions — if applicable	All new configuration items correctly identified		
	All new configuration items properly stored		
	All stakeholders informed of new configuration items		
Remarks			
Event observer informed by		Date	
CCB Signature		Date	

Figure 8-8 *Full Event Life Cycle Registration Form—High Degree of Formalism (continued)*

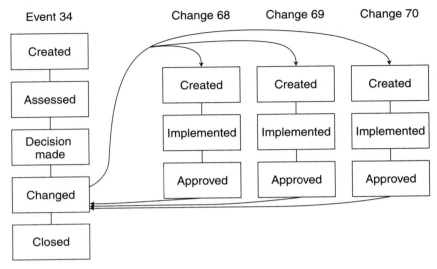

Figure 8–9 *Change Requests Derived from an Event Registration*

no problem to trace when a one-to-many relationship occurs. The former are more frequent at the beginning of a project. The further in the life cycle, the more complex the items and, hence, the more frequent the one-to-many relationships. In informal contexts, change requests may also arise spontaneously. In any case, all corrections must be documented.

Life Cycle and Responsibility

A change must go through a defined life cycle, as indicated above. Typical phases may be creation, implementation, and approval.

Content

A change request should contain these data elements:

- The change: identification, identification of the underlying event, configuration item concerned, and priority
- Phase information for the change: phase, date and time, name of the person responsible, description

Identification

Every change request must have a unique identification; this will typically be a number in a specified series.

Event

Every change request must have a unique reference to the event registration that caused it.

Configuration Item

Every change request must have a unique reference to the configuration item it concerns. A change request should never have more than one item attached to it, unless it can be ensured that this does not make registration and reporting of progress unnecessarily difficult.

A change request always gives rise to the identification of a new configuration item in which the change must be implemented—typically a new version of the item to be changed. This reference may be to the new as well as the old item and must be as precise as possible—preferably with the unique identification of the configuration item(s).

Priority

Every change request should be given a defined priority, such as a number on a scale from 1 to 5, with 1 as the highest priority, or indications like "Immediate," "Urgent," and "Convenience." It's important to specify the indications of priority used and to define their meanings clearly.

Phase Indication

See the description in the previous section.

Date and Time

See the description in the previous section.

Created

In this phase, the rest of the data elements may have the meanings shown in Table 8–4.

Implemented

In this phase, the rest of the data elements may have the meaning shown in Table 8–5.

Table 8–4 *Data Elements for a Change Request in the Creation Phase*

Data Element	Meaning
Name of the responsible person	The name of the person responsible for the whole change request; this will typically be the project manager or a group manager.
Description	A description, as exhaustive as possible, of the required change. This may also contain an estimate of the resources required to carry out the change, such as in calendar time or man-hours

Table 8–5 *Data Elements for a Change Request in the Implementation Phase*

Data Element	Meaning
Name of the responsible person	The name of the person responsible for implementation of the change in the configuration item concerned
Description	A description, as exhaustive as possible, of the change that has been made. This should contain a precise indication, given in the same unit of measurement as the estimate, of the resources required to implement the change.

Approved

In this phase, the change has been approved and is accordingly closed. The person responsible for this phase will be the person who has approved the correct implementation of the change. This may be the person responsible for test or quality assurance. This description may be important, especially if the change is not approved and the change request is sent back into the life cycle.

New Events

It may happen that while carrying out a change, one comes across new events. One may find mistakes in the configuration item being worked on or in other related items. These events must be registered just like all other events, with the type "internal" or the like.

Examples

This section contains two examples of change registration forms, one for a configuration management system with a low degree of formalism and one for a high degree of formalism. In systems of the lowest formality, e-mail may be used to communicate change requests based on events.

Low Degree of Formalism

Figure 8–10 shows an Excel workbook used to register and follow change requests derived from events. All project members may access the book, and change entries may be sorted by any of the columns to produce various overviews of the information. The file c1.doc may contain a further explanation of the change.

High Degree of Formalism

Figure 8–11 shows a change request form. A form should be used to follow each accepted change during its life cycle and can be used for signatures for documentation of progress. Since the life cycle of changes may be quite complicated, a procedure describing the life cycle and how to register information is useful.

As in the case of event registration, a change request today will seldom be on paper. Figure 8–11 gives an idea of what information to collect and communicate for a change to be implemented and may also serve as inspiration for the layout of a full change request report.

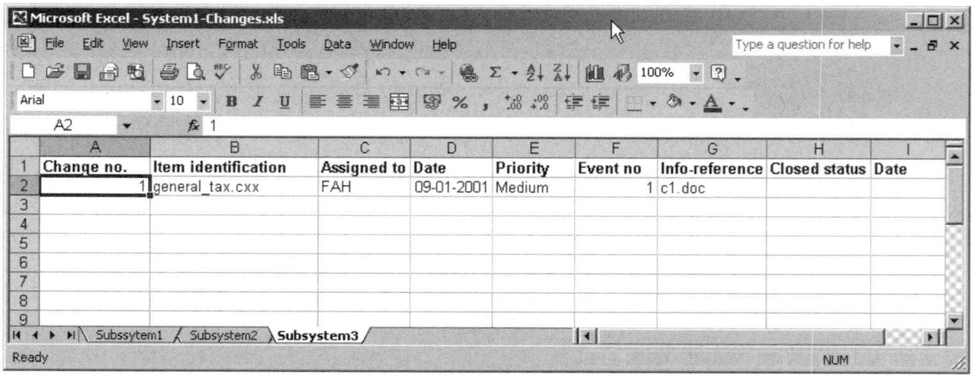

Change no.	Item identification	Assigned to	Date	Priority	Event no	Info-reference	Closed status	Date
1	general_tax.cxx	FAH	09-01-2001	Medium	1	c1.doc		

Figure 8–10 *Excel Workbook Used for Change Request Registrations*

Change Request Form		
Change Number		
Related Event Registration		
Configuration Item Name		
Version		
Priority	Immediate / Urgent / ASAP / Convenience	
Change Life Cycle		
Status = Created		
Request created by		Date & time
Comprehensive description of requested change	Include references to attachments, if any.	
Estimated change effort		
Status = Implemented		
Change implemented by		Date & time
Comprehensive solution description	Include references to attachments, if any.	
Actual change effort		
Implementer's Signature		Date
Status = Approved		
		Date & time
Remarks		
Approver's Signature		Date

Figure 8–11 *Change Request Life Cycle Registration Form—High Degree of Formalism*

Chapter 9

What Information Is Available for Configuration Items

The result of status reporting is the production of required status reports. Each company will have to decide, possibly for each project, which reports it wishes to produce. It's important in defining metadata to try to imagine what status reports will be needed and hence which data to collect.

9.1 EXAMPLES

Examples of report types are given below, but many other types could be produced. In these examples, the format has been changed to fit the format of this book. XX is the acronym for the product. Where applicable, the user requirement document is XX_URS.doc, _URS is the type acronym for a user requirement specification, and .doc is the file type.

Release Note

Figure 9–1 shows a release note for a delivery configuration item. The example in Figure 9–2 is downloaded from the Internet and shows an ongoing release note for a product.

Release: XX_URS.doc, v.3.0

Date of issue: 10-31-97

Previous released version: 2.0

Responsible: POL

The following changes have been implemented since the last release version:

Change Request	Where	Responsible	Comments
XX_CR_105	Page 54	FAH	Req. 10.4.1.5 Reworded
XX-CR_109	Page 106	FAH	Req. 10.6.2.10 Split in two
XX_CR_110	Page 106	FAH	Req. 10.6.2.11 Removed
XX_CR_116	Page 223	FAH	Req. 11.3.4.7 Reworded

Figure 9–1 *Release Note Example 1*

[10 Sep 2000] PGP 7.0 released

NAI has released PGP Desktop Security 7.0 for Windows and MacOS. This is a commercial release. A freeware version is expected soon. Stay tuned…

[2 Sep 2000] PGP 6.5.8 command line available for download

PGP 6.5.8 command line is now available for Windows NT/2000 and for various Unix platforms.

[25 Aug 2000] PGP 6.5.8 available for download

PGP 6.5.8 has just been released, and is available for download now (Windows & Macintosh). This release fixes a nasty bug in PGP 5.5.x and 6.x regarding the ADK (Additional Decryption Key) feature. For more information on the ADK bug, see the CERT advisory and the security advisory from NAI.

Figure 9–2 *Release Note Example 2*

Item Status List

Figure 9–3 shows a status report for a configuration item.

Item History List

Figure 9–4 shows a history report for a configuration item. The table in the figure shows the history for a user requirement specification for a given product.

Item Composition List

Figure 9–5 shows a composition report for a configuration item. The item is a delivery, itself composed of several subdeliveries. The report breaks each subdelivery down into individual configuration items. Only an extract is shown.

Status: XX_URS.doc

Report date: 10-20-97 18:02

Newest version: 3.dB

Release date: 10-19-97

Responsible: FAH

Distribution:

To	Purpose	Date	Responsible
Review-board	Official review	10-20-97	HIL

Outstanding Event Registrations:

Event Registration	Status	Date	Responsible	Change R.
XX_ER_135	Decided	20-10-97	PET	XX_CR_133

Outstanding Change Requests:

Change Request	Status	Date	Responsible
XX_CR_133	Coded	10-20-97	FJG

Figure 9–3 *Item Status List*

History: XX_BKS.doc

ER: Event registrations   **CR:** Change request

Version	Status	Date	Respons.	Released	ER	CR
1.dA	Draft	01-08-97	FAH	02-13-97 Review board	XX_ER_23 XX_ER_24	XX_CR_23 XX_CR_24
1.dB	Draft	02-13-97	FAH	04-01-97 Internal review	—	
1.0	Released	02-28-97	POL	03-01-97 Architectural design-basis 03-01-97 System test- basis	—	XX_CR_76 XX_CR_77 XX_CR_91
2.dA	Draft	03-28-97	FAH	08-05-97 Review board	—	
2.0	Released	08-31-55	POL	09-05-97 Detailed design- basis 09-06-97 System test- basis		XX_CR_105 XX_CR_109 XX_CR_110 XX_CR_116
3.dA	Draft	10-18-97	FAH	10-17-97 Review board	XX_ER_131	XX_CR_132
3.dB	Draft	10-19-97	FAH	10-20-97 Internal review	XX_ER_135	XX_CR_133
3.dC	Draft	10-21-97	FAH	10-21-97 Internal review	—	
3.0	Released	10-31-97	POL	11-10-97 System test 12-09-97 Acceptance test		XX_CR_342
3.1dA	Draft	12-27-97	AMJ	12-27-97 Review board	—	
3.1	Released	12-30-97	POL	12-30-97 Customer		XX_CR_581
3.2.dA	Draft	08-28-98	AMJ			

Figure 9–4 *Item History List*

Delivery: XX

Milestone: Completion of system test

Version 1.2

Date: 11-30-97

Responsible: POL

The delivery is composed of: [for clarity, only part of the delivery is shown]

Configuration Item	Version	Status	Date	Responsible
Project plan	4.1	Released	11-28-97	POL
CM plan	4.0	Released	11-28-97	AMJ
Test plan and specification ⇓	5.2	Released	11-28-97	JOH
Requirement specification	3.0	Released	10-31-97	MDC
Architectural design ⇓	1.3	Released	08-31-97	MWG
Detailed design ⇓	1.2	Released	10-31-97	MWG
User guide	1.1	Released	11-28-97	HIL
Complete system ⇓	1.0	System test	11-30-97	TGH

⇓ Indicates that the configuration item is in itself a delivery, whose composition is described below.

Delivery: Complete system

Milestone: Completion of system test

Version 1.0

Date: 11-30-97

Responsible: TGH

The delivery is composed of: [for clarity, only part of the delivery is shown]

Configuration Item	Version	Status	Date	Responsible
Susbystem 1 ⇓	1.1	System test	11-30-97	PIU
Susbystem 2 ⇓	1.1	System test	11-27-97	MWG
Compiler	4.3	Approved	01-02-97	TGH
Linker	7.2.5	Approved	01-02-97	TGH

⇓ Indicates that the configuration item is in itself a delivery, whose composition is described below.

Delivery: Subsystem 1

Milestone: Completion of system test

Version 1.1

Date: 11-30-97

Responsible: PIU

The delivery is composed of: [for clarity, only part of the delivery is shown]

Configuration Item	Version	Status	Date	Responsible
modulex.cxx	3.5	System test	11-28-97	AMJ
moduley.cxx	2.4	System test	11-27-97	JOH
....				

Figure 9–5 *Item Composition List*

Trace Report

Figures 9–6 and 9–7 show an extract of a trace report between a user requirement specification and the corresponding system test specification. The report was originally produced in Access. Similar reports may be produced for all pairs of configuration items that are traced to each other.

In Figure 9–7, a section number and running number identify the requirement and test cases. These reports may seem "bare" but are quite useful. Where work is done on a test case, for example, the unique identification of the test case will be known, and the identification of the requirements traced to it can easily be found in the list. The unique identification of the requirements serves as a key to the entire requirement. It may be expedient to provide a title or more information for each requirement and test case, in addition to the unique identification numbers, but this takes up more space and makes the lists less handy.

Introduction

Tracing: XX_BKS.doc, v.1.2 and XX_STS.doc, v.1.0.

The report contains the following lists:

- A list that for each test case identifies the requirement(s) that the test case is testing. This list is used to verify that the test case covers the identified requirement().

- A list that for each requirement identifies the test case(s) in which the requirement is tested. This list is used to identify which test cases to perform to test a given requirement completely.

- Lists of untraced requirements and untraced test cases. These lists are used to verify that nothing has been forgotten and nothing is superfluous.

Figure 9–6 Trace Report, Part a

Tracing from test cases to requirements

<u>1.1 (1)</u>
10.3.1.6 (80)
10.4.1.1 (86)
10.4.1.2 (87)
10.4.1.4 (89)
10.4.1.5 (90)
10.4.1.8 (93)

<u>1.2 (2)</u>
10.3.1.6 (80)
10.4.1.1 (86)
10.4.1.2 (87)
10.4.1.4 (89)
10.4.1.5 (90)

<u>1.3 (4)</u>
10.4.1.4 (89)
10.4.1.6 (91)
10.4.1.8 (93)
10.6.2.1 (110)

<u>1.4 (32)</u>
10.6.2.8 (126)
10.6.2.9 (127)
10.6.2.10.a (129)

Tracing from requirements to test cases

<u>9.1.1.2 (4)</u>
8.3 (25)
<u>9.1.1.4 (7)</u>
6.9 (52)
<u>9.1.1.5 (8)</u>
2.4 (45)
<u>9.1.2.1.a (14)</u>
5.1 (10)
<u>9.1.2.1.b (15)</u>
5.3 (13)
5.4 (14)
5.5 (12)

Untraced requirements

3 untraced requirements have been found:

9.3.3.2 (54)

10.4.1.3 (88)

10.4.1.12 (219)

Untraced test cases

0 untraced test cases have been found.

Figure 9–7 *Trace Report, Part b*

9.2 CONFIGURATION MANAGEMENT AS SUPPLIER OF MEASUREMENTS

Configuration management is an outstanding source for measurements for metrics connected to other processes. Both metadata and change control data for configuration items may be used to extract information. It's therefore advisable, when defining metadata and change control data, to have a good grasp of the requirements from all processes regarding metrics. Likewise, it's important to define reports so these data can be presented as useful information. Those in charge of the processes are responsible for expressing their requirements. The person responsible for configuration management may, of course, also contribute suggestions.

Below are a few examples of how configuration management data may be the basis for the collection of measurements. Only the imagination and the usability set the limits for the measurements, but there is no reason to collect measurements if nobody is going to analyze them and act in accordance with the results.

Configuration management data may be used to collect or calculate measurements in the following categories: estimation, event frequencies, and effectiveness of quality assurance activities. The latter two may be made as specific as required in view of available data.

Estimation

Estimated resources for implementing changes may be part of the information on a change request. The number of change requests may itself give rise to estimates for implementation and approval of changes. To improve accuracy, estimates should be compared with actual data after the activities are completed.

Estimates may also, with reservations regarding their reliability, be used for activities in the company in general. In such cases, estimates for implementing and approving changes should be taken into account—something all too rarely done.

Event Frequencies

Events may be analyzed according to frequency, such as appearances over time or for specific items. To give an example, a person responsible for testing may calculate the frequency of already identified failures. This could enable prediction of the test course and possibly a decision about when to stop testing.

Somebody may also be interested in knowing the distribution of events, such as in relation to configuration item type, producer, or time of production. Do we create more faults on Mondays? Just after a long holiday? In large items or small ones?

Likewise, it may be interesting to analyze events in relation to who observed the event or who made and approved related changes. Is one user better at finding failures in the system? It might be interesting to discover why.

Effectiveness of Quality Assurance Activities

Quality assurance activities may be reviews, inspections, and various types of tests, such as module or system tests. The effectiveness of these activities may be calculated at any time as the relation between events found during each activity and the total number of events that could have been found.

To give an example: four faults are found during a module test. After three months in production, a defect is identified, resulting in the isolation of one more fault. This gives an effectiveness for this module test of 4/5, or 80%. It may be argued that it takes quite a while before effectiveness can be calculated, but this is nevertheless a metric much used in the testing field.

Ideas for Process Improvement

If analyzed correctly, all measurements may be used as inspiration for process improvement. The more precise the measurements, the better they are as a basis for process improvement. Measurements connected to clearly defined configuration items provide the best possibility for analysis. Furthermore, they may stimulate ideas as to how faults may be avoided in the future. Much literature is available on the definition of metrics and the collection and analysis of measurements. CMMI gives many examples to determine the status of activities for processes defined in the model.

Part III

Roles in Configuration Management

A (software) project is like a play: all roles must be filled. Some are big, some are small, but all are important.

Real people must fill the roles. Real people have personalities—a fact of life that's almost impossible to change. Technical skills you can learn, but your personality is to a large extent fixed when you reach adulthood. Different people fill roles in different ways, and these differences may be used to advantage if the basics of team roles are known.

This part discusses the human aspect of configuration management. The focus is not on individuals, however, but on their roles in connection with software development and maintenance. Describing the roles is important to the general understanding of the work. Processes and procedures may be described thoroughly, but only when activities and tasks are connected to roles—and thereby to people—do they become meaningful.

The roles are arranged within an organizational structure. This may, of course, vary from company to company. One or more people may fill one role, just as one person may fill one or several roles.

Chapter 10

People and Configuration Management

Many people influence and are influenced by configuration management during the development and maintenance of software products. Configuration management may be your main occupation or a tool among others in your main occupation, such as programming or project management. In each case, you need to work in teams. Teams have certain dynamics that influence the way work is performed.

10.1 CONFIGURATION MANAGEMENT AS A CAREER

Configuration management is an ignored discipline in software development. It doesn't have the same sex appeal as writing fantastic code—a fate this discipline shares with other processes such as quality assurance and testing. Options for education in configuration management are few at institutions offering instruction in information technology.

No doubt many people wonder why anyone would consider configuration management as a career. But it may be technically exciting as well as managerially challenging. It offers the opportunity to follow products through their entire life cycles and to get to know all levels and types of colleagues and customers, from top management to the newest developer.

Configuration management is a discipline in progress. The industry is becoming more aware of the significance of increasing maturity and structured and targeted process improvement work. The demand for quality is growing, as is the need for more and more people with a solid knowledge of and experience in configuration management. Initiatives are already being undertaken to provide more education in the subject, so that configuration management and its significance will be taught with other software development disciplines.

The experience of more than ten years working with maturity in the software industry indicates that companies wanting to face the growing pressure of time-to-market, better quality, lower prices, and more reliable pricing (the latter especially for custom software) will need a better understanding of the importance of configuration management, and hence people with a solid knowledge of the discipline.

Roles in configuration management consist of the person responsible, the librarian, and members of the configuration control board. These roles are described in the next chapter.

Qualifications

Configuration management is an administrative discipline, and special demands are made on people who want to specialize in it. Among other things, it demands that you have

- A general overview
- Attention to detail
- Meticulous work methods
- Diplomacy
- The ability to communicate with many types of people
- The ability to "sell" configuration management in the company
- A thorough knowledge of software development in general

As can be seen from the preceding list, the best team roles (discussed below) for a configuration management professional are—in order of preference—completer/finisher, implementer, specialist, and coordinator.

10.2 MANAGING CONFIGURATIONS IS EVERYONE'S JOB

Configuration management is an inevitable part of everyday life for anyone who deals with developing and maintaining software products. No matter which role you have it will involve configuration management activities. These activities may take up a lot of room or a little room in your life, but everybody will benefit from the results and will have to contribute to the performance. This is described in Chapters 12–14. The extent of its influence depends, among other things, on its scope and degree of formalism. If no configuration management is performed in a certain context, you risk, for instance, having to redo something that has already been completed.

As indicated earlier, configuration management is an administrative discipline that makes special demands on people. This means that everyone on a project must know which configuration management processes exist for the activities he or she is responsible for performing and what the process descriptions contain.

10.3 UNDERSTANDING TEAM ROLES

Dr. Meredith Belbin and his team of researchers at Henley Management College, England, have studied the behavior of managers from all over the world for over nine years. Managers taking part in the study were given a battery of psychometric tests and put into teams of varying composition while engaged in a complex management exercise. The exercise assessed their core personality traits, intellectual styles, and behaviors.

Results of this research showed that a finite number of behaviors, or team roles, define certain patterns of behavior adopted by various personality types. A team role, as defined by Dr. Belbin, is "a tendency to behave, contribute and interrelate with others in a particular way." The team roles are

- Action-oriented—shaper, implementer, and completer/finisher
- People-oriented—coordinator, teamworker, and resource investigator
- Cerebral—plant, monitor/evaluator, and specialist

Table 10–1 shows further details for each role.

Table 10–1 *Belbin Team Roles Descriptions*

Team Role Type	Contributions	Allowable Weaknesses
Plant	Creative, imaginative, unorthodox. Solves difficult problems.	Ignores incidentals. Too preoccupied to communicate effectively.
Coordinator	Mature, confident, a good chairperson. Clarifies goals, promotes decision-making, delegates well.	Can often be seen as manipulative. Offloads personal work.

(continues)

Table 10–1 *Belbin Team Roles Descriptions (continued)*

Monitor/evaluator	Sober, strategic, and discerning. Sees all options. Judges accurately.	Lacks drive and ability to inspire others.
Implementer	Disciplined, reliable, conservative and efficient. Turns ideas into practical actions.	Somewhat inflexible. Slow to respond to new possibilities.
Completer/finisher	Painstaking, conscientious, anxious. Searches out errors and omissions. Delivers on time.	Inclined to worry unduly. Reluctant to delegate.
Resource investigator	Extrovert, enthusiastic, communicative. Explores opportunities. Develops contacts.	Over-optimistic. Loses interest once initial enthusiasm has passed.
Shaper	Challenging, dynamic, thrives on pressure. The drive and courage to overcome obstacles.	Prone to provocation. Offends people's feelings.
Teamworker	Cooperative, mild, perceptive and diplomatic. Listens, builds, averts friction.	Indecisive in crunch situations.
Specialist	Single-minded, self-starting, dedicated. Provides knowledge and skills in rare supply.	Contributes only on a narrow front. Dwells on technicalities.

Putting Teams Together

When putting a team together for a task, it's important to analyze the type of task and what team roles are best represented on the team. The contributions and weaknesses of each role must be considered, and the team role of each member should be known. A well-formed team is a strong team, and a team tailored for the task is the strongest team you can get. The bibliography gives the Web address for more information about Belbin team roles, how to identify your own team role, and how to benefit from working with team roles.

Chapter 11

Configuration Management Roles

The roles in this category are centralized and specialized configuration management roles, typically supporting more than one organizational unit, if not an entire company. One or more of these roles may also be connected to a specific organizational unit, such as a large project.

The roles are filled formally in companies of a certain maturity level, but no matter what the level, it's always a good idea to consider where these responsibilities should be placed. If this is not done, this work will either be carried on informally, possibly as "invisible" work not appearing in any plan or accounting of time, or it will fall between two jobs not being done at all.

These roles do not have to be full-time jobs, but they shouldn't be less than 25% of a person's time, since other duties might interfere with doing a proper job. In highly automated configuration management systems, the workload for some roles may have to be minimal but should not be underestimated.

11.1 CONFIGURATION CONTROL BOARD

The configuration control board carries overall responsibility for change control of configuration items. The board is hence responsible for

- Evaluating event registrations
- Creating relevant change requests

- Following up on event registrations and change requests though their respective life cycles
- Providing feedback to the person who registered the event and other stakeholders
- Coordinating with other related configuration control boards
- Coordinating with project management or other relevant management

A board's role is to represent all stakeholders in the configuration items. It must have a chairman who has the mandate for making decisions—including decisions that have economic consequences, so that the decisions of the configuration control board may not be reversed.

The board may delegate responsibility for changes—for example, the project manager may know or be able to identify which configuration items are affected by an event registration. Or the producer of a given configuration item may perform an analysis of the effect of a change on the product. But the overall responsibility lies nonetheless with the board. This also means that the board's decisions cannot be appealed. Therefore, it's important to pay attention to the constitution of the board(s).

A board may consist of a single person, such as the producer of an object or the person responsible for quality assurance, if the person with overall responsibility has granted this person the authority to make appropriate decisions. This typically happens in production, where a document or piece of code is first written and work can be performed relatively informally, without bureaucracy and heaps of paper.

Where the configuration item has a wider impact, a board may consist of a number of people, such as the project manager, customer representative, and the person responsible for quality assurance. This may be where a requirement specification forms the basis for the design or the final delivery to the customer.

Skills and Knowledge

The configuration control board exclusively decides the fate of an event registration. It's therefore important that the board has the competence and will to make the necessary decisions, especially where these decisions may be unpopular.

The board must know the general purpose of the product and possibly related products, along with the company vision to an extent that allows competent assessment of the consequences of changes. The board must of course also have a general knowledge of configuration management as it's performed in the given context, especially regarding procedures for change control. It must know what information is available about configuration items and how to access it.

Configuration control boards are best constituted by people with a variety of team roles, preferably coordinator and monitor/evaluator. At least one member must have a good measure of diplomacy and courage.

Multiple Boards

A company may have more than one board, handling different types of configuration items and/or connected to different organizational units. This is illustrated in Figure 11–1. The figure also shows how configuration items may have an impact on different organizational units, such as the producer, project, entire company, or customer. Depending on where the impact of the item is, different boards may be responsible for change control. (Figure 11–1 shows only an organizational aspect, not a time aspect.)

Multiple boards are unusual, but they should not be found only in the formal end of the spectrum. It would be advantageous for relatively informal configuration management to graduate the formality of the change control process by the use of different types of boards. Many companies think they should have only one board and that it must be large and formal. Therefore they give up on the idea of having a board at all. This is a shame, because they could easily benefit if they had multiple boards with a variety of constitutions. It's the responsibility of the company to decide on the constitution of the boards for various configuration items. You do, however, have to be careful not to end up with a swarm of boards.

Each board, where more than one exists, must have a clearly defined area of responsibility, limited to the relevant configuration items. Possible interfaces must be clarified, such as if an event registration has to be handed over to a different board or an item must be handled by two boards.

Managing Configurations of CCB Work Products

Configuration management activities may also be performed for products produced by the configuration control board, but this doesn't often happen.

References

It may be of special interest to members of configuration control boards to read Chapters 1—Change Control, 7, 8, 9, and 17—Configuration Management.

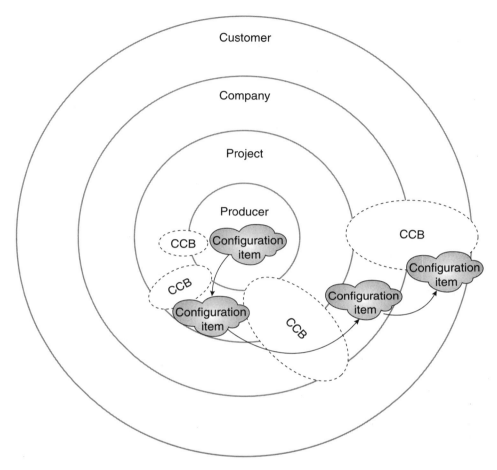

CCB = Configuration control board

Figure 11–1 *Multiple Configuration Control Boards*

11.2 LIBRARIAN

The librarian is responsible for establishing the configuration management library or libraries and for maintaining each library's internal integrity and possible integrity between libraries. The analogy to an ordinary librarian is precise—the librarian takes care of the structure (shelves and categorization systems) and adherence to the settings (the correct labeling and positions of the books) but not the contents of the books. This is the responsibility of the authors and publishers.

The librarian role may also be compared to that of a bookkeeper. The librarian makes sure all the practical aspects of the configuration management hang together and work properly. The person holding this role must therefore have extraordinary attention to detail and a meticulous method of working.

The person acting as the librarian must be good at communicating with many different types of people. This person must be able to stick to principles, including in time of crisis, and at the same time be flexible and have the breadth of vision to be able to circumvent principles when necessary. The best team role for the librarian is implementer, followed by completer/finisher.

The librarian's activities depend highly on the degree of formality with which configuration management is performed. For a high degree of formalism, activities include performing or supervising the following:

- Establishing the configuration management library—a controlled master library for storing configuration items
- Maintaining and controlling the contents of the library
  - Placing items in storage based on item approvals
  - Creating and maintaining metadata
  - Releasing items for usage based on release requests
  - Releasing items to production
- Communicating contents of the configuration management library
  - Producing templates for status reports
  - Extracting information for and producing status reports
  - Extracting ad hoc information, such as measurements for other processes
- Controlling the configuration management library
  - Controlling the integrity of metadata
  - Possible ordinary database administration activities, such as compressing data
  - Possible backup activities

Where the degree of formalism is low, many of the librarian's activities will be delegated to other roles and/or automated. This doesn't mean that the activities are not performed—in all circumstances, the responsibility for them must be placed somewhere. The librarian must have a solid knowledge of configuration management in general, as it's performed in the company, and for his or her area of responsibility. In many cases, the librarian will cooperate in production and the improvement of processes for configuration management with the person responsible for configuration management and/or process management.

The responsibility of a single librarian is typically limited to either a single product or project or to a specific type of cross-organizational product, such as assets for reuse or development tools. Even though the area of responsibility is limited, various librarians or libraries may cooperate, such as where a borderline exists between a project and an IT department concerning configuration management of tools.

Tools

Smaller or larger parts of the librarian's activities will be supported or taken over by tools. The librarian must therefore have a solid knowledge of the tools in use. This may be a database administration system, which the librarian must be able to tune or use for production of report templates.

It is also advantageous if the librarian is interested in investigating new possibilities for tool support and thereby contributes to improving the configuration management system. Knowledge of available tools falls under this area as well. The librarian will often have to cooperate closely with the person responsible for tools or may even hold that role as well.

Managing Configuration of Library Work Products

The librarian seldom has products of his or her own to place under configuration management. The person holding this role may contribute with estimates and information for plans for the appropriate organizational unit(s) and cooperate in the producing procedures, as mentioned above, but apart from that, the librarian does not usually produce objects that may be placed under configuration management.

References

It may be of special interest to a librarian to read Chapter 1—Storage, 5— Examples, 15— Emergency Changes, and 21.

11.3 PERSON RESPONSIBLE FOR CONFIGURATION MANAGEMENT

The person responsible for configuration management implements, maintains, and improves configuration management within the framework provided by management. The holder of this role may also be responsible for the use of tools to support configuration management. This person may have overall responsibility for configuration management in the company or limited responsibility within an organizational unit, such as a product or project.

The person responsible for configuration management has to cooperate with many people inside and outside the company or the organizational unit. He or she refers directly to management or a project manager. This person should have a close working relationship with the person responsible for process management regarding processes relevant to configuration management.

The person responsible for configuration management must have a distinct sense of order and a sense for details as well as broad outlines. The person must have management skills and be good at communicating with many different types of people—also in adverse situations.

This person must have thorough knowledge and understanding of configuration management and the theoretical and technological states and trends for the discipline. The person must also understand the company's needs and be capable of transforming them into practical processes. The person should also have some knowledge of management disciplines, such as risk analysis, estimation, calculation of profitability, and metrics, as well as up-to-date knowledge of relevant technology and available tools.

This person must also be able to "sell" the idea of configuration management in the company or organizational unit, which may require a certain amount of stamina. The role is best filled by a person with one (or more) of the team roles completer/finisher, implementer, specialist, or coordinator. Activities for the person responsible for configuration management include

- Transforming the company's needs and requirements for configuration management to relevant, practical procedures, resources, and tools
- Selecting and testing configuration management tools
- Updating information about new versions of existing tools and new tools
- Following up on the performance and efficiency of configuration management
- Making status reports to management with data analysis and recommendations for improvement

All other roles may, to a larger or smaller degree, look for leadership to the person responsible for configuration management, depending on how responsibility is divided and the degree of formality. In some companies, this person may also need a close working relationship with the person responsible for tools. This may entail splitting activities between them differently from the way described in this book. As long all activities are covered, this is fine.

Planning Configuration Management

Configuration management must be part of the activities included in planning and budgeting a product or a project. To facilitate this, the person responsible must work closely with project management in producing relevant configuration management plans—either as independent documents or as parts of an overall project plan.

Managing Configuration Management Work Products

The products that the person responsible for configuration management produces may also be placed under configuration management. The person holding this role may set a good example by adhering to applicable configuration management procedures.

References

The person holding this role should be familiar with the entire book as well as other literature and sources of information described in the bibliography.

Chapter 12

Organizational Roles

The roles described here are typically part of the organizational structure in the company. Project-related roles are discussed in the next chapter. Descriptions of roles here focus on their relationship with configuration management. These sections contain a certain amount of repetition. It's not the intention that everybody should read through all of them from one end to the other. Choose the sections relevant to you and read only those.

12.1 MANAGEMENT

Management is responsible for ensuring that the company has a policy for configuration management that effectively supports the company's business goals. This is to say that management should consider how configuration management is to be performed to provide the best possible benefit relative to the cost involved.

Such a policy may be layered. This means that it may be expressed on the project level as well as on the level of cross-organizational activities in the company. Cross-organizational activities may for instance be reuse or maintenance of the company's infrastructure. Configuration management may be performed by an organization-wide functional unit, like a process office, or locally in the projects. It may be done with a higher or lower degree of formalism.

Managers have a great responsibility in terms of being role models for employees and thereby signaling company values. Managers contribute indirectly to the performance of configuration management in general by performing configuration management

149

on the objects for which they are directly responsible, such as master plans. This enables management to get a feeling for what configuration management is and what the benefits are for the company. Management also contributes by requiring, and allocating resources to, configuration management on other cross-organizational objects, such as sales material.

Defining and Tracking Goals

Based on a general knowledge of configuration management principles, management should establish goals for configuration management in the company and track fulfillment of those goals. As part of the support for the goals, it's management's responsibility to provide

- ◆ Active support of implementation or improvement of configuration management
  - — Asking for configuration management plans and tracking progress
  - — Allocating and prioritizing necessary resources for both people and infrastructure
- ◆ Active support for employees working with configuration management
  - — Producing job descriptions for configuration management roles
  - — Including configuration management activities in other job descriptions
  - — Defining career possibilities in configuration management with the company

Benefits

A company gains many benefits in performing appropriate configuration management, from the top manager being able to track master plans and visions to the newest developer or administrative assistant being able to find and trust the processes describing their tasks.

References

More details on related subjects may be found in Chapters 5 (especially Examples), 6—Types of Objects in Cross-Organizational Perspective, and 25.

12.2 PERSON RESPONSIBLE FOR ASSETS

The holder of this role is responsible for assets, or components for reuse, that are produced and used in product development. This includes ensuring that assets fulfill the requirements expected of them and maintaining them under configuration management. Configuration management of assets is essential, because changes to these may have far-reaching effects on products and projects.

Configuration management should be part of activities taken into consideration while planning and budgeting in an organizational unit that deals with developing assets or components for reuse. The person responsible for the assets must ensure that necessary resources for people and infrastructure are included in the planning and are actually provided.

The person responsible for assets is in contact with many people, who may have contradictory requirements for the assets. Therefore, it's important from a configuration management point of view for the person holding this role to have solid knowledge about

- Principles of configuration management in general
- The company's way(s) of performing configuration management
- The products, projects, and objectives, at a level that allows effective assessment of the consequences of change requests
- The fundamental rules of diplomacy in dealing with people

All configuration management activities must be performed for assets. It's essential to be aware of the following:

- Asset descriptions must be defined. Presumably more than ordinary metadata is needed for useful assets to be easy to find.
- Evaluation and acceptance of new assets is crucial to maintain quality.
- All users of assets should be given detailed information when an asset configuration item is released in a new version, so they can decide whether to use it.

Different Process Descriptions

Configuration management may be performed differently in different places in the company. Differences may be culturally or historically defined and/or defined by tools. Although it might be desirable for these differences to be as small as possible or nonexistent, differences do occur in most companies. They become even clearer in connection with configuration management of assets, where technical interfaces cross organizational borders.

It may be naming conventions, which have to be defined in relation to naming conventions for different products. It may also be that procedures for placing products in storage or releasing them for usage are different. Therefore, the person responsible for assets must be careful when producing the relevant process descriptions.

References

More details on related subjects may be found in Chapters 5, 21—Internal Asset Development (Product-Line Approach), and 23.

12.3 PERSON RESPONSIBLE FOR OPERATION

The person responsible for operation ensures that products run in production or operation as they're supposed to and that configuration management is performed during operation. Operation will typically be sustained by a special department, but other organizational units may also be responsible, such as the unit that uses the product while carrying out its tasks. Operation may involve products the company has produced itself or has bought externally. Operation may be internal to a company using the products itself or a service to a customer.

The person responsible for operation receives a product for operation at some point in its life cycle. It should be clearly agreed when this person takes over responsibility for a product and what the responsibility covers. This person starts the operation of new products or new versions of products. This also implies a responsibility for being able to roll back to a defined state in case the start of operation reveals that the product doesn't work properly.

This person should have clear instructions for how to treat older versions of a product when a new version is put into operation. Does the new version replace the older one immediately, or should they operate in parallel for a specific time?

Configuration Management Responsibility

The person responsible for operation may share this responsibility in various ways, such as with the development department and/or a maintenance function. One extreme could be that this person takes full responsibility for the product maintenance and therefore the corresponding configuration management. The other could be that this person acts as a user, to make sure the product is accessible to other users.

In some situations, the entire operation environment must be placed under configuration management with the product in operation. In this case, ordinary configuration management principles apply, depending on the types of configuration items. For instance, platform, network, and corresponding software products may form the delivery for operation.

This person's responsibility toward other users must also be clarified, such as whether to undertake all registration of events only on his or her own behalf or on behalf of other users as well. On average up to 50% of events occurring during a product's lifetime are found during operation, so this responsibility must be clearly defined, as well as how these events will be registered and progress through the configuration management system. Events may also include follow-up on product efficiency during operation, such as with metrics.

References

See also Chapter 16—Operational Use.

12.4 PERSON RESPONSIBLE FOR PROCESS MANAGEMENT

The person responsible for process management typically works in an organizational unit that runs across ordinary project organization in a company, such as a department for methods and tools or a quality assurance department. This person ensures that the processes used in projects and other organizational units meet the company's needs and satisfy its demands effectively. Parts of these processes are configuration management processes. This person also places the company's processes (products produced under his or her responsibility) under configuration management.

The person responsible for process management has contact with many people who may have contradictory requirements for processes. Therefore, this person should have solid knowledge about

◆ The culture, values, and objectives of the company

◆ Software development in general, and specifically in relation to the company

◆ Principles of configuration management in general and as it's performed in the company

Implementing and improving processes in a company, not least the configuration management processes, poses special demands in terms of skills and knowledge by the person responsible. Among other things, good sales ability and cooperation are required. Process work must be carried out in close connection with the person responsible for configuration management—the same person may even fill both roles. For the part of this role that has to do with processes for configuration management, activities may include

- Compiling a general process description for configuration management
- Compiling guidelines for the tailoring of process descriptions to the needs of individual projects
- Reviewing the tailored process descriptions for configuration management
- Defining a measurement plan for performance of configuration management in the company
- Collecting and analyzing measurements according to the measurement plan
- Adjusting process descriptions based on analysis of the measurements
- Performing pilot projects for new process descriptions
- Possibly educating other employees in configuration management

Managing Configurations of Process Management Work Products

All configuration management activities must be performed for the processes for which this person is responsible. The following are especially important:

- This person may set a good example by following the required configuration management procedures.
- The configuration control board or change control for process descriptions must provide rapid responses to event registrations.
- All users of a process should receive comprehensive information when the process description is released in a new version.

Configuration management of the process description for which this person is responsible must be considered during planning and budgeting. The holder of this role must see that necessary resources for people and infrastructure are planned and allocated.

References

More details about related subjects may be found in Chapters 5, 11—Person Responsible for Configuration Management, 21— Quality System, Including Process Management, 23, and 25.

12.5 PERSON RESPONSIBLE FOR ENVIRONMENTS AND TOOLS

The person responsible for environments and tools ensures that the required tools are available and work appropriately. This person often performs support in connection with tool use. This person must be aware of the interfaces between these tools and those used in other connections (such as registration of hours). The responsibility for these interfaces should be clarified. This person may also perform configuration management for the company's configuration management tools and products belonging to them, such as manuals, installation scripts, and data exchange scripts.

The person filling this role must be good at identifying and coordinating common needs to obtain uniform implementation. This person should be good at cooperating with others and able and willing to function as a mentor. The person must have an interest in new technology, especially related to configuration management.

This person must have a solid knowledge of configuration management, both generally and in the company. This person must also know the borderlines and interfaces with other processes, such as quality assurance, and other tools used in the organization. Quite possibly this person should have some knowledge of programming, as most tools must be adjusted to the organization in one way or another. The activities of this person in relation to tools available for configuration management may include the following:

- Installing and implementing tools
- Producing necessary support tools or connections between tools (such as scripts)
- Maintaining installed tools, including communication with suppliers
- Supporting users of configuration management tools
- Possibly educating other employees in the use of tool(s)

Managing Configurations of Environments and Tools

All configuration management activities must be performed for the tools and products for which this person is responsible, according to the extent to which they're placed under configuration management. The following are especially important:

◆ This person may set a good example by following required configuration management procedures.

◆ All users should receive comprehensive information when a tool is upgraded or changed.

Configuration management of tools should form part of the planning and budgeting for this person's work. The holder of this role must see that necessary resources for people and infrastructure are planned and allocated.

References

More details about relevant subjects may be found in Chapters 5, 21—Company Infrastructure, 23, and 26.

12.6 SUPPORT/HELPDESK

The support department guides and advises users of a system. It also forms the connection between users and those responsible for maintaining the system by registering and possibly following up on relevant events. Support personnel must have thorough knowledge of the configuration management tool(s) used for registering events and extracting information in the metadatabase(s). They must also know about information available for configuration management items and event registrations, and how fast it can be obtained.

The staff of the support department or helpdesk may take advantage of information in configuration management to solve their support tasks. Their activities typically include

◆ Registering relevant events with a correct statement of required information

◆ Following up on registered events to the extent required of them. This may involve handing over ownership of the event registration to the configuration control board.

- ◆ Gathering information from the configuration management system(s) when answering inquiries and registering events. This may be
  - Information on registration of similar events
  - Identification of configuration items in use
  - A temporary solution for a problem (workaround)
  - A change history for a configuration item (a complete system or part of a system)
  - Information on contents of deliveries
  - Progress of an event registration

References

More details about relevant subjects may be found in Chapters 7 and 8—Event Registration.

Chapter 13

Project-Related Roles

The roles described here are typically connected to implementation of a project and are related to one project at a time. The focus is on their relation to configuration management—knowledge of the roles' subject areas are not included.

As an illustration, performance of configuration management by a designer requires a certain sense of order, although this may not be significant for the person's ability to be a good designer. Not all roles are necessarily filled in any given project, or the level of activity for a role may be small. The amount of work depends on the degree of formalism. These sections contain a certain amount of repetition. It's not the intention that everybody should read through all of them from one end to the other. Choose the sections relevant to you and read only those.

13.1 ANALYST

Analysts, also referred to as systems engineers, carry out early activities in the life cycle of a product, producing requirement specifications, such as for software, and other documents, such as user manuals. Analysts also maintain these documents throughout the lifetime of the product, producing new versions according to change requests. Analysts use the configuration management system for analysis activities to the extent that configuration management is performed.

Analysts must have configuration management in mind when working. This may include requirements regarding variants, which should be handled in conformity with the current configuration management system. Analysts contribute to the performance of configuration management by

- Identifying relevant configuration items
- Placing relevant items in storage after due approval
- Producing appropriate event registrations for the items used in connection with analysis (such as contracts or user requirement specifications)

Analysts may also be involved with configuration control boards in evaluating event registrations in later development activities.

Benefits

On top of the benefits of placing their own products under configuration management, analysts may benefit from configuration management by

- Extracting related configuration items as the basis for producing analysis objects, such as contracts or user requirement specifications
- Getting information about the status and history of these items
- Getting trace analysis results toward these items, to ensure the analysis covers all requirements

References

More details about relevant subjects may be found in Chapter 16— Documentation Activities (Specifications and Design).

13.2 DESIGNER

Designers produce architectural and detailed designs and maintain these documents throughout the lifetime of the product, producing new versions according to change requests. All configuration management activities must be performed for the design activities for which this person is responsible.

Designers must keep configuration management in mind when design work is done. This may be in the form of designing with a view to making changes as easy as possible to implement and making design items easy to place under configuration management, both individually and as deliveries. Designers contribute to the performance of configuration management by

◆ Identifying relevant configuration items (design documents)

◆ Placing relevant configuration items in storage after due approval

◆ Producing appropriate event registrations for items used in connection with design work, such as user requirement specifications and software requirements specifications

Designers may also be involved with configuration control boards in evaluating event registrations in later development activities.

Benefits

On top of the benefits of placing their own products under configuration management, designers may benefit from configuration management by

◆ Extracting related configuration items as the basis for producing design items, such as software requirements specifications

◆ Getting information on the status and history of these items

◆ Getting trace analysis results toward these items, to ensure that the design covers all demands

References

More details about relevant subjects may be found in Chapter 16—Documentation Activities (Specifications and Design).

13.3 PROGRAMMER

Programmers perform all programming activities, producing source code and related objects, such as system data and build scripts. They also maintain these programming objects during the product's life cycle, producing new versions according to change requests. They may also be responsible for the testing of their own code, such as performing module tests, and possibly also for integration tests.

All configuration management activities must be performed for coding and other activities for which this person is responsible, such as testing. Programmers contribute to the performance of configuration management by

◆ Identifying relevant configuration items (source code and object files)

◆ Placing relevant configuration items in storage after due approval

◆ Producing appropriate event registrations for items used in connection with programming, such as requirement specifications or design

Programmers may also be involved with configuration control boards in connection with evaluating event registrations. Programmers' contribution to laying a good foundation for configuration management should not be underestimated.

Benefits

On top of the benefits of placing their own products under configuration management, programmers may benefit from configuration management by

◆ Extracting related configuration items as the basis for producing programming objects, such as software requirement specifications and design

◆ Getting information on the status and history of these items

◆ Getting trace analysis results toward these items, to ensure that the code and related objects cover at least the design and possibly also explicitly all software requirements

References

More details about relevant subjects may be found in Chapters 16—Coding, Integration, and Test, 18—Managing Configurations in Different Development Models, and 22— How to Get Started from Nothing.

13.4 INTEGRATOR

Integrators integrate source code (or rather the derived object files) into larger and larger subsystems, concluding with the whole system. Integrators also re-create integrated (sub)systems for later retests or regression tests during the product's life cycle.

The contents of a product begin to assume definite form in connection with integration. Accurate identification of a product's contents is essential to further treatment in testing and registration of events. Integrators should use the configuration management system in all integration activities.

Integrators play a central role in connection with configuration management. This person contributes to configuration management by

◆ Identifying relevant configuration items (build scripts and, not least, deliveries in the form of larger and larger subsystems)

◆ Placing relevant items in storage after due approval

◆ Producing appropriate event registrations for items used in connection with integration, such as source code

Integrators should have a good overview of the system and information on the configuration items it contains. They may contribute to the auditing of configuration items because, by virtue of their overview, they can ensure that whatever must be included in a delivery is in fact included.

Benefits

On top of the benefits of placing their own products under configuration management, especially deliveries, integrators can benefit from configuration management by

◆ Extracting related configuration items as a basis for integration, such as architectural design, development plans, and test plans

◆ Extracting configuration items from which their own items must be produced

◆ Getting information on the status and history of these items

References

More details about relevant subjects may be found in Chapter 16—Integration.

13.5 TESTER

Testers test a system according to the applicable test plan. Testing can be performed at various levels, but all levels are treated together here. Testers also perform later retesting or regression tests throughout a product's life cycle. Testers are responsible for using the appropriate configuration management system in performing all test activities, and they have a central role in connection with configuration management. They contribute to the performance of configuration management by

◆ Identifying relevant configuration items (test plans, descriptions, scripts, and data, and releases for an entire test, including test environment)

◆ Placing relevant items in storage after appropriate approval

◆ Producing appropriate event registrations for items used in connection with testing, such as source code or (sub)systems

Benefits

On top of the benefits of placing their own products under configuration management, testers may benefit from configuration management by

- Extracting related configuration items as the basis for testing, such as individual configuration items or, more important, deliveries in terms of integrated (sub)systems
- Getting information on the status and history of these items
- Getting information about relevant event registrations and their progress

References

It may be of special interest to a tester to read Chapter 16—Test.

13.6 PROJECT MANAGER

The project manager has overall responsibility for a given project and the product created. This person is responsible for planning configuration management according to project requirements and seeing that it's performed. This includes partly what the employees produce and partly what the project manager produces (project plans).

To be able to define and scope configuration management, the project manager must understand its requirements and be able to administer them, with respect to both the company and to customers and suppliers. The project manager must also understand the relevance of configuration management and be able to pass on this understanding to those working on the project. It's also an advantage if the project manager has a good knowledge of configuration management in general, not just as it relates to the project.

Configuration management should be part of the activities included in planning and budgeting a project. The project manager must ensure that necessary resources for people and infrastructure are included in the planning and are actually provided. For the part of the task related to configuration management, activities may be

- Producing and updating a configuration management plan in agreement with the overall project plan
- Identifying necessary configuration management roles for the project
- Assigning responsibility for configuration management activities in accordance with identified roles

- Allocating resources for configuration management
- Following up on planned configuration management activities

These activities are important in getting configuration management implemented and properly performed, either in a project or in a company. The project manager's active and visible use of configuration management benefits described below may be a strong incentive to employees in their performance of configuration management.

Benefits

On top of the benefits of placing their own products under configuration management, project managers can use configuration management and the information held therein in performing daily project management work. The project manager may use

- Status reports from the configuration management system concerning configuration items
- Information about event registrations and their progress
- Measurements produced from the configuration management system, concerning both configuration management itself and other processes

Managing Configurations of Project Management Work Products

All configuration management activities should be performed as appropriate for products produced by the project manager.

References

More details about relevant subjects may be found in Chapters 1—Change Control, 5, 9, 17, 23, and 25— Metrics for Control of the Performance of CM.

13.7 PERSON RESPONSIBLE FOR QUALITY

The context here is the person responsible for quality in a given project. This person ensures that quality assurance activities are sufficient to fulfill the requirements for them and for the product generally. This person also ensures that quality assurance activities are performed as they should be, by auditing quality records and configuration management and its products and performing requirements inspections, code reviews, and so on. This person might also ensure that other processes in the project are being followed as they should be.

To audit configuration management, the person responsible must have a good knowledge of configuration management generally and for the project in particular. This person must also have a good knowledge of measurements configuration management can produce and how they can be used. For the part of the task related to configuration management, activities may be

- Establishing requirements concerning the quality of configuration management activities and their results
- Following up on the quality of the planned configuration management activities and their results, such as producing a configuration management plan; identifying, storing, and using configuration items; and handling change requests
- Creating event registrations for related configuration items, if events are observed
- Reporting and summarizing results of achieved quality

Quality assurance activities and configuration management activities overlap, among other things in connection with the approval of configuration items. Here it must be clarified who is responsible for what, so the responsibility doesn't fall between two job responsibilities.

Managing Configurations of Quality Assurance Work Products

Configuration management activities should also be performed for products the person responsible for quality produces, as appropriate. This person can set a good example by following relevant configuration management processes.

References

More details about relevant subjects may be found in Chapter 17—Quality Assurance.

13.8 PERSON RESPONSIBLE FOR CUSTOMER CONTACT

The person responsible for customer contact ensures that customer cooperation is satisfactory according to contract. Often the project manager carries this responsibility; only in a large project would a special person be assigned this responsibility.

This person must understand the customer's requirements for configuration management and make sure they're fulfilled, which demands a talent for cooperation. The borderlines between configuration management of the project and of the customer must be clear, as well as how these lines may be crossed if necessary. This person's job may concern how event registrations are handled during the course of development or how project material is transferred to the customer's configuration management at delivery.

To be able to cooperate with the customer about configuration management, this person must have good knowledge of the principles of configuration management generally and as it's carried out in the company and the project. The types of activities depend on how cooperation with the customer takes place (closely or loosely). Depending on the contract, activities typically include

- Producing documentation to fulfill the customer's configuration management requirements
- Receiving and possibly performing quality assurance on deliveries from the customer, such as user requirement specifications, and possibly performing internal configuration management on them
- Possibly forwarding event registrations to the customer
- Receiving event registrations from the customer, such as in connection with a review of documentation or with early user or acceptance tests

References

More details about relevant subjects may be found in Chapters 14—Customer and 20—Multiple Stakeholders.

13.9 PERSON RESPONSIBLE FOR SUBCONTRACTOR CONTACT

The person responsible for subcontractor contact ensures cooperation with possible subcontractor(s). For each subcontractor, a contract is required, whose terms must be monitored during development and at final delivery. This person must make sure that the subcontractor's configuration management activities fulfill the requirements.

Borderlines between configuration management in the project itself and of the subcontractor must be clarified, as well as how these lines may be crossed. The subcontractor may place his or her material under configuration management independently of the rest of the project, but it must all be transferred to the project's configuration management system in connection with delivery.

To be able to cooperate with the subcontractor about configuration management, the person responsible for subcontractor contact must have a good knowledge of configuration management principles generally and as they are carried out in the company and the project. The person filling this role must also understand the subcontractor's method of working and configuration management and have the necessary knowledge to formulate requirements regarding the subcontractor and follow up on them. This of course also demands a talent for cooperation.

The types of activities depend on the nature of the cooperation with the subcontractor. A close cooperation will often involve substantial contact with the subcontractor, while a more isolated subdelivery may require only a single contact. Depending on the contract, activities typically include

- Defining requirements for the subcontractor's configuration management system
- Maintaining contact between the subcontractor and the project
- Following up with the subcontractor to ensure that configuration management requirements are fulfilled
- Receiving and performing quality assurance on subdeliveries and forwarding these to internal configuration management
- Forwarding event registration and possibly change requests to the subcontractor for configuration items for which the subcontractor is responsible
- Receiving event registrations from the subcontractor

References

More details about relevant subjects may be found in Chapters 14—Subcontractor and 20—Multiple Stakeholders.

Chapter 14

External Roles

Configuration management is not always limited to the company that develops and maintains a product. In the context of this book, this company may be regarded as the contractor. Both customers and subcontractors may have a say in the contractor's development and maintenance of the product. Figure 14–1 shows the relationships between the concepts of customer, contractor, and subcontractor and the way deliveries normally occur.

However some communication in connection with configuration management often occurs and may flow in both directions. Therefore, all parties should have clearly defined interfaces for exchanging both deliveries and configuration management information.

14.1 CUSTOMER

This section describes the customer's configuration management role in connection with the contractor's development and maintenance of a product. It also describes the interfaces between the customer's and contractor's configuration management. This is not directly about the customer's own configuration management. If the difference between the customer's and the contractor's levels of configuration management is large, it will require an extra effort from both parties to make the cooperation work.

The customer is responsible for making sure the contractor has a level of configuration management that satisfies the customer's requirements and for making these

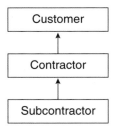

Figure 14–1 *Customer, Contractor, and Subcontractor*

requirements clear to the contractor. The customer is also responsible for living up to the obligations for configuration management specified in the contract. Especially with regard to large projects, it may also be the customer's responsibility to have his own configuration control board, which possibly communicates with the contractor by means of a common configuration control board.

A customer must have knowledge of configuration management in general at least to the level the contractor is required to fulfill, and preferably further. A customer must be able to study, understand, and use the contractor's configuration management to the extent required for cooperation and establishment of a contract. Depending on what is agreed to, customer activities may include

- Participating in one or more configuration control boards
- Creating event registrations
- Approving produced configuration items

In some cases, the customer (or a third party contracted by the customer) takes over operation and maintenance of a product. Here, the party who takes over operation must perform all the usual configuration management activities connected with product maintenance. In such cases the requirements for configuration management in the activity must be made clear beforehand, just like the interfaces in connection with delivery.

References

More details about relevant subjects may be found in Chapters 13—Person Responsible for Customer Contact and 20—Multiple Stakeholders.

14.2 SUBCONTRACTOR

This section describes the subcontractor's configuration management role in connection with a subdelivery and the interfaces between the contractor's and subcontractor's configuration management systems. This is not directly about the subcontractor's own configuration management, though in many cases the subcontractor's level will define the upper limit for requirements that can be fulfilled. If the difference between the contractor's and the subcontractor's levels of configuration management is large, it will take an extra effort from both parties to make the cooperation work.

The subcontractor must live up to the obligations concerning configuration management that are specified in the contract between him and the contractor. A subcontractor must have knowledge of configuration management at least to the level the subcontractor is required to fulfill, and preferably further. A subcontractor must be able to study, understand, and use the contractor's configuration management system to the extent required for cooperation and in the contract. A subcontractor must also be able to implement and use a configuration management system at the level required by the contract. The subcontractor's activities will depend upon what is agreed upon but may in principle include all configuration management activities. If cooperation is close, the subcontractor may follow the same rules as the contractor and possibly even work on the same configuration items. This could be seen as parallel or multisite development.

In the case of a more separated development process, the focus will often be on the contents of the delivery and on change control, especially documentation of changes from an earlier delivery and their consequences. Here, the interface between the two configuration management systems might influence the form and the contents of the subdelivery and the connected history of change.

The contractor often delivers event registrations or change requests (depending on the form of cooperation) to the subcontractor. The opposite may also happen, especially when cooperation is close; however, a subcontractor rarely creates change requests to the contractor.

References

More details about relevant subjects may be found in Chapters 13—Person Responsible for Customer Contact, 20—Multisite Development, 20—Multiple Stakeholders, and 20—Parallel Development.

Part IV

Configuration Management in Practice

There's no getting around it: configuration management is hard work—you have to do what you have to do. It starts out gently, and more and more is added as the project progresses—but it all has to hang together.

This part discusses how configuration management is actually performed once decisions have been made about what to place under configuration management, and when and how. The decision-making aspects are discussed in Chapters 5 and 6. When these decisions have been made, all you have to do is get on with it.

Most systems do, however, have a fair amount of built-in complexity. In configuration management, it's rarely enough to look at an item from one angle. Figure IV–1 illustrates this. When considering how to perform configuration management for an item, all the aspects shown in the figure must be taken into consideration: item type, project type, product type, special conditions, and degree of formalism required. Consequently, it's not enough to look under one heading in this book for inspiration—you have to identify all aspects of the case and read all relevant sections.

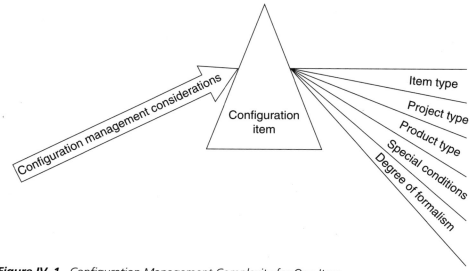

Figure IV–1   *Configuration Management Complexity for One Item*

Chapter 15

General Principles

This is a collective treatment of some general principles for configuration management in practice—principles that hold generally for what is discussed in the following chapters.

15.1 MILESTONES

Milestone deliveries are important. They must be planned in good time and must always be placed under configuration management. As the name implies, they are always deliveries—configuration items composed of other configuration items, which may be either single items or other deliveries.

Milestone deliveries often become more and more comprehensive throughout the development process, because they should always consist of the preceding milestone delivery (in new versions, if necessary) as well with the new delivery from the concluded delivery. However, milestone deliveries need not develop this way; this will happen mainly where configuration management is performed with a fairly high degree of formalism. Table 15–1 shows the possible development in milestone deliveries.

Identification

A delivery must be identified just like any other configuration item. The unique identification of milestone deliveries may be built up this way: PPPP MMM.nn. Table 15–2 describes the function of each element.

Table 15–1 Development in Milestone Deliveries

Included Configuration Item	Closing of Requirements	Closing of Architectural Design	Closing of Detailed Design	Closing of Module Test	Closing of System Test	Final Acceptance of System Test
				Milestone		
Project plan	1.0	2.0	3.0	4.0	4.1	4.1
Configuration management plan	1.0	2.0	3.0	4.0	4.0	4.0
Test plan and test specification	1.0	2.0	3.0	4.5	5.2	6.3
Requirement specification	1.0	1.2	1.3	1.4	1.6	1.6
Architectural design	—	1.0	1.2	1.3	1.3	1.3
Detailed design	—	—	1.0	1.1	1.2	1.3
User manual	—	—	—	1.0	1.1	1.1
Subsystem 1	—	—	—	1.0	1.1	1.2
Subsystem 2	—	—	—	1.0	1.1	1.2
Compiler	—	—	—	4.3	4.3	4.3
Linker	—	—	—	7.2.5	7.2.5	7.2.6
Complete system	—	—	—	—	1.0	1.1
Release note	—	—	—	—	—	1.0

Table 15–2 *Unique Identification of Milestone Deliveries*

Element	Function
PPPP	The project or product to which the configuration item belongs (e.g., PCM for Professional Configuration Management)
MMM	Milestone designation (e.g., "CURS" for "Closing of User Requirement Specification"). For further inspiration, see the headings in Table 15–1.
.nn	Version designation, expressed by "." followed by running number (two digits).

It's important to define authorization for milestone deliveries: whom each delivery is produced by, under the responsibility of, and approved by. Often, the producer will be responsible for development or the like, while final responsibility should rest with the project manager. It may be an advantage to include an impartial quality function to carry out auditing and general approval of milestone deliveries, such as by checking that all components are present in the correct versions and approved. Milestone deliveries can be traced to a project or development plan in which the milestones have been planned.

Generic Content Lists

The components of a milestone delivery must be identified correctly and precisely, taking the entire unique identification into account. It may be a good idea to keep a generic list of the components—for example, to have a list showing that the contents of the generic delivery "Printer driver" are the generic configuration items "Print card," "PLD," "EPROM," and so on. But when a specific delivery is made, both the delivery itself and all components must be explicitly identified, using the correct and complete unique identification.

Where deliveries are defined like this from generic lists or inherit their contents from earlier versions, it's important that they not contain components that are no longer relevant. This means that stray items must be recognized and removed from the identification of deliveries.

Storage

An individual configuration item is physically placed in storage and has associated metadata. A delivery will also have associated metadata but will not necessarily be present as a physical item in its own right. Part of the metadata for a delivery is a list of the components. This refers to physical configuration items—at least eventually, when the entire hierarchy has been resolved. Furthermore metadata points out how the delivery is to be assembled, typically by referring to a make-file or packing list.

Where a delivery doesn't exist in physical form, it will be constructed at the time of release. This will take place according to the production description. To give an example, it may be the release of a software product, where the source code, tools, and build script are stored in the configuration management library. The delivery consists of an executable file produced at the time of release and not kept in storage.

It may be necessary to place a proxy item in the configuration management library, especially if metadata are maintained together with the items and the tool used for the library requires items to handle the metadata. Typically, a proxy item is an ASCII file with a text like "I am a representative of hardware item XYZ, which is physically to be found at xxx." This provides registration without the need to place tools, for example, under configuration management. Proxy items and their meta-data must be included in status reports and the like for the physical item.

A delivery may be assembled in a physical item, such as an apparatus with embed-ded software. A list of components should still accompany such an item. A delivery may be a mixture of the above two cases—consisting of both a physical item and refer-ences to configuration items that are already present. An example could be an appara-tus with an electronic user manual under configuration management.

Change Control

Typically, a milestone delivery will be definitively defined shortly before the final review associated with it, such as the closing of design activity. The person who is to approve the activity (typically the customer or a general product manager) will receive the delivery for approval. At this stage, events may occur that require changes in one or more components before approval. This means that a milestone delivery often does not change at all, or just a little, in connection with final approval. However, change control must be carried out for milestone deliveries.

Actually, events are registered for deliveries more often than for individual con-figuration items. For these items, the configuration control board will often consist of people on a relatively high level in the organization.

During analysis of an event registration, change requests will be produced for relevant items, which are subsequently changed for the delivery to be released in a new, changed version composed of the new, changed versions of some or all of the components. An example could be an error in a delivery *A*, v.1.2. Analysis identifies an error in building block 4, v.3.5. This is corrected, and building block 4 is released in v.3.6. Delivery *A* is subsequently released in v.1.3. If building block 4 is part of other deliveries, this is a multivariant situation.

Changing components in a milestone delivery after approval of the milestone should not affect earlier deliveries. They must function as fixed snapshots that must not be changed retroactively. New versions of components will become part of future milestone deliveries. The processing speed for events and changes should be high for milestone deliveries, to facilitate progress.

Status Reporting

A report template should be available that can produce reports listing metadata for the components of milestone deliveries, together with, naturally, metadata for the milestone delivery itself. The degree of detail for such reports should be considered, as milestone deliveries often consist of deliveries in several layers.

15.2 DOCUMENT HANDLING

In a product's lifetime, many documents are created at different times and in different contexts. For instance, plans are created in connection with project management, and specification documents are created in connection with analysis and design. However, when talking about configuration management, documents are not generally the main consideration. The subject of this section is document handling in general. This means that the principles hold no matter when in the life of a product the documents are created and placed under configuration management.

Configuration Items or Deliveries

A document can be a single configuration item, but it can also be a delivery consisting of a number of components that are individually under configuration management. Such components may be general text, specific components (requirements, test cases, single chapters, sections), or drawings and diagrams. Figure 15–1 shows a document in the form of a delivery with components under configuration management.

The smaller the units with which one chooses to work, the more precisely one can refer to the items and manage them, and the more precisely one can carry out tracing between them. On the other hand, with increasing granularity the amount of configuration items and metadata will increase, as will the amount of work.

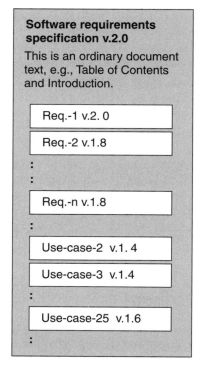

Figure 15–1 Document Delivery

Identification

Documents under configuration management must be identified. Because configuration items may appear on several levels in connection with documents, conventions must be defined for unique identification of these levels, which may be whole documents or components (requirements, drawings, and so on). Identification for these levels is described in detail below, as are the other aspects of identification.

Unique Identification of Documents

The unique identification of whole documents may be built up this way: PPPP_NNN.TTT n.n. Each of these elements has the function described in Table 15–3. The unique identification should be used in the file name for the document concerned and/or in the storage structure, according to conventions. It's up to each individual company to define details for each element, such as a list of permitted document types and rules for use of version and release designations.

Table 15–3 Unique Identification for Documents

Element	Function
PPPP_	Project or product to which the configuration item belongs
NNN	Document type, e.g.:

NNN	Means
URS	User requirement specification
VVP	Verification and validation plan
OP	Operation plan

Element	Function
.TTT	Reference to the production tool expressed by "." followed by a reference, e.g., "doc" for documents in Word
n	Version designation expressed by a running number
.n	Release designation expressed by "." followed by a running number or a letter. A convention may be used saying, for example, that as long as a document is in the form of a draft, letters are used in the release designation, while numbers are used when the document has been approved. In this way, a document may have these designations of version and release consecutively: 1.A, 1.B, 1.0, 1.1, 2.A, 2.0, 2.1, and so on.

Unique Identification of Components

The affiliation of components must form part of the unique identification. This affiliation may be implied in the physical placing of the component—a requirement written directly in a requirement specification document. The affiliation may also form part of the component identification, by including identification for the document of which the component forms a part. This may be the case if a component belongs only to one document and is stored in a database, for example. Where a component belongs to several documents (or other types of deliveries), the delivery must carry the relation "consists of," as described under metadata.

The unique identification of components themselves may be built up this way: BBBB h.h.h (nn) b.b. Table 15–4 describes the function of each element. Each company must define details for the single elements, such as in a list of permitted types of components and rules for unique numbering.

Table 15–4 *Unique Identification of Subitems*

Element	Function
BBBB	The component type: *requirement* or the like. This element is not often included, as the component type is normally implied in the context.
h.h.h	Number of paragraph or drawing or the like, specifying where the component is to be found in the document.
(nn)	The component's unique number within the context, to be used for tracing. The paragraph number (h.h.h) and this unique number (nn) must be independent of each other, for flexibility in the item's location and integrity in tracing. This makes it possible to move a component to another place in the document without having to change trace information.
b.b	Version and release designation for the component. This may follow the designation of version and release for the document, so a component may have the same or a preceding designation relative to the document, but this need not be the case. Components can have a life cycle quite independent of the one that holds for the document.

Authorization

Authorization for documents must be defined: whom each document is produced by, under the responsibility of, and approved by. Documents are often produced by several people who are experts within their own fields. Authorization information for document configuration items will often be stated in the document itself, on the front sheet or on a special sheet reserved for this information. Space may be left for signatures and dates. Electronic signatures may also be used where documents are only electronic, but this seldom occurs.

Tracing

Often it will be necessary to carry out tracing for document configuration items in a tool that is not the same as the storage tool, such as a separate database. This requires considering how the identification of single items can be exchanged between the storage tool and the tracing tool.

Storage

Documents are often available in files that are not ASCII format, such as documents written in Word or drawings produced with various tools for design and drawing. It may be complicated to find a configuration management tool that can store such configuration items, as most tools can handle only ASCII files. In such cases, it's necessary to build the file structure to handle the configuration management one wishes to perform.

It may be practical to create independent directory branches for each version and restrict the rights on the structure and the individual files. A whole branch can be made "read-only" when the delivery associated with it is approved and placed under configuration management.

It may be a good idea, for registering metadata and consistent status reporting, to create proxy configuration items for documents in the tool used for storing other types of items. This creates a bit more work with registration but provides an easier overview and facilitates status reporting.

Change Control

Event registration and handling of changes should be performed the same way for documents as for other items. Maybe this sounds self-evident, but it's not general practice to carry out document event registration with the same degree of accuracy as for, say, source code. Nor is it general practice to handle event registrations for documents in the same tool as other event registrations.

Status Reporting

In defining status reports for documents it's important to realize that information may be spread over several media. Metadata may be found in the documents themselves, and the documents may be stored in other places and in other media than are other configuration items. For this reason, one must expect extra work gathering and coordinating information from several sources.

15.3 EMERGENCY CHANGES

In special situations, it can be necessary to break all rules and carry out an emergency correction. This may occur in all development activities in a product's life, but it's probably most common in maintenance.

Examples

A company has issued a document in version 1.01 as an updated version after review. The document is many hundreds of pages. Afterward, the author discovers he or she has forgotten a correction on page 43. The correction has been approved and only has to be entered. Should she just make the correction and bring out a new page 43 in version 1.01, or must the entire document be issued in version 1.02, as prescribed by the procedure?

An engineer is going to install a new version of a software system far from home. A serious error is discovered in the delivery shortly before the engineer is to leave. If the error is corrected in the prescribed way, the engineer will miss his plane and the installation will be postponed at least a week, with considerable damages forthcoming. If the error is not corrected, the engineer's trip will be in vain, and the company will still have to pay damages for late delivery. What can be done?

A large system is running in ordinary production but goes down in the middle of the night. The programmer is sent for and finds an error in a program. Should she get the system to run straightaway, or should she wait for the next working day and have the event treated in accordance with existing guidelines, which say that the chairman of the configuration control board must sign the event registration? The guidelines don't say she's allowed to wake the chairman at three o'clock in the morning!

Principles for "Cheating"

A company may have substantial reasons to bypass configuration management in special situations, and a way to identify and allow handling of exceptions should be built into the processes. What is important is that things appear exactly as they are, with nothing swept under the carpet. It must be clear to everybody involved that processes are being bypassed. When deciding whether this can be allowed in a given situation, the following must be considered:

- Does it contribute positively to the company to bypass processes—or does it give a short-lived gain that will be detrimental in the long run?
- How can the way processes have been bypassed, and the reason, be made unmistakably clear to everybody?
- How can existing processes be changed to handle this type of situation?

Allowing processes to be bypassed in special cases may contribute to acceptance of configuration management, by diminishing the idea of the system as existing for its own sake.

Avoid Cheating

Bypassing processes must never become a habit. If it seems necessary to bypass processes too often, and especially the same processes time and again, something is seriously wrong. An unnecessary bottleneck may be built into a process, such as if approval must be obtained from a person who is only rarely accessible or if it takes too long to handle an event registration. One should not close one's eyes to the fact that exceptions occur, because such cases are a good source of inspiration for improving the system.

Examples Again

In the first of the examples of emergency changes, the solution could be to issue page 43 in version 1.02, together with relevant new pages, such as the document identification page (typically the front page) and history page, both with an indication of the new version and its grounds. The change in the process description is that it takes into account the possibility of issuing single pages in a new version.

The solution in the second and third examples could be to obtain oral permission from the proper people to correct the error if this is in any way possible, correct it, and afterward get the necessary registration work done. This could be a posthumous event registration and the ensuing handling of a change request—a registration of decisions and actions after they have actually been performed. The change in the process description is the addition of guidelines for such cases.

Chapter 16

Configuration Management in Development Activities

In many companies, coding is closely connected with module test. Also, integration, integration test, and system test are performed in a way that can make it difficult to keep them clearly apart. This makes good sense, as in the end it is all a matter of the delivery of complete and tested systems.

Configuration management, however, distinguishes between coding, integration, and test. Coding produces code, which is integrated into systems to be delivered. Integration produces assembled (sub)systems for delivery. Testing produces test-related items, which do not necessarily have to be delivered. Therefore, this chapter distinguishes between these activities, with each one treated in a section below. (Although test levels and types may be categorized in many ways, from the point of view of configuration management these differences are not significant; therefore, all test levels and types are treated as one in the section on testing). Each activity requires the capability for unique identification, authorization, tracing, storage, change control, and status reporting, although these are not repeated in each case except where they merit special mention.

16.1 DOCUMENTATION ACTIVITIES (SPECIFICATIONS AND DESIGN)

Documentation activities are the first activities in product development, up to coding. These may be preliminary study, user requirement activity, and analysis and design. The activities are widely different, but, from the point of view of configuration management, the products they create don't differ much. Therefore, these activities are treated collectively here.

Identification

Table 16–1 shows document type designations for various configuration items. The unique identification must be in accordance with a general definition and details for each type.

Table 16–1 *Document Types*

NNN	Designation
URS	User requirement specification
SRS	Software requirement specification
HRS	Hardware requirement specification
ADS	Architectural design specification
DDS	Detailed design specification

Figure 16–1 shows a small section of a requirement specification: a single requirement, number 54, with attached paragraph number, version "Stage 1," and the requirement text itself.

Please refer to Chapter 15—Document Handling for more information on this topic.

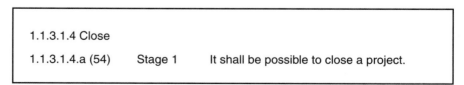

Figure 16–1 *Single Requirement*

16.2 **CODING**

Coding typically produces single configuration items, but it may be a good idea to define deliveries for modules. This implies defining a corresponding module delivery for each source code module, consisting of source code, associated header files and include files, and tools. Alternatively, a module delivery may consist of the compiled item (.obj file), but not all configuration management tools can handle compiled items. As a further alternative, the tool could indicate what belongs to a piece of source code, so it can be included in the delivery.

Unique Identification

The unique identification of source code and related items may be built up this way: PPPP NNNNNN.TTT n.n. Table 16–2 describes each of these elements.

Table 16–2 *Unique Identification for Coding Items*

Element	Function
PPPP	The project or product to which the configuration item belongs.
NNNNNN	Item name. It must be defined in terms of a maximum number of characters, depending on the platform(s) used (e.g., 20 alphanumeric characters at most). Names must be descriptive of the items and, if the design contains a subsystem structure, must reflect the position of items within it. It's not a good idea to name the source codes after the players on the national football team, even if the system is an administration system for the local football club. It is a good idea to name related files in the same way, so that, for example, source code and the corresponding object file have the same name.
.TTT	Reference to the type, expressed by "." followed by a reference (e.g., "psc" for source code written in Pascal, or "obj" for compiled items).
n	Version designation, expressed by a running number.
.n	Revision designation, expressed by "." followed by a running number.

Authorization

It's important to define authorization for these configuration items—that is, describe who each item is produced by, under the responsibility of, and approved by. Configuration items produced in the coding activity will typically be produced by a single person—a programmer or the like.

The responsibility for these configuration items normally rests with a person responsible for development, a group manager, or the project manager depending on the size of the project. It may be an advantage to include an impartial quality function for the final approval of these configuration items. Approval may be a peer approval, in which a colleague at the same level as the producer approves the item, or the approval may be performed by a person responsible for quality on the basis of test results or the like for the module.

Tracing

Source code or modules must be traced to detailed design. This will be a one-to-one tracing if the detailed design is broken down to the module level. Source code or modules may also be traced directly to the software requirements, to ensure that the producer has met them. This type of tracing is rare, but it can do wonders in helping the programmer understand what he or she is actually coding.

Storage

Source code and related items are often stored by means of a tool. Modules may be extracted for usage in connection with approval, such as for review or test. Moreover, it may be useful to be able to release items from coding for usage as support for other items to be tested, such as modules that function as stubs or drivers.

Change Control

The earlier source code is placed under configuration management, the easier the task of registering the events ought to be for the person having to do it, as more errors will presumably appear earlier than later. These early errors may be a source of valuable information on the design and coding processes.

16.3 INTEGRATION

All items one could place under configuration management for integration are deliveries. This will typically be "integration subsystems," "subsystems," and "the complete system." The size and composition of these configuration items depend on which types of single items one places under configuration management and the degree of granularity one prefers for the integration systems.

In this context, an "integration subsystem" means a subsystem that cannot be delivered as is but is used for integration test. It may consist of anything from just two pieces of source code with corresponding configuration items to almost a whole (sub)system, with all its configuration items. A "subsystem" or "complete system" is an assembly that can and may be delivered.

It's important to note that the composition of integration deliveries under configuration management is determined by the design. Finding out what such deliveries should consist of is not a configuration management task; the job is only to track the components once they've been defined. But in actual practice, the person who takes care of configuration management may be involved in audits of deliveries on behalf of the person responsible for quality. In any case, the audit task should not fall between two jobs.

Production Time

A configuration item from integration may consist of all relevant single types of configuration items. At release, the integration subsystem, subsystem, or complete system is produced when the relevant make-files and/or build scripts are executed. The configuration item may also be produced and placed under configuration management as a whole and released for usage on request. It may be practical to do this rather than placing all the items for producing a (sub)system under configuration management individually.

Unique Identification

The unique identification of integration subsystems, subsystems, and complete systems may be built up this way: PPPP NNNNNN n.n. Table 16–3 describes the function of each of these elements.

Table 16–3 Unique Identification for Integration Items

Element	Function
PPPP	The project or product to which the configuration item belongs.
NNNNNN	The name of the system. It must be defined in terms of a maximum number of characters of well-defined types (e.g., 20 alphanumeric characters at most). The names must be descriptive of the items.
n	Version designation, expressed as a running number.
.n	Revision designation, expressed by "." followed by a running number.

Tracing

(Sub)system configuration items should preferably be traced to both the detailed design and software requirements. This way, the subsystems inherit tracing from these items. Analyses of tracing must be performed on the complete system, to establish that all requirements have been met.

Storage

As described earlier, deliveries are rarely stored as one physical configuration item. But at least a reference to a given delivery must be stored, to provide an overview of the delivery's content and a description of how it's produced for release (when the constituent modules are to be integration tested). As with coding, it may be practical to release such items as support for other items to be integration tested, i.e. stubs or drivers.

It's not unusual for integration subsystems to be removed as configuration items when the complete system has been delivered. This may be sensible for reasons of space but unwise if retesting or regression testing will need to be done. What is most suitable in the given situation must be thoroughly considered. The complete system is released for usage for the first time when it's to be system tested or acceptance tested.

Change Control

As the configuration items that are handled in this development activity are deliveries, they are changed when their components are changed. For this reason it's important, when preparing change requests for source code, to include the relevant change requests for (sub)systems. At this point, the fanning effect should be noticed: an event registration may produce a number of change requests for source code and the like, whereas all this may create only one change request for the affected (sub)system. It's therefore important for the configuration control board to have the necessary overview and/or access to status reports that provide the overview.

16.4 TEST

Deliveries

A good many items produced during test are deliveries, in the sense that they're documents, which may be composed of test cases. It may be useful for later retesting and regression tests to define deliveries composed of the test object and the associated test configuration items, especially the test environment. As an example, a module might be assembled with associated test cases, driver, stubs, and test data into a module test delivery—one configuration item. Likewise, a test delivery will often be defined as the entire system, including the system test specification, associated test data, test hardware, and so on.

Drivers and Stubs

Drivers and stubs are source code that simulate how a test object is activated and other modules it uses. Real modules (actual modules to be delivered, rather than specially made drivers or stubs that are not delivered) may be used as drivers or stubs and should be under configuration management. If drivers and stubs are developed, they should be placed under configuration management like all other types of source code. Their unique identification should be defined so that it's apparent to which test item a driver or stub belongs.

Tracing

Tracing for test specifications may be and should be performed to any relevant preceding documentation and at as detailed a level as possible. This aspect should be taken into consideration when planning the granularity of the objects placed under configuration management. Figure 16–2 shows tracing for test-related configuration items performed according to the classic waterfall development model.

Accept test	<->	User requirements
System test	<->	Software requirements
Integration test	<->	Architectural design
Module test	<->	Detailed design

Figure 16–2 *Test-Related Tracings*

Storage

Storage should be performed in the same manner and in the same place (in the same structure) as for corresponding configuration items from other development activities—documents, source code, and hardware. It may be necessary and useful to "store" (build and maintain) completely independent test environments (hardware, directory structure, and so on) to ensure having them later, when they are needed. It may be worth the effort and cost to build and maintain a system test or acceptance test environment as a complete copy (perhaps with reduced size for data) of the real production environment. It's a configuration management activity to describe and maintain such environments.

Change Control

Change control should preferably be in place for modules, integration system, sub-systems, complete systems, and related documents before test activities start. Change control must also be in place for test-related items, since events may also occur for test specifications, for example.

16.5 OPERATIONAL USE

Operational use is, from the point of view of configuration management, the ultimate release for usage. What is considered operation in this connection is the packing, delivery, and installation of the product either at a customer's site or in an internal operation department, as well as the following ordinary use or running. Another kind of operational use is the packing and sale of off-the-shelf, or shrink-wrapped, products subsequently used privately by individuals or in companies.

New single configuration items are not created in this activity. Here, if not earlier, deliveries are defined that constitute the entire system to be released. Most often, such deliveries will be defined in integration, so final approval and any necessary changes can be performed immediately before the product is deployed. As the last part of the test, it's a good idea to test the delivery to be deployed, to be sure it's complete and can be installed and run. It may be useful to define a delivery consisting of the system in operation together with the operating and/or development environment. Special attention is required for variants of the product.

Configuration Management Considerations

In operation the configuration management system will stand its final test:

- Have the deliveries been composed and specified such that everything (and not too much) is included?
- Are the procedures for release in order, so everything required is generated and delivery takes place at the correct time, to the correct destination?
- Are the corresponding status reports adequate, so the operations staff or the customer can check up on the product and deploy it in operation?
- Is it possible to go back to an earlier operation version if a new operation startup goes wrong?
- Is it possible to register events for the product?
- Is it possible to extract information on running versions and existing event registrations?

All this must be planned and tested before the first operation starts and sustained throughout the product's lifetime. This is especially important if the start is complex and installations must be made on several platforms that must work together, such as client-server systems running on a mainframe, workstations, or Web systems.

Release

The operations staff themselves may take out the finished system for operation start, but most often it will be handed over more or less formally, assembled and packed for operation. This is especially true if operation takes place at a customer's site or from sale of off-the-shelf products.

Event Registration

The most important configuration management activity in operational use is registration of events, especially in the running-in period. This period can vary from product to product or user group to user group. Internal or external users (customers) as well as operations staff will presumably observe events and must be able to register and handle them. Ideally, they have access to the facility in which events for the product are registered, but this is not always the case. Access must allow both registration of new events and searching for events that are already registered.

Several levels of support functions may be placed between the ultimate user and the event registration itself. The first level might be with the customer himself and the second with the operations organization. The support function must never be performed directly by developers without event registration and a configuration control board. How events are registered and handled must be defined.

Status Reporting

The operations organization must know which configuration item the running system is—its unique identification and composition. It must be possible to extract relevant information from the status reporting facility or facilities. It may also be important to extract information on which users (customers) are running which configuration items (systems) and which events are already registered for a given item.

Organizational Considerations

Operation is usually placed elsewhere organizationally than development and test—even where operation is within the developing company. For this reason, it's important to define the interfaces between development/test and operation, so that it's clear when the responsibility for configuration management is transferred from one organizational unit to the other.

For off-the-shelf products, the responsibility remains in the company—certainly if the product must be maintained. When a product is transferred to a customer who is to be in charge of the operation or will involve a third party, it must be clear whether the configuration management responsibility is transferred and if not, who will carry which parts.

If the entire life of a product lies in an operations department, the responsibility is transferred to operations or may remain in development, so operations has only the responsibility for operation itself and possible event registration of observations. In such cases the operation environment should be isolated from other environments, such as development and test. Other reasons for isolating the operation may be security, reliability, and performance issues.

Backup

Backup of systems in production, including data, is a major responsibility for operations. This is not a configuration management task, though freezing the data contents, to be able to re-create it if necessary, resembles storage in configuration management. However, the two activities must be kept apart, since they require different procedures and information.

16.6 MAINTENANCE

Maintenance is the introduction of relevant changes—corrections or enhancements— to preserve the system's integrity. The starting point for maintenance is event registrations. On the basis of event registration, maintenance requirements must be put in order of priority, distinguishing between correcting errors and making desired improvements. They may also include requirements for adding facilities, such as new or more printers.

Maintenance of a product is generally regarded as a series of small projects in themselves, each running through the traditional development activities—requirement specification, design, coding, and test—but usually on a smaller scale than the original development.

New Versions

Each company must decide when and how to release new versions. In some companies, especially where the company itself is the customer, new versions are released on a running basis as event registrations are received and handled. Other companies gather event registrations and resulting change requests and release new versions at previously defined intervals, such as quarterly. It may be an advantage not to send out new releases too frequently, because of the learning curve for the users. Emergency situations may naturally arise.

Configuration Management Considerations

Configuration management during maintenance is fundamentally the same as during production. Identification of new configuration items must take place, both entirely new ones that are now needed (maybe in the form of a patch) and new versions of existing ones. New items must be placed in storage and released for usage. New events will be observed and must be handled. New status reports must be produced. And so on, until the product is no longer maintained. This may be more distant than the original developers think. How many developers who made software in the seventies and eighties imagined that their products would live to see the millennium?

Example

A company had to make a small correction for the millennium in a system from 1985. They had access to the source code and even the original programmer, but the question was whether they would be able to create a new version. Would there be a compatible PC, the correct operating system, a suitable diskette driver, the correct compiler and run-time library, and so on? There was, but this was sheer luck.

In some cases, the only way to ensure that a product can be reproduced ten or more years later is to take a full development environment, with everything that belongs to it, and place it in a corner. This may be a waste of resources—but it may also be a company's sheet anchor. Moreover, one should check that the environment functions in isolation, so that it does not depend on, say, an Internet connection.

Chapter 17

Managing Configurations for Project Support Functions

Project-support or life-cycle-independent functions are operative throughout a project's lifetime. This does not have to be—and rarely is—identical with the lifetime of the developed product. Often, a product will go through several projects, such as a proposal and contract project, a development project, possibly an independent test and delivery project, and an operation and maintenance project. This chapter discusses how configuration management can be performed for the objects produced in these functions. The principles apply to any type of project.

17.1 PROJECT MANAGEMENT

Project management includes defining, planning, and organizing a given project, as well as defining activities, interfaces, and resources. Project management also consists of, among other things, analyzing risks, estimating, and doing detailed planning of activities, as well as following up on progress and doing relevant updating of the plan.

Project management produces mostly documents. The types of objects that might be placed under configuration management for project management are proposals, contracts, the project plan, development plan, quality assurance plan, test plan, and configuration management plan. The tools employed may also be placed under configuration management, primarily word processors, drawing tools, and planning tools.

Example

A large Danish company that develops instruments with a great deal of software in them places all plans and budgets for products and their attached projects under configuration management. This permits managers to follow the progress of a project closely and gather experience about the development process.

Deliveries

Configuration items produced in connection with project management are rarely deliveries in themselves, as it's not often necessary to place sections, drawings, or diagrams in a plan under configuration management individually. Configuration items for project management should be part of all milestone deliveries in the project's lifetime. These items often change considerably from milestone to milestone, especially if they're produced iteratively, so that for each milestone they contain details for the next development activity and only general guidelines for the following ones.

Connection with Other Processes

As implied in the list of possible configuration items, project management and other processes may overlap, in the sense that these processes may be responsible for placing their own plans under configuration management. For instance, quality management may be responsible for the quality assurance plan. It's important to have well-defined interfaces, so that it's clear where responsibility is placed, which information should be transmitted from one area to another, and which conventions must be agreed upon.

The person responsible for configuration management may also be responsible for producing the configuration management plan and placing it under configuration management. The information that in this case must be transmitted from one area to another may be the total resource expenditure for configuration management, which must be consolidated in the general project plan. Conventions may include the naming of documents, which must be the same no matter whether the document (the plan) is identified by the project manager or the person responsible for configuration management.

Identification

Table 17–1 describes document type designations that are relevant to project management items.

Table 17–1 *Project Management Document Types*

NNN	Designation
PRO	Proposal
GPP	General project plan
QAP	Quality assurance plan
GTP	General test plan
CMP	Configuration management plan

Tracing

Plans can and should be traced to a contract, so it can be documented that the contractual obligations are being kept. Some configuration items for project management may trace to each other—for example, a test plan or configuration management plan may trace to the project plan. Otherwise, the same considerations apply to configuration items for project management as to configuration items of the document type generally.

Change Control

For plans, the producer often puts forward an event registration, which may be followed by a single change request for the configuration item—the plan (or the like) he wants to update. The configuration control board(s) for these items should be composed of representatives for external stakeholders, such as the customer or a marketing department.

Status Reporting

Generally, these configuration items have no great need for status reporting during a project. In large projects with subprojects, however, it may be important to obtain status information for all project documentation. Summarizing reports, with information for process improvement, may also be needed.

17.2 CONFIGURATION MANAGEMENT

Configuration management in itself produces items that may be placed under configuration management, Except for a high degree of formalism, with highly critical systems, it's rare for this to include anything but the configuration management plan and some status reports (tracing reports and delivery descriptions).

Change control is rarely needed for forms and the like produced under configuration management. Some forms, such as release requests, do not change at all. Others such as change requests, change in a controlled way according to a (defined) life cycle.

A person responsible for configuration management may prepare the configuration management plan, but it may also be the project manager. Quality assurance interfaces with configuration management in connection with the approval of objects and the reporting and handling of observations. Quality assurance produces item approvals and event registrations, both of which are input for configuration management.

Milestone Deliveries

Status reports, such as tracing reports and delivery descriptions, form part of milestone deliveries. They may change to some extent at the time leading up to the milestone (and maybe just after) if the relevant configuration items change. A milestone at the conclusion of the software requirement analysis may, for example, contain a report on tracing between the user requirement specification and the software requirement specification, together with a delivery description indicating which configuration items form part of the delivery, and in which versions.

If, say, the user requirement specification must be changed and is issued in a new version in connection with final approval of the milestone, both the tracing report and delivery description must be changed accordingly. This means that change requests must be prepared for these items if they are kept under configuration management.

Storage

In some companies, the configuration items from configuration management itself (and maybe from quality assurance) are stored separately from the rest of the configuration items for the project, partly because they are often on paper.

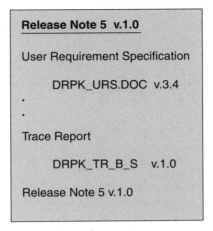

Release Note 5 v.1.0

User Requirement Specification

      DRPK_URS.DOC v.3.4

.
.
.

Trace Report

      DRPK_TR_B_S v.1.0

Release Note 5 v.1.0

Figure 17–1 *Release Note for Full Delivery (Excerpt)*

Change Control

Changes of configuration items discussed here will most often be derived changes, as described earlier. Of course, plain errors may occur in a report under configuration management. In such cases, one must be able to undertake change control.

Status Reporting

Items produced under configuration management are unlikely to need separate status reporting. However, these items form part of delivery descriptions. Figure 17–1 shows the delivery report for the user requirement specification scenario described above under Milestone Deliveries. The release note in this example is recursive—it includes itself as part of the delivery.

17.3 QUALITY ASSURANCE

Quality assurance covers validation and verification of a system. Management should set up quality goals with the person responsible for quality. Quality assurance should be part of project planning.

    Validation answers the question "Have we made the right thing?" This is answered by, among other things, analyzing tracing reports, to ascertain that all requirements have been met, or by usability assessments, to determine the usability of the system.

Verification answers the question "Have we made it properly?" Here, activities depend on what is to be quality-assured. Verification may include activities such as review, inspections, walkthroughs, and tests. In this section, only non-test activities are discussed.

Quality assurance produces documents. Items that might be placed under configuration management are the quality assurance plan, quality assurance reports (review reports, audit reports, and the like), item approvals, and event registrations. Except for a high degree of formalism, with highly critical systems, it's rare for this to include anything but the quality assurance plan.

Connection with Other Processes

A person responsible for quality assurance may prepare the quality assurance plan, but it may also be the project manager. Quality assurance interfaces with configuration management in connection with approval of items to be placed in storage, auditing of configuration items to be released for usage, and reporting and handling of observations. Quality assurance produces, among other things, item approvals and event registrations, both of which are input for configuration management. Such items are rarely placed under configuration management.

17.4 SUBCONTRACTOR MANAGEMENT

Subcontractor management is necessary when parts of a product are produced by another company or organizational unit with which an agreement on delivery of specified components has been formed. Components delivered by subcontractors may represent small parts of a product or the whole product, which the company assembles.

Either way, it's important to select well-qualified subcontractors and create an agreement containing a clear definition of the extent of the work, its progress, and the conditions of collaboration. An agreement on configuration management requirements and related interfaces should not be omitted.

It's important to study how subcontractors perform configuration management and how subcontractors' process descriptions—if they exist, which they hopefully do—match the company's. It may be necessary to adjust the configuration management processes between the company and the subcontractors, but who should adjust to whom cannot be stated definitively. Some companies deliberately choose subcontractors who are more mature than they are, to enhance their own maturity.

Everything that can be placed under configuration management may—in principle—be delivered by subcontractors, or vice versa. When a company defines what must be placed under configuration management, it must take into consideration what is delivered by subcontractors and how configuration management is performed by subcontractors internally. It should be specified clearly to the subcontractors which objects must be placed under configuration management, and when, and the degree of formalism required.

Identification

Items placed under configuration management with a subcontractor must be identified like all other configuration items. Special conventions for identification might be necessary, so that the identification will indicate which subcontractor has delivered a given configuration item. It should also be possible to transfer configuration items to the company's own configuration management system if required, without complications from the unique identification.

Storage

Who is storing what, and where, must be made clear. Where subcontractors deliver whole, self-contained subsystems a problem will not usually arise with storage, which can take place at the subcontractor's site until delivery. Where subcontractors deliver parts with many interfaces to parts developed elsewhere, storage may be similar to storage for geographically distributed development.

Change Control

Interfaces for change control must also be made clear. Ideally, the company and the subcontractors will use a common event registration system, so all events are registered in the same place. The configuration control boards will channel change requests to those responsible, whether in the company or with a subcontractor.

However, it's not always possible to give everybody access to such a common event registration system. It must be agreed how subcontractors should register events and how these registrations are to be consolidated within the company. Composition of the configuration control boards in relation to subcontractors must also be determined—which boards can be composed locally by a subcontractor and which must have representatives of other stakeholders (the company, other subcontractors, and/or the customer).

Status Reporting

The company must clearly define its requirements for subcontractor status reporting. It may be advantageous for the company to be able to extract status reports itself, but this is not always possible. Channels of command should be decided for preparation and delivery of status reports. Moreover, the need for consolidation of status information must be considered.

Delivery

One day, items produced by the subcontractor must be delivered to the company. It should be specified clearly when such delivery must take place and what the requirements are for configuration management in this connection:

- How much is to be delivered? All versions, all metadata, and all information concerning configuration management, or only some of this—and, if so, which parts?
- Does the company take over the responsibility for maintaining the components delivered, or does it remain with the subcontractor?

Chapter 18

Managing Configurations in Different Development Models

Development and maintenance of a product may be organized in one project or a number of projects under different management during a product's lifetime. Each subproduct may follow its own development model—the software subproduct may follow an iterative development model while the hardware subproduct follows a waterfall model. The development model always coexists with other factors, such as the product type or special conditions. This, of course, adds to the complexity.

It's important to separate the valid factors for a project or a product, define how each factor is to be handled independently, and then define how the combination of factors should be handled. This chapter discusses different development models and development philosophies, ordered alphabetically.

18.1 AGILE DEVELOPMENT

Agile software development centers on four values identified in the Agile Alliance's Manifesto:

- Individuals and interactions over processes and tools
- Working software over comprehensive documentation
- Customer collaboration over contract negotiation
- Responding to change over following a plan

Agile development is not a development model as such, but the values are used in a number of development models and frameworks, of which the most commonly known are perhaps the eXtreme Programming (XP) model, Crystal Methodologies, and SCRUM. The keywords in agile development are, in short, change and communication. This makes configuration management one of the more important areas of activity if agile development is to succeed. Iterative development models are strongly related to the agile development philosophy, though not all of the values are found in the more commonly used iterative models.

Configuration Management in Agile Development

The words "configuration management" are hard to find in the literature about agile development. Configuration management is, however, an undercurrent in many of the twelve principles defined for agile development. Those that touch on configuration management are listed and discussed below:

- Welcome changing requirements, even late in development. Agile processes harness change for the customer's competitive advantage.
- Deliver working software frequently, from a couple of weeks to a couple of months, with a preference for the shorter timescale.
- Business people and developers must work together daily throughout the project.
- Build projects around motivated individuals. Give them the environment and support they need, and trust them to get the job done.
- Working software is the primary measure of progress.
- Agile processes promote sustainable development. The sponsors, developers, and users should be able to maintain a constant pace indefinitely.

Empowered Teams

The best emerges from self-organizing teams giving continuous attention to technical excellence. Agile development will not work with only inexperienced people. Only when you know the principles of what you're going to do and have some experience can you loosen formality and get better results.

Technical excellence in software development encompasses configuration management. It should be a natural part of forming self-organizing teams to share their experience, including configuration management, and agree on processes and practices to follow—at least at the start of the process, since processes are also subject to change in agile development. The general principles of configuration management (identification, storage, change control, and status reporting) should be observed and tailored to the product type and other determining factors, observing the principle of working smarter, not harder.

Process Handling

Agile development does not mean that no processes are defined or followed. On the contrary, processes are agreed upon and accepted among participants—management, developers, and customers (or businesspeople)—on equal terms. At regular intervals, the team reflects on how to become more effective, then adjusts its behavior accordingly. This means that processes are revised by agreement and new processes are immediately communicated to those involved. The detailed planning horizon in agile development is naturally not long. The focus is on continuous replanning according to needs, with only short-term detailed planning.

This is also valid for configuration management: only short-term, detailed configuration management planning should be performed. However, it's both necessary and possible to plan and define configuration management processes in more and more detail as the project progresses. The way to perform configuration management for the relevant types of objects produced should be planned as early as possible—how to identify and store objects and how to control the changes to come.

In agile development, changes to the product are the norm, and so are changes to the processes. You'll rarely find company-wide processes in such an environment, but the teams should be encouraged to share their experiences and inspire each other—and maybe also inspire company-wide processes, if possible.

Environment and Support

Part of keeping good people motivated is to give them the work environment and support they need. This includes providing facilities to perform necessary configuration management: people, tools, hardware, and access to appropriate company processes. This is not to say that configuration management should be imposed from management but that it should be carefully organized, including providing sufficient people to fulfill configuration management roles. In agile development, the responsibility for configuration management will be shared in the teams, and it's a good idea to have responsibility for the more administrative and tedious tasks, such as a frequent build of the system, circulate among team members.

Professional configuration management requires sufficient support and a good working environment. It's not easy, for example, to work fast with good configuration management if it's impossible or difficult to control the physical storage facilities (e.g., inability to separate development, test, and production environments). Keeping large portions of the system separate in specific development workspaces is important to the success of agile development.

Requirements Management

Agile development welcomes changing requirements, even late in development. Requirement management is therefore of utmost importance for creating a stable and valuable product. Requirements come in many shapes and forms, not least in agile development, where the emphasis is on understanding the requirements, rather than having them elaborately documented. However, it's necessary for the teams to agree on a way or ways of getting and keeping requirements identified.

It's a good idea to be aware of the granularity of configuration items related to the requirements. Are changes going to be documented in terms of story cards, use cases, detailed requirements, overall business requirements, or another category? Don't make the granularity too fine too early, but adjust the granularity from coarser to finer as need and knowledge grow. In any case, don't just use a few high-level business requirements as the basis. Tracing requirements to software code and test specifications is essential. This enables fast identification of the implications of changes to requirements during the product's life cycle.

Working Together

Business people and developers must work together. This means that business people and developers are constantly making decisions together. An important decision to make often in agile development is prioritization of requirements, but decisions could also be in terms of changes to requirements or to interpretations of requirements. Decisions determine the direction of a product and are part of active change control.

Business people and developers should agree on a way of documenting decisions they make relative to configuration items—to requirements and software code and the traces between these—as this information is valuable for sustainable, fast development. If decisions are not captured, even the best teams run the risk of getting into an unstable situation, where decisions are made and remade.

Frequent Delivery of Working Software

Working software is the primary measure of progress and should be delivered frequently. To do this, the group must be able to build working versions of the system as easily as possible. This is such an important issue, it's discussed separately in the following paragraphs.

Communication and Documentation

Lack of communication within a project has been identified as a root cause for problems. Communication underlies the values for agile development. Communication is between people and should embrace not only developers but the business people involved. Agile development values working software over documentation. This doesn't mean there is no documentation but that documentation is kept to a minimum. Configuration management should focus on using source code as the means of communicating and capturing information. Coding standards, which the teams should form and agree on, should support this.

Coding standards and supporting templates may well include facilities for managing identification (including all necessary metadata—not least tracing information), event registration, and change request handling. Also, test specifications should be self-documenting in terms of identification, including trace information.

Status Reporting

Status reporting is perhaps not too important in an agile environment, especially not as formal reports, because frequent builds and deliveries of working products document the progress. It should, however, be possible to easily extract information for making decisions, preferably online. This is primarily trace information for source code and test specifications and customer-related documentation.

18.2 FREQUENT-BUILD TECHNIQUE

The frequent-build technique, also known as build-and-smoke-test, daily builds, continuous integration, or personal builds, is an integrated part of agile and iterative development. It may also be used for sequential development during coding and integration. The purpose of frequent-build is to build and test the entire system or the available part of the system often, possibly daily. This is to say that all source files are compiled and linked to build an executable system. Some sort of test is then performed to see if the product works. This test may vary from superficial to thorough, according to the needs and possibilities.

Planning Considerations

It's a planning decision to include frequent-build in development activities. Successful use of this technique depends on cooperation between the involved roles: development, integration, test, quality assurance, and configuration management. Frequent-build includes the following steps:

- Establish a build group. This must be done in cooperation with configuration management.
- Build as often as meaningful—as often as new changes may be synchronized.
- Test every build. Make it a first priority to make sure every build works, or fall back.
- Introduce reprisals if a build doesn't work—but don't make it buying a cake if you want to stay slim.

As with other techniques, frequent-build should be performed even under pressure. People make more mistakes under pressure, and it's in these situations that the technique may prove its worth.

Configuration Management Considerations

Frequent-build poses special requirements for configuration management. However, these requirements are not difficult to fulfill, and most tools support them. When items are placed under configuration management often—when change cycles are as short as one day or the time it takes to make a useful change—the configuration management system must be able to handle a large storage volume. For the sake of development speed, consider also how registrations and subsequent extraction of metadata may be performed as quickly and smoothly as possible and, perhaps most important, how fast builds can be made. It may be a good idea to invest in a good, sturdy, fast database tool.

Frequent Builds Are Not Frequent Storage

The frequent-build technique should not be confused with the frequent placement of items in storage. Only finished and approved configuration items—items that provide a tested solution for a specific task—may be placed under configuration management. Intermediate "solutions" are private!

Identification

Builds must be identified as precisely as possible. This is often done by adding a running build number to the identification: System XZ, version 2.03.743, where 743 is the build number. It may also be in the form of a date: System ZY, version 3.5-01.04.11, where 01.04.11 indicates that this version was built on April 11, 2001. Configuration items that are part of the build are "ordinary" items and should be identified according to their type.

Building

Building a system is a type of release for use. The test is the use, and its purpose is to ensure internal consistency. It has to be easy to establish a new version of the product, composed of the latest version of all relevant configuration items. It's a great advantage if this work can be done fast, such as by performing an optimized build.

A good build procedure is necessary. It's a good idea to produce a generic build script, which automatically includes the latest version of the relevant configuration items. Furthermore, the script must produce a list of the contents with full identification, so it's possible to see which versions of the configuration items are included in a given build.

Frequent-build depends on the test. The test specification needs to be changed as frequently as the build, especially if the test is to touch all parts of the product in a convincing way. It's therefore advantageous to place test scripts and so on under configuration management with the rest of the configuration items in the build.

Storage

Placing the version of the system being built under configuration management can be done by placing its build script under configuration management as a proxy item for the system. This will save space and in most cases it will be easier to handle the build script than if the executables were placed under configuration management. In this way, it's possible to rebuild a version of the system if this should prove necessary (provided that the individual items are available).

Backtracking

Frequent-build ensures the quality of what is being developed and placed under configuration management, and it should be an exception for a developer to ruin a build. Microsoft is infamous for equipping its developers with a pager, to call them to work even in the middle of the night if they've caused a build to fail. Builds do fail, and if a major problem is introduced, it may be necessary to fall back to the previous version.

Change Control

As mentioned above, it should be an exception for a build not to pass the test, and it should be taken seriously if it doesn't. The event(s) connected with the failure must be registered, treated like other events, and given highest priority. For frequent-build to fulfill its purpose of ensuring the earliest identification and correction of errors, it's important to follow build test events closely and get them out of way before a new build is done.

Example

The following example has kindly been provided by Mr. Bjarne Månsson from Baan CRM in Denmark. During development of a new product, Baan CRM used the frequent-build technique, as described below. All source code was version-controlled in Microsoft Visual SourceSafe (VSS)—source code was checked into VSS daily. Source code of a full build was labeled with a unique label, so a particular version could always be rebuilt. Development and build environments were saved as an "image" of the PCs—that is, there was no saving of individual development tools. All components were integrated into a full system on a daily basis, including an automatic regression test.

Initially, a problem was identified: that source code was checked into VSS on a daily basis—that is, the "morning" build was performed on the latest (but maybe not tested) code. Figure 18–1 shows the results of the daily builds of the product's seven components. The points above the x-axis indicate failed builds, so Figure 18–1 shows that of the 87 builds from August 14 to December 12, 68 have points lying above the x-axis. Only 19 don't have points above the x-axis and were therefore entirely successful.

The beta release was on December 4, 2000; only around this time could improvement be spotted. This prompted a new approach: building on "promoted" code only, which was tested against other components before promotion, as illustrated in Figure 18–2.

The advantages of this were that the developer promoted the code only when it was stable, it was tested against other promoted code, and the code for the build was

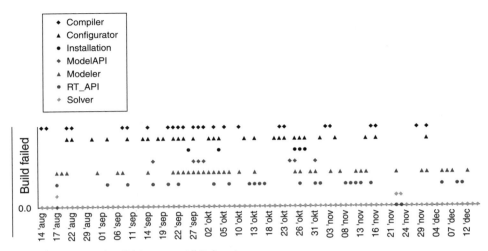

Figure 18–1 Initial Build Success, All Subsystems

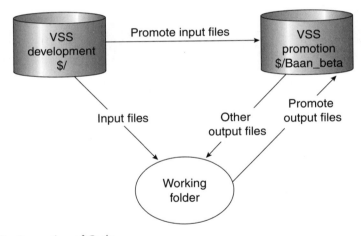

Figure 18–2 Promotion of Code

stable. The disadvantages were that the build code might be a week old, and the promotion process needed tuning. However, this approach did provide much more stable builds, as illustrated in Figures 18–3 and Figure 18–4.

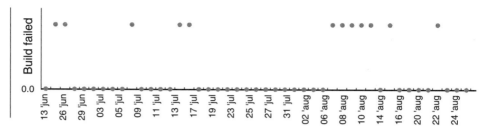

Figure 18–3   *Configurator Subsystem Beta Release August 24, 2001: 75% Successful*

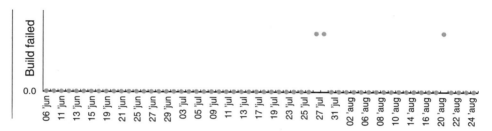

Figure 18–4   *Salespoint Subsystem Beta Release August 17, 2001: 95% Successful*

18.3 INTEGRATED PRODUCT DEVELOPMENT

The Software Engineering Institute (SEI) defines integrated product development (IPD) as

> a systematic approach to product development that achieves a timely collaboration of necessary disciplines throughout the product life cycle to better satisfy customer needs. It typically involves a teaming of the functional disciplines to integrate and concurrently apply all necessary processes to produce an effective and efficient product that satisfies the customer's needs.

SEI developed and supported an IPD-CMM (capability maturity model) for integrated product development that is now part of CMMI. The field of IPD is characterized by cross-functionality and holistic thinking, which is becoming more relevant as products become more complex. Products may be composed of subproducts, such as

- ◆ Software—the application(s)
- ◆ Hardware—boxes and/or PCs and/or peripherals
- ◆ Network—LAN or the internet

◆ Data—system data or parameter values
◆ Services—intangible deliveries such as training and maintenance

IPD requires considering a product's entire life, from conception to destruction—from the initial idea to disposal of all the parts. This is especially interesting for products that create nuclear waste, where destruction may take hundreds or thousands of years.

Products are also more than just the product, since they includes processes—for design, test, logistics, manufacturing, and so on—that make the product possible.

Organizational Considerations

Integrated product development is an organization-wide decision. The definition of IPD already presented has an impact on the way an integrated configuration management system is set up: the teaming of functional disciplines to integrate and concurrently apply all necessary processes.

Configuration Management Considerations

A configuration management system for integrated product development must take all the aspects of this philosophy into account and ensure that all the items defined for an integrated product can be placed under configuration management in an integrated and concurrent way. This is not easy.

Approach

Existing configuration management system(s) must be identified:

◆ For the full product and all subtypes (e.g., software and hardware development)
◆ For all defined lifecycle development activities (e.g., preparation, design, and production)
◆ For all processes (e.g., process management)

If a configuration management system does not exist for one or more of the aspects or if it's not complete, the missing parts must be defined. The processes involved must be analyzed to identify overlaps and conflicts, which must be resolved. It's unrealistic to imagine that no borderlines will exist between configuration management of the various types of items, but they must be made as smooth and imperceptible as possible.

18.4 ITERATIVE DEVELOPMENT

An iteration is the controlled reworking of part of a system to remove mistakes or make improvements. Iterative development is a collective term for development models where some or all of the activities are repeated in short cycles. Specific iterative models are the RAD Model by James Martin and the Spiral Model by Barry Boehm. The stages in iterative development, shown in Figure 18–5 (after James Martin), are

- ◆ Project initiation—determining the vision and objectives of the product
- ◆ Development—a set of iterations, refining and expanding the product
- ◆ Deployment—cut-over and use of a part of (and eventually) the full product

Each of the stages may contain iterations, though only the development stage is shown with iterations in Figure 18–5. Frameworks supporting iterative development

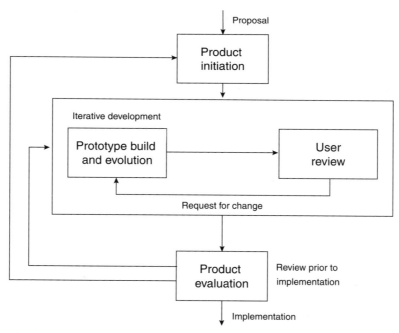

Figure 18–5 *Stages in Iterative Development*

are, for example, Microsoft Solution Framework, Dynamic Systems Development Method, and Rational Unified Process.

Developing a product using iterative development is a planning decision. This decision has a strong impact on the configuration management performed during the product's life cycle. Project planning must take configuration management into account at an early stage.

Configuration Management Considerations

In iterative development, frequent releases are planned, and changes are not only planned but actively encouraged. This means that well-thought-out configuration management is important, not least if iterations overlap—if iteration $n + 1$ starts before the result of iteration n is deployed. This occurs often, as a way of optimizing resources. Designers start the design of iteration $n + 1$ based on the design of iteration n while developers and testers are working on the release of iteration n.

Requirements Management

The part of configuration management concerned with requirements, often called requirements management, is particularly important for iterative development. The requirements are the basis for the product. In iterative development, the requirements in the total pool of requirements are constantly undergoing changes:

- Requirements are added to the pool.
- Requirements in the pool are changed.
- Requirements are taken out of the pool for implementation in a specific iteration.
- Requirements dedicated to a specific iteration are changed.
- Requirements dedicated to a specific iteration are implemented.
- Requirements dedicated to a specific iteration are tested.
- A specific iteration fulfilling requirements is released.
- Requirements dedicated to a specific iteration are postponed (rerouted to the pool).
- Released requirements are changed (in the pool) and need reimplementation.

All this requires strict and swift configuration management of the requirements. In iterative development, the coding stage is not early enough to start configuration management. Configuration management must start at least with requirements and preferably with high-level visions and objectives.

Identification

It's important to be able to identify versions and other historical information for configuration items in iterative development, where each new iteration is an expansion of the previous version. For planning and implementation, identification should include information about which iterations a requirement has been implemented in and which it is going to be implemented in. Tracing between requirements and other related configuration items is therefore part of identification that must be carefully considered, planned, described, and performed.

Storage

Since iterative development entails frequent restructuring of design and code, configuration management must facilitate easy fallback to a previous version of any item. Configuration management should also cater to frequent builds for fast extraction of configuration items, especially delivery items. Also, the configuration management system should cater to extracts for production, since the whole idea is to keep changing and expanding the product.

Change Control

Since changes are the norm, the relevant configuration control board(s) must be defined early on. Special care should be taken to make these accessible and fast working, able to make decisions and carry them through, and representative of as many stakeholders as possible. It may be worthwhile to simplify event registrations and change requests, but documentation of the connected decisions must not be compromised.

Status Reporting

Status reporting should be comprehensive and fast, not least concerning requirements, because an overview of the requirements and their progress through their life cycle is an indispensable tool for iterative development. Reports concerning deliveries are also important, especially so customers and users can comprehend what is included in a new iteration and what is not.

18.5 SEQUENTIAL DEVELOPMENT

"The waterfall development model is dead," claim many of today's developers and researchers. But it isn't. Experience shows that many companies still follow some variation of a sequential development model, of which the waterfall model is the origin.

A sequential development model is one where development activities follow each other in a forward sequence. This is illustrated in Figure 18–6 in a waterfall model for a simple, pure software project. The work flows from one development activity to the next, and each development activity has to be finished—the planned work products approved—before the next starts.

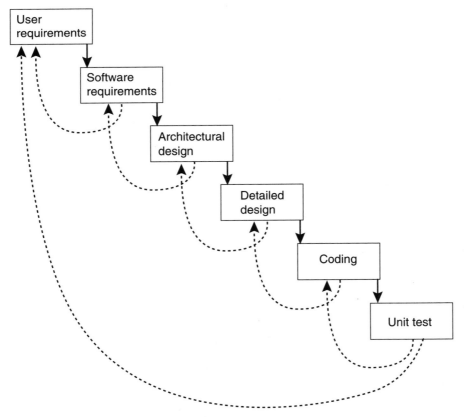

Figure 18–6 *Pure Waterfall Development Model*

However, some backpass from a development activity to a previous development activity always occurs, as indicated by the dotted lines. Not all possible backpasses are shown—just a few examples. This happens because changes of mind are as inevitable as are mistakes, so both new knowledge and error corrections will contribute to backpasses. A waterfall model with backpass is different from an iterative model, in that backpass is considered an exception, and the aim is to conclude each activity before starting the next, even when going through a backpass.

W-Model

The so-called W-model, shown in Figure 18–7 and widely used today, is an extension of the classical waterfall model and the V-model. The principle of the V-model is that testing is performed as a number of different test types, according to different test objects, shown as the right "arm" in Figure 18–7. This means that testing is not just one test at the end of the project but a number of tests performed as early as possible, starting with the unit test. This is based on the detailed design and is performed on individual units as soon as they are ready. The unit test is followed by an integration test, system test, and acceptance test.

The extra principle in the W-model in relation to the V-model is that each test is prepared as soon as the basis for it is ready. For example, the acceptance test is planned and specified along with the user requirements—preferably in parallel, but at the latest as soon as the requirements are finished. This is shown as the right part of the left "arm" in Figure 18–7. The results of the tests are documented and reported; this is shown as the right part of the right "arm."

Figure 18–7 does not include the backpasses, but this doesn't imply there are none. On the contrary, this model has even more than the pure waterfall model, since the early work on test specifications creates awareness of both necessary enhancements and errors to the basis for the test specification (e.g., the architectural design).

Configuration Management Considerations

It may look as if configuration management is not important when you are using one of the sequential models. They usually involve few planned releases and at least the theoretical assumption that everything is done right the first time. This is not the reality, as the inclusion of one or more test activities indicates and as experience shows (illustrated in the backpasses). Hence, configuration management is relevant as a support function for sequential development but perhaps a little easier than in agile models.

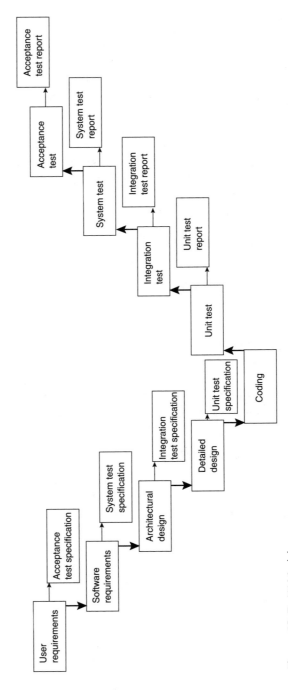

Figure 18–7 *W-Model*

Identification

Tracing, both vertically and horizontally, is an important part of the sequential development model, especially the W-model. The vertical trace ensures that everything in a development activity is catered to in the next development activity; this is an important contribution to "doing it right the first time." It also ensures that the product doesn't grow—isn't gold-plated with unwarranted functionality or features. This is an important contribution to keeping the plans.

The horizontal trace—between the test basis and the test specification (such as user requirements and acceptance test cases) ensures that everything is testable and is going to be tested. This trace also contributes to "doing it right the first time" and to keeping the plans. To be able to perform and register these traces, the objects involved must be placed under configuration management early. This means at least having identification procedures in place when new objects are created and, as part of this, a good and easy trace procedure.

Change Control

A project must be prepared for changes and have a change-handling procedure ready, even when using sequential development. Events should not come as a surprise, and the configuration control board(s) should be constituted as early as possible. Changes must be catered to in planning. Even if the intention is to do everything right the first time around, planning must allow for changes, not least as part of test activities. Experience shows that project management is often surprised by the number of errors found in testing and the time involved in finding and resolving them.

Status Reporting

Usually, it's important for project management on sequential development models to follow up closely on project plans. Status reporting from the configuration management system can provide valuable information. Therefore, it's important to ensure that status reporting is fast, comprehensive, and reliable. Trace reports can reveal the state of completeness for each development activity in turn, as can reports on event registrations and change requests. A development activity is not complete until the trace is complete and the number of open event registrations and change requests has reached an acceptable level.

Chapter 19

Managing Configurations for Different Product Types

Configuration management to be performed for a given product depends on the nature of the product. Products may be relatively simple or complex, or something in between. They may be harmless, with no great impact on human lives or other companies, or extremely safety-critical, or something in between. As indicated in the previous chapter, any product has a combination of these attributes or factors that coexist with other factors, such as the development model, that must be taken into consideration singly and together.

19.1 COMPOSITE SYSTEMS

Composite systems are products that consist of many types of configuration items, such as software, hardware, and documents. Figure 19–1 shows an example of a composite system. It's a network print server, consisting of a print card with various components on it. Several components on the card contain software: (1) is the program memory, which is neatly labeled with configuration information; (2) and (3) both contain pure hardware functions (logical circuits). These may, however, both be configured by the means of software, but only one of them (2) has controlled configuration. Moreover, a change in the delivery can be seen in the form of a "louse" at (4).

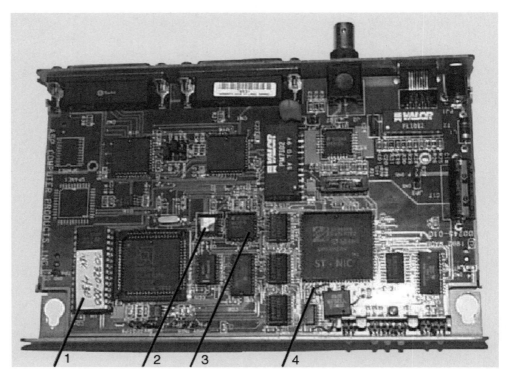

Figure 19–1 *Composite System—Example*

Design Considerations

The architecture for a product is a design decision that determines which functionality is to be implemented in software and which in hardware. However, this distribution is likely to change during development.

Configuration Management Considerations

It's important, when handling composite systems, to make clear what is what. When software and hardware are mixed, items that should have been placed under configuration management may easily be forgotten. Each type of item must be identified separately, and deliveries must be defined for collections. This means that it's no good to place a piece of hardware with software in it under configuration management as a single configuration item. It must be placed under configuration management as a single hardware item, a single software item, and, moreover, as a delivery consisting of these two items in combination.

Identification

All configuration items in composite systems must be identified. The item type should appear from the unique identification—hardware, software, or something else. When defining conventions, consider how software identification could be related to hardware identification for items that are naturally related. It may be necessary to create proxy items to represent hardware items in a database, as hardware items cannot be placed in the database themselves. Tracing information must define which part of functionality is implemented in which parts of the system.

Storage

Deliveries consisting of hardware with embedded software are stored like hardware items—produced in a number of copies that are stored physically and physically released for usage.

Change Control

Careful change control is necessary for composite systems. The same processes should be employed for all configuration items in these systems, whatever the item type. It's necessary to account for emergency changes, as shown in the "louse" in the previous example. It's especially necessary to maintain tracing information to reflect functionality transferred from a hardware item to a software item, or vice versa.

Status Reporting

Status reporting should include information that is as highly integrated as possible for all types of configuration items.

19.2 MULTIPLATFORM

Multiplatform problems arise when products must be developed, used, and maintained on different computers and/or operating systems. Multiplatform products may be those that must run on both UNIX workstations and Windows PCs, for example, or those that must "merely" run on different versions of UNIX, (SunOS, HP-UX), or different versions of Windows (Windows 98 or NT). Multiplatform problems are also found in embedded systems, where the software is developed and maybe tested on a PC platform and subsequently placed in an apparatus. Multiplatform products may be created in connection with initial requirements or with maintenance, where a product must be transferred to a newer platform.

Configuration Management Considerations

Multiplatform development is a special form of multivariant development (where configuration items are developed centrally) and/or multisite development (where configuration items are "owned" by a platform). Although multiplatform products will naturally be developed with some degree of decentralization, it's practical to perform configuration management centrally. This may be done by choosing one platform from which configuration management takes place. Some tools support this.

Identification

When defining conventions, it should be possible to use the names on all the platforms—the number and types of permitted characters must be considered specially.

19.3 MULTIVARIANTS

Multivariants or just variants occur when what may seem to be a single configuration item (from a functional point of view) appears in different, almost identical versions simultaneously. This may arise because of

- Language requirements (e.g., Danish and English)
- Hardware requirements (e.g., different processors in the same family of products)
- Legislation requirements (e.g., concerning registration of personal information in different countries)
- Communication protocols
- Customer requirements (e.g., the demand for an "economy" model and a "deluxe" model)

Examples

Variants of a Single Configuration Item

A company sells accounting systems all over the world. The system consists of a kernel and a number of modules that may be added to the kernel. One of these modules is calculation of sales tax (ST) to be added when an item is being sold. The legislation in this field varies from country to country, and the module exists in a number of variants. All these variants have the same interface to the kernel, so the complete product can be delivered in different variants.

Variants of Delivery

A company sells a product that may be bought with varying functionality depending on the needs (and the money). The complete product can be delivered with a varying number of configuration items.

Requirements Considerations

Variants are created as a consequence of requirements for the complete product. Analysts may facilitate configuration management by making clear as early as possible which variants are expected and which combinations may occur.

Design Considerations

The creation of variants is a design decision, not a configuration management decision. But the configuration management system must be able to cater to variants when they occur. The design of items that may appear in variants should take maintenance and configuration management into account. This may be done by placing as much as possible of the common functionality in items that do not appear in variants.

In the tax example previously given, the tax module for Denmark should contain only what is strictly relevant to Denmark. This reduces the risk that changes will affect many items. The variants will, however, always have something in common—the interface at least.

The number of variants may also be reduced by introducing parameter control for a common item, so the variants are tailored to the customer on the basis of a common product. In the example of the product with varying functionality, the deluxe system may be delivered as an economy system by closing off access to "extra" modules. A solution of this kind may, however, result in a need for variants of a parameter file, and then we're back where we started.

Another way of reducing the number of variants is to use conditional compilation (e.g., #ifdef). This may be a good solution when delivery is to different hardware platforms. In the two examples already given, the benefits of simpler configuration management must be weighed against the disadvantage of moving the complexity to the code and thereby also to test and maintenance. Designers may facilitate configuration management by making clear as early as possible how variants will be handled as regards design.

Configuration Management Considerations

Variants may cause configuration management to be complex indeed. Variants of single configuration items must be considered. But variants are always reflected in deliveries: if the configuration items contain variants, the deliveries will too. Furthermore, the deliveries may have variants without variants in the single configuration items, as in the two examples already discussed.

Each variant in a family must be treated as a single configuration item—that is, it must be possible to release new versions of the item independently of the other variants. For example, the newest version of the sales tax software for Denmark may be 2.3, while the newest version for the U.K. may be 1.8. Variants rarely appear as branches of a configuration item, but it may happen. It may also happen that variants melt into one configuration item, but this is rare for genuine variants. Both these situations are handled as parallel development with regard to configuration management.

Identification

Naming conventions must take variants into account. It must be clear from the metadata for a configuration item that this item is part of a variant family, and which one. Especially for deliveries, the combinations of variants must be considered. A product may, for example, be delivered as PROD_UK-deluxe, PROD_UK-minimum, or PROD_DK-minimum.

It must also be clear from the metadata which configuration items are related variants. It may be necessary to introduce an extra data element to register the family, but this may often be solved by the name alone. In the sales tax example already discussed, the family might be called CALC_ST and the names of the variants could begin with CALC_ST. The variant part of the name could be _aa, where aa follows the international standard for country codes.

Tracing must be performed with care, so that common requirements implemented in all variants are traced to all variants, while requirements pertaining to one variant are traced only to that item.

Storage

In principle, all variants must be stored individually as configuration items, like all other configuration items. It may be an advantage to store different variants in different master libraries, so that variants belonging to Denmark are placed in a Danish master library and the French variants are stored in a French master library, while common items are stored in a common master library. Such a solution may also be combined with multisite development. Separate libraries may make the production of deliveries easier and more secure but may also make it more difficult to handle metadata—that is, to produce information about families.

When collecting deliveries, the proper variants must be included in each one. This applies to deliveries both for test and for operation. Each delivery variant will often have a special production procedure (make-file or the like). It's important to know which variants have been released to whom, so changes may be communicated to relevant stakeholders, and only to them. It may, for example, not be terribly relevant for a Danish user to be informed that the German variant has been updated.

Change Control

Change control must be performed with special care when variants are involved. The configuration control board must have access to information about variants: the board must be able to make out if a given configuration item is a variant and, if so, which other items are in the same family. On the basis of this and relevant tracing information, the board must decide if an event has an effect on all variants in the family, some, or only one. Variants must also be included in an analysis of the consequences of an event. It may not be feasible to introduce a change in a variant if it has significant adverse consequences on other variants.

Status Reporting

Status reporting must take variants into account. It must be possible to get a report that identifies all variants in a family on the basis of a single variant. It must also be possible to identify to whom the variants in a family of deliveries have been released. Furthermore, it must be possible to give a statement of status and history for each variant in a family independently of the others.

19.4 SAFETY-CRITICAL PRODUCTS

Several classifications regarding criticality apply to software products. Table 19–1 shows an example.

Table 19–1 Safety Criticality Classification Example

Type	Level (Weight)			
	A **(100,000,000)**	**B** **(100,000)**	**C** **(100)**	**D** **(1)**
Safety	Many people killed	Human lives in danger	Damage to physical objects; risk of personal injury	Insignificant damage to physical objects; no risk to human beings
Economy	Financial catastrophe (the company must close)	Great financial loss (the company is threatened)	Significant financial loss (the company is affected)	Insignificant financial loss
Security	Destruction/ disclosure of strategic data and services	Destruction/ disclosure of critical data and services	Errors in data	No risk for data
Environment	Comprehensive and irreparable damage to the environment	Reparable, but comprehensive damage to the environment	Local damage to the environment	No environmental risk

Examples

At level A are found systems for air traffic control and military systems. At level B are found fire-fighting systems and integrated financial systems. At level C are found fire alarms and financial systems in isolation. At level D are found office automation systems and entertainment systems. A system may of course be of different levels for different types of risks. The combined weight determines the final classification.

Configuration Management Considerations

There are no unambiguous rules for the kind of configuration management that must be performed as a result of a product's criticality level, but the need for formality and automation increases with the level of criticality. For the majority of products on levels A and B, standards apply that include requirements for configuration management. For this reason, it's practical to follow the standards (see Chapter 3).

19.5 SIZE OF PRODUCT (LARGE AND SMALL)

Everything is relative. A final definition of what is a small product and what is a large product cannot be given. What may seem large in one company may seem of ordinary size, or even small, in another. A company's own definition determines whether a product is regarded as large or small.

Small Systems

When is a product too small for configuration management to be profitable? A short answer to this question is: never! But of course the amount of work is generally less with small products than with larger ones. No matter how few items are contained in a product and no matter how few people are involved in development, employees leave and employees forget. People cannot hold more than seven to nine things in their heads at a time, and if they must do so, the quality of what they are doing will be reduced. Therefore, critical items in even the smallest products must be placed under configuration management. One could ask oneself, "Would the possibility of delivering the proper system on time and within the budget be affected if a certain item were lost, destroyed, or used the wrong way or in the wrong version?"

Large Systems

Big numbers are terrifying. The size of a product does not in itself make configuration management more complicated, but the task may seem overwhelming. Moreover, the need for formality increases with the number of people involved in development. It's always a good idea to break down large products into smaller pieces that are then placed under configuration management individually. It's also a good idea to break the project itself into smaller (sub)projects or activities and plan for one development activity at a time. This also makes the configuration management task more manageable. Sufficient resources to accomplish the task are required, especially an increased need for tool support.

Identification

When defining conventions for unique identification, one must take care not to define numbers and acronyms that may run out. This applies to small systems as well as large ones. It's impractical if a series of numbers has only one character and the need arises for ten configuration items in the series. It's equally impractical if a series has five characters and the need arises for 100,000 items in the series.

Storage

In the case of large products, it's important to secure sufficient storage for saving many versions of many files. It's also important to optimize the time it takes to extract configuration items for usage, (especially to produce large deliveries, such as for test), because the size of the product can have a significant influence on this.

Change Control

No specific considerations apply to change control in connection with product size, except that large products may require a special comprehensive overview by configuration control boards. For small products, one must take care that change control does not become too informal.

Status Reporting

Neither do any special status reporting considerations apply with regard to product size, except that status reporting must be able to meet volume requirements in connection with large products. For small products, one should not reduce the possibilities of producing status reports.

Tool Considerations

For large products, tool support is inevitable. Requirements for handling large volumes should enter into considerations with regard to the choice of tool. Most serious tools tolerate almost unlimited scaling, but it's important to make sure that this scaling applies to the tool one ends up choosing. For small products, tool support should be carefully considered, to obtain optimal performance while not cracking a nut with a sledgehammer and taking on unnecessary functionality.

19.6 WEB APPLICATIONS

Web development involves applications that can be used via the Internet or a local intranet. In many ways, Web development is similar to traditional development, but there are some differences:

- Time-to-market is small: new versions may be produced in less than a week, or indeed in less than an hour.
- The number of configuration items is much larger: a Web application may consist of 100,000 items (including all graphic details), while a classic software system consisting of 10,000 items is usually regarded as extraordinarily large.
- It's easy to release a new version—all you have to do is move the item to the server (if it's not developed right there). This is both an advantage and a serious threat to control.
- Iterative development is common, and maintenance is part of development: you design a little, develop a little, test a little, release, and so on.
- WWW = wild, wild Web or wild, wilder, wildest: people who make Web systems often have a background different from that of other software specialists.
- Generally, companies that develop Web systems experience considerable staff turnover.
- To a large extent, and increasingly, Web applications involve components developed by others. Earlier companies suffered from the "not-invented-here" prejudice, which meant that everything had to be developed from scratch. Now, the attitude "stolen with pride" prevails.
- Techniques and platforms are totally new (and untried) and change all the time.

Configuration management processes and tools must be able to cope with these special conditions.

Examples

Examples of Web systems are numerous: e-banking, sites for companies or organizations, e-commerce such as amazon.com or the local supermarket, search sites like Google, travel sites like Shellstar, and so on. Just connect to the net and start surfing!

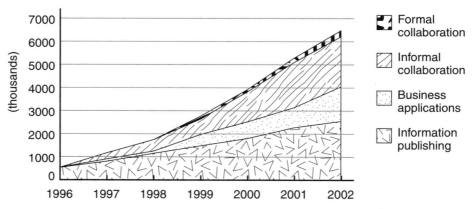

Figure 19–2 *Web Usage*

Content Management

Configuration management for Web applications is also known as content management. This partly refers to the fact already mentioned—that Web applications are usually composed of a large number of small items: a large list of contents. It used to be that changes in Web applications were largely performed by replacing entire items rather than just by making changes to them. This picture is different now, as Web applications develop from being pure showcases to supporting business functionality.

Figure 19–2 shows the increase in servers, grouped according to their primary use. The figure illustrates that the use of Web software as pure publishing of information (showcase) is stagnant, while the use of real systems that can "do something" (functionality) is increasing. Systems with functionality are shown in the three groups: business applications (such as e-commerce), informal collaboration (such as the possibility of entering gas meter reading), and formal collaboration (such as interactive control of a remote production system).

Content management is, however, also configuration management. The new name may also be a sign of old virtues coming into fashion again. As the new "wild" developers experience the cost of lack of configuration management, they begin to realize that configuration management may be overlooked but is certainly not obsolete.

Configuration Management Considerations

In "Notes from the Front Lines: How to Test Anything and Everything on a Web Site," Ted Fuller says,

Lesson #1: Testing Web applications is completely different from testing any other software.

Lesson #2: Testing Web applications is no different from testing other software.

Lesson #3: Nothing in your QA experience prepares you for working on a Web project.

Lesson #4: Everything in your QA experience prepares you for working on a Web project.

No doubt the same applies to configuration management! The change in the nature of Web applications, as illustrated in Figure 19–5, also means that quality requirements for the systems have grown, as have requirements for configuration management.

Identification

It's important to clarify how the many external pieces used in Web systems should be identified: whether they should be identified internally, at the risk of their development not being sustainable (because the link to the external development may be cut off by changing the identification), or whether their original identification should be used, at the risk of its fitting badly into the local identification conventions.

It's also important constantly to take care that the composition of deliveries is correct. New versions of deliveries often inherit their content description from earlier versions, but Web deliveries especially may be so fast-moving that one risks not including everything or getting stray items that are no longer necessary. The case where everything is not included will presumably be found quickly in a test. In the opposite case, deliveries contain a large number of items that nobody will acknowledge and nobody dares to remove.

Composite deliveries must be expressed explicitly, so one does not get newer versions of single configuration items without wanting or knowing it. A newer version of a configuration item than the one expected may completely smash up a Web system.

Storage

Separate libraries, or environments, are essential for production, test, and operation. Much too often these environments are mixed in connection with Web applications, so that test and even development take place directly in the operation environment. For the sake of mobility between various environments, design must be performed with an eye to configuration management, using relative links, so changes do not have to be made whenever something is moved.

Change Control

Change control is a special problem for Web development, because everything must go so fast, especially regarding registration and error correction. The process for event registration must be easy to use, and handling speed must suit the overall speed requirements for Web development. However, one must not allow oneself to be tyrannized by the demand that everything must go fast. One should not reduce one's demands for change control—not even for Web development.

Status Reporting

For Web systems, status reports should be clear and able to be produced quickly. Therefore, it may be advantageous to produce different types of reports with less information in each one or to provide for convenient search directly in metadata.

Chapter 20

Managing Configurations under Special Conditions

A number of factors may cause special problems or add complexity during a product's life cycle and thereby pose special requirements for configuration management. More of these factors may be present in some projects, and they always coexist with other factors, such as the development model and product type. As indicated earlier, these factors must be taken into consideration singly and in combination.

20.1 MULTISITE DEVELOPMENT (GEOGRAPHIC DISTRIBUTION)

Multisite or geographically distributed development means that different parts of a development group are in different locations, which implies that everybody does not have direct access to all configuration items. Typically, source code is shared among several development sites, but it may be all types of configuration items. The principles are the same: information must be doubled and synchronized.

Example

A company has been developing software in Denmark for many years. As part of the company's expansion plans, it buys two minor competitive companies, one in the United States and one in Europe. Staff policy dictates that each development project have participants from all three offices. It's not economically and technically possible to establish connections so staff members outside Denmark can work directly on the server in Denmark. Figure 20–1 illustrates the situation.

Figure 20–1 *Multisite Development—Sharing Items*

All development sites need all configuration items, but each office is responsible for the circled items. The offices do not have direct access to each other's machinery; all configuration items must therefore be accessible in all three places simultaneously.

Organizational Considerations

Multisite development is an organizational decision. When a company decides on multisite development, a number of derived decisions must be taken, especially

- How the connection between the development sites should be organized
  - Over the Internet, and with which bandwidth
  - Offline, via the postal service
- How the responsibility should be distributed
  - For configuration items
  - For synchronization
  - For processes that must be followed
  - For machines and their connections
- How much language and culture matter
  - In which language(s) should procedure descriptions be written
  - How should procedure descriptions be formed to make them as useful as possible
  - Which language(s) should a possible tool support

Configuration Management Considerations

The key words in connection with configuration management and multisite development are ownership and synchronization. The need for formality and automation increases with the time (different time zones or shift work) and distance that divide the people involved and with the degree of competition among them.

All development sites must follow the same processes—the same (described) procedures. This is the first thing that must be in place. If one does not agree on how things must be done, multisite development will never work. If it's not possible to synchronize processes thoroughly, the differences must be made clear, as well as how these differences should be handled. Who is responsible for maintaining the processes must also be clear.

Identification

Identification of configuration items should follow the same conventions on all development sites. In any case, the merging of the unique identification for different items should definitely be avoided. An item's identification should indicate which site is responsible for it. Each item must be owned by one site only.

Storage

What is really complicated in connection with multisite development is storage, as it's necessary to double the controlled library on each site and take care that all copies of the library are synchronized. At the same time, a site must not by accident be able to changes items the site is not responsible for. Access to all such configuration items must be for release to usage exclusively, never for production or placement in storage (access must be read-only).

The method of synchronization between the sites should be carefully considered. This may entail the transfer of changed configuration items via tape or disk sent by ordinary post to the most sophisticated automated synchronizing mechanisms. Several configuration management tools support multisite development, offering various solutions to the synchronization problem. The appropriate solution depends on the company's needs and financial capacity.

In the above example, the Danish office makes changes in the configuration items it's responsible for. These changes must be distributed to the other offices. The changes made by the other offices to items they are responsible for must be distributed as well. This is shown in Figure 20–2, where the arrows illustrate synchronization. It must be clear to everyone when synchronization takes place.

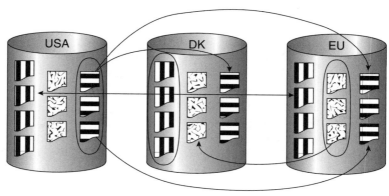

Figure 20–2 *Synchronization of Multisites*

Change Control

Change control must be performed centrally. The sites should not have local configuration control boards unless these boards are explicitly arranged and well motivated. On the other hand, configuration control boards with members from several or all sites will often be needed. These groups may use e-mail or Web-enabled systems.

In the ideal situation, all sites will use a common event registration system. The relevant configuration control board must treat all event registrations and channel change requests to the relevant sites. All those affected by an event registration should be informed of the progress, as well as those at a site other than the one where a change is performed.

Status Reporting

All information should be synchronized in the same way as the configuration items themselves. This will often make it possible to extract relevant status reports where needed.

Example

The following example has kindly been provided by Mr. Bjarne Månsson of Baan CRM in Denmark. The company has two development sites: Golden (Colorado, USA) and Herlev (Denmark), each developing individual components of the product. Visual SourceSafe (VSS) is used for version control of the files. Local components are built locally on a daily basis and distributed to the other site after a successful regression test. Synchronizing the components between sites means, with the eight-hour time difference, that local components in Herlev must be ready for build by noon (4:00 A.M. Golden time) and in Golden by 10 P.M. (6:00 A.M. Herlev time). Figure 20–3 shows the synchronization process.

A full build has components from both sites, since local components depend on components from the other site. A build consists of both binaries (compiled components .dll, .exe), Web files (.html, .js, .asp, .xml), and a database (.mdb). This is illustrated in Figure 20–4. The full synchronization and build process consists of the following steps:

- Getting the latest binaries and Web files from the other development site
- Building (compiling) the latest source code from the local development site
- Making an installation file on all binaries and Web files

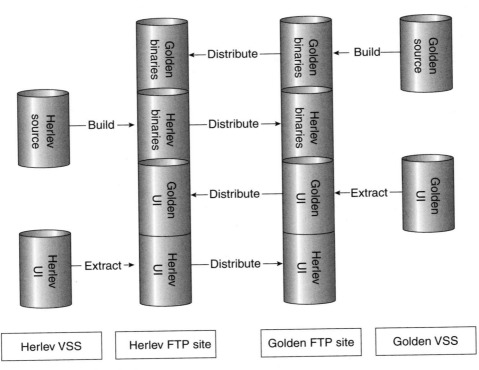

Figure 20–3 Synchronization

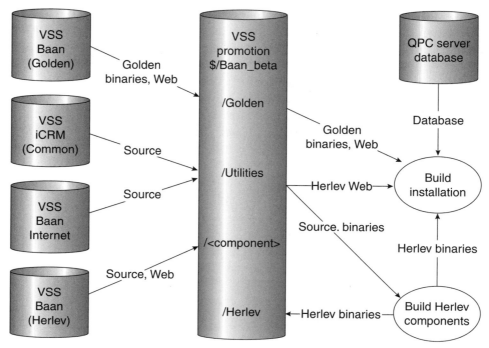

Figure 20–4 *Multisite Build*

Note that binaries are also stored in VSS—this facilitates a rebuild of a particular version. The code is identified in VSS by the build number after a build, using VSS's labeling function.

The release (final build) requires an extra round of distribution, because every local build depends on changed code from the other site. So the final build consists of these steps:

- At Golden (build number $n - 1$): build with changed Golden and changed Herlev code (of build number $n - 2$)

- At Herlev (build number $n - 1$): build with changed Golden (of build number $n - 1$) and changed Herlev code

- At Golden (build number n): build with same Golden and changed Herlev code (of build number $n - 1$)

- At Herlev (build number n): build with same Golden (build number n) and same Herlev code

- At Golden: test installation of build number n
- Release build number n

20.2 MULTIPLE STAKEHOLDERS

Every project should undertake a stakeholder analysis. Stakeholders who may be important to the performance of configuration management may be

- Customers or authorities with special requirements for the use of standards, such as military, space travel, medical, or other safety-critical systems
- Customers with their own standards/ideas
- Subcontractors with their own standards/ideas
- Other departments in the company, such as test or operation

The more stakeholders in a given project, the more complicated the work may be. But the work may also become easier if one or more of the stakeholders has clear requirements about how to perform configuration management.

Get an Overview of the Requirements

In a project with many stakeholders, it's important to ascertain the influence each stakeholder has or wants to have. One could ask oneself these questions:

- Who has indispensable requirements for configuration management, and which requirements?
- Who has requests concerning configuration management, and what are they?
- Who has requirements or requests for interfaces to their configuration management system, and what are they?
- Who can help accomplish the task, and how?

It may be a good idea to produce overviews of the requirements for each stakeholder independently and compare these in a more or less formal way, possibly including priorities.

Analyze the Requirements

Requirements can first be divided into generic requirements and explicit requirements. An example of a generic requirement (from [PPS-05-09]) is "SCM09 The identifier of a configuration item shall include a version number." An example of an explicit requirement is the format for a unique identification. Investigate which explicit requirements match which generic requirements and whether requirements conflict (and if so, which have the greatest weight).

Describe the Fulfillment

On the basis of the requirements analysis, prepare a fulfillment matrix showing how the configuration management system employed by the project meets the requirements. Where the requirements suggest better solutions, the project's configuration management system must be adapted.

Conflict of Authority

Conflicts of authority may arise between different stakeholders, such as departments, in connection with configuration management. It's essential to make borderlines clear and establish how cooperation can take place across them. It may be complicated, for example, for a project to include tools in configuration management that are under the jurisdiction of an operations department. In this case, metadata could merely refer to the tools.

20.3 PARALLEL DEVELOPMENT

Parallel development occurs when people have to work on the same configuration item at the same time—when branches have to be formed from one item (the trunk), and the results are merged. The need for parallel development may be caused by time pressure, shift work, or distribution of expertise.

Example

A company has to produce a large requirement specification, which includes both a graphical user interface and communication protocols. Different experts will have to work on different parts of the requirement specification at the same time. The requirement specification is therefore divided during this work and merged into the final document near the end of the activity. Figure 20–5 illustrates this process.

   If the experts have worked on separate parts, like a chapter each, the merge is probably not difficult. It may, however, be complicated indeed, especially if time pressure is the driving force and a number of people are working in more or less the same places in the items. Fortunately, some tools support the merging of configuration items.

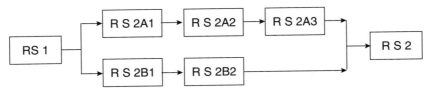

Figure 20–5 *Parallel Development and Merge*

Planning Considerations

Parallel development is a planning decision and is therefore the responsibility of the project manager or development manager. Consider carefully whether parallel configuration items should be placed under configuration management or the parallel development should take place outside the configuration management system, in the production environments.

What needs to be considered is whether the intermediate versions—R S 2A1 through R S 2A3 and R S 2B1 through R S 2B2 in the example—should be made public and whether it's necessary to know their individual history, or whether it's only of interest to know the history from R S 1 directly to R S 2. In the latter case, development is not parallel from a configuration management point of view, but the actual parallel development must of course be catered to in planning, and the merge must be performed before the final result is placed under configuration management.

Parallel development under configuration management should be limited to an absolute minimum. To avoid it, it might be advisable to make changes to the design and split an item into more independent items. It might also be worth considering the XP practice of pair programming and let two developers do two changes together, instead of splitting the work between them.

This section is about "genuine" parallel development, where branches are placed under configuration management. However, some of the discussions are also valid if parallel development is done outside configuration management. Where parallel development can't be avoided, frequent merges should be planned, to make the branches as few and as short as possible.

Configuration Management Considerations

Where parallel development can't be avoided parallel individual configuration items must be considered. Parallel development may work its way through to deliveries, so parallel deliveries will have to be produced. If something is really parallel development, however, it must be made clear whether the result is a merger into a single configuration item or if it's variants.

Identification

Identification should reflect parallel development, so that metadata indicates whether an item is a branch in parallel development and, if so, which item it originates from and possibly which item the branching will end up in. Figure 20–6 shows good and bad examples of version designations for parallel development.

An extra data element may be necessary in the metadata to register the trunk in a branching, but most often this can be solved by the name alone. Tracing must branch off and merge with the items themselves. It's important to know at all times which functionality is maintained where—which part of the trunk each of the branches is responsible for. Two branches should not share responsibility for any part of the trunk.

Storage

Configuration items that are branches must be stored individually, on an equal footing with all other items. Branches that exist as independent configuration items are stored as described in the Multivariants section, above.

Change Control

Change control must be done with extra care in parallel development. The configuration control board(s) must have access to branching information, to determine whether an item is a branch and, if so, which item is the trunk and what other

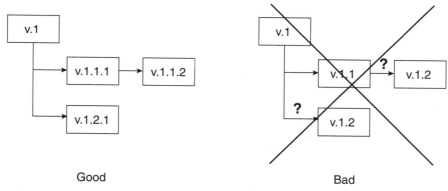

Good   Bad

Figure 20–6 *Naming Conventions in Parallel Development*

branches exist. Based on this information and relevant trace information the board(s) may decide if an event is to enter into a branch or maybe wait until the merge has taken place.

Status Reporting

Status reporting must take any possible parallel development into consideration. It should be possible to produce a report that identifies all branches from a trunk and to identify who has received which branches between merges. Status and history for each branch should be presentable independently of other branches from the trunk. Even after the merge, it's important to be able to get information about each of the branches.

Tool Considerations

Several configuration management tools offer a variety of comparison and merge facilities. However, most tools are not able to perform a reliable merge of items with conflicting differences. This could be changes to the same piece of source code in two different ways (for two different, but valid, reasons) from the same trunk. In these cases, the board responsible for the trunk and the result must step in and decide how such a merge is to take place, if at all. This may be done with tool support, though it requires a final human judgment.

20.4 TOOL SUPPORT

Most projects use some form of tool support. Development tools range from the simple, such as an editor, compiler, and linker, to the most complex integrated development environments (IDEs) or fourth-generation development languages (4GLs). Which tool(s) to deploy is a high-level management decision in a project or company-wide. It should not be made in isolation, but in connection with other needs, including configuration management.

Configuration Management Considerations

Configuration management of items developed in simple environments does not usually pose significant problems. In this context, work is done on ordinary files, most often in ASCII format, that are directly accessible and under full control of the developer (and the operating system). It's far more complicated to place items developed in, for example, a 4GL environment under configuration management. These tools organize their working files in internal libraries that do not provide direct access and control.

Part of the selection process for a development tool should be how the tool handles configuration management in context. If the development environment fulfills the requirements, these built-in facilities should be used and fitted into the configuration management process. It may be necessary to export metadata for the sake of status reporting, but that is usually possible.

If the development environment does not fulfill the requirements, the tool(s) may be able to cooperate with the configuration management system, especially the configuration management tool(s). If not, reconsider the choice of tool. IDE and 4GL systems, which can't cooperate with configuration management tool(s), tend to increase the risks of product development rather than reducing them.

Chapter 21

Managing Configurations for Cross-Organizational Functions

21.1 COMPANY INFRASTRUCTURE

The complexity of configuration management of the infrastructure is much higher than in the days of mainframes, when everybody in a company used the same version of the editor, for example. Many people are unfamiliar with the details of the infrastructure they use during their daily work. In many cases, this is not important. For some products, however, it may be crucial for parts of the infrastructure to be placed under configuration management like the rest of the product, such as when it is necessary to re-create earlier versions of the product. Every part of the infrastructure may be placed under configuration management: machines, peripherals, networks, operating systems, and tools.

Organizational Considerations

Most often, responsibility for configuration management of the infrastructure is placed with an internal IT department. Interfaces to the other organizational units, typically projects or other departments that develop products, must be clear. This is to ensure that what should be placed under configuration management actually is, and in a way useful for everybody affected. It does happen, however, that tools are placed under configuration management with the product for whose production they are deployed. Interfaces to suppliers and subcontractors must also be made clear.

Identification

Needless to say, the parts of the infrastructure that are to be placed under configuration management must be identified. It may be necessary to agree on a special convention or conventions for some parts. This could be in connection with a product that has strong external requirements for identification or to avoid conflicting unique identifications. It's rarely possible to perform tracing for infrastructure. This is possible only if the company has an explicit IT strategy to which traces may be provided.

Storage

Storage is special for the infrastructure, since configuration items are mostly distributed and in use. An important part of storage is registering where individual configuration items are "stored"—where a specific workstation is placed, and which workstations have which versions of which tools installed. This task may be extensive and difficult, especially if the responsibility for the infrastructure is distributed or unclear.

An important aspect of storage is maintaining older parts of the infrastructure that are still under configuration management. How long to keep old configuration items must be agreed upon with users. A large public organization still has a need for running recalculations on some systems that are more than 30 years old, including printing special reports. This is possible only on an equally old printer, since newer printers are not wide enough. Keeping the old printer in storage eliminates the need to rewrite large trunks of the old reporting subsystem.

Change Control

Event registration will most often be in the form of upgrades or enhancements to the infrastructure. These may be requests from management, employees, or from the outside in connection with projects with special needs. Event registration may of course also be for faults in items.

Event registrations from different parts of a company concerning the infrastructure may often conflict. The configuration control board(s) in charge of events and change handling for the infrastructure should therefore include representatives of as many stakeholders as possible. Everybody using the infrastructure should be informed when changes are implemented. One consideration is whether to adopt all changes immediately or to use an older part even if a new one has been released.

The project plan and/or development plan must take into consideration whether new parts of the infrastructure are to be adopted during a project. Such changes can cause a lot of trouble in a project; such as if a customer can't handle documents written in a new version of a word processor or if some construction in the code is not acceptable anymore.

Status Reporting

Employees must be able to get a quick overview of the configuration of the infrastructure they use. This may include the infrastructure's composition as well as any pending event registrations or change requests.

21.2 CROSS-ORGANIZATIONAL OBJECTS

Cross-organizational objects are artifacts produced and used across projects involved in product development and maintenance. These are mostly in the form of documents. Typically, high-level or cross-organizational units carry the responsibility for such objects, such as department management or a sales division. Many people use cross-organizational objects more or less independently of their roles in connection with product development and maintenance.

One or more responsible people must be appointed for cross-organizational objects. The objects may be divided into groups, for which different units carry the responsibility, as long as no object falls between two job responsibilities.

Configuration Management Considerations

It's uncommon for cross-organizational objects to be placed under configuration management. These objects are rarely used as the starting point for other objects, and changes do not often occur. It may, however, be a good idea to assess which objects are used by many people and at least place these under configuration management, so an old version can be re-created and so the history of the objects and reasons for changes will be accessible. It may also be useful to place high-level plans under configuration management, as a basis for documenting various courses of events.

Identification

It's important to define standards for unique identification so that it's clear which type of object one is dealing with. Clashes in unique identification must be avoided between cross-organizational configuration items and other items, such as other cross-organizational items, components for reuse, or product-specific items.

Storage

It may be useful to establish separate configuration management libraries for different types of cross-organizational configuration items (such as staff information, sales material, and business plans), under different people's responsibility. Cross-organizational items must under no circumstances be stored with items for specific products or components for reuse.

Change Control

No specific considerations apply to change control of cross-organizational items, apart from general principles. Configuration control board(s) may be difficult to form and to make function, but nevertheless, it's important to have board(s) that represent the relevant stakeholders.

Status Reporting

Status reports for cross-organizational items must be accessible to everybody with access to or an interest in the items. This may warrant access control for direct search in metadata, if many types of cross-organizational items are handled in the same place (e.g., using the same tool).

21.3 EXTERNAL REUSE COMPONENT DEVELOPMENT

External reuse refers to items developed and maintained entirely outside a company, such as those bought from other companies or downloaded from the Internet. External components that are changed within the company become either internal components or product-specific configuration items. This will change the way the items are treated from a configuration management point of view. The handling of external components is related to the handling of internal components for reuse that are developed and maintained in the company.

External components should be owned centrally, even if they are (initially) only used in one project. Central ownership is administration—no changes are connected with it.

Examples

In connection with Web applications, it's becoming more usual to use external components of the "Flash plug-in" type, for animated graphics. External components with ready-made graphics are also used extensively, such as pretty buttons with various functionality. Another example is the buying of complete class libraries for specific purposes, such as scientific or economic data handling, where the classes are used in the company's products.

Configuration Management Considerations

Only limited configuration management may be performed for external components. However, it may be important to the stability and maintenance of the company's own products to place external components under internal configuration management on a more or less equal footing with items developed internally. Configuration management of external components should be performed centrally.

Identification

It may be useful to define an internal unique identification for components. The supplier's identification must still follow the component, but that should not be used internally, to ensure unique identification within the company and avoid clashes with other components and items.

Extended metadata may accompany external components from the supplier, such as information about deployment and interface. These metadata must be made available to possible users of external components. When registering metadata, make sure it is connected to the correct component—for example, that the storage location is correct, especially where components are accessible only in executable form (as .exe files), which makes it impossible to check them directly.

Storage

External components should always be in controlled storage centrally. An external component may never be stored in more than one place. External components may, of course, be released for usage and kept in any number of copies in static libraries (depending on license agreements). They may be released to form the basis for production, such as if a component is needed to support a test or a local object is to be based on a component. A new version of the components must not be produced internally. If the need (or the temptation) for this arises, the new objects must be treated as independent internal objects—and not necessarily internal components.

Change Control

Change control of external components is special, in the sense that the company doesn't directly influence the implementation of changes. Configuration control boards must be especially careful in handling event registrations where external components are in use, creating special registrations if necessary. The boards are responsible for creating such registrations the way the supplier wants them and directing them to those responsible for external components, either at the company or at the supplier, if possible.

Change requests cannot be created for external components, as decisions for changes in these components will always be outside the company's jurisdiction (at least formally). A special effort may be necessary to describe workarounds for problems originating in external components.

It's not always possible to communicate directly with a supplier of external components, so that information about new versions of external components accrues automatically. Often, a company must keep itself informed about changes and take new versions in, such as from the Internet. External components should always be taken into the company at a central place, preferably with an acceptance test procedure to approve them before distribution to the rest of the company.

Registration of who has which external components will identify those who should be informed of changes. Projects that use these components should always be informed of new versions, but deploying them must be a local decision. New versions must never be automatically released into unsuspecting projects.

Status Reporting

Status reporting is as important for external components as for internal configuration items, though the nature of the reports is different. It may be a good idea to provide a special status report in the form of a catalogue for available components, with extended information (purpose, prerequisites). Status reports may also include a usage matrix (as in Figure 21–1) or similar stakeholder matrix about who has which components.

Product	External component								
	1	2	3	4	5	6	7		n
1			X	X			X		
2	X		X			X			X
3			X	X	X		X		
n	X	X				X			X

Figure 21–1 *Usage Matrix*

21.4 INTERNAL ASSET DEVELOPMENT (PRODUCT-LINE APPROACH)

Many companies have embraced the idea of development for reuse, instead of producing each system from scratch every time. This is a sign of a more mature industry, since only mature companies have the foresight, energy, and resources to look for and find patterns in what they are doing. This applies to processes as well as products. Development for reuse is known under a number of names: development of internal assets, development of components, and product-line approach. (The product-line practices initiative, driven by the Software Engineering Institute, provides good guidance on this subject at the Web address given in the bibliography.)

In this section, the term *component* will refer to objects developed for reuse under the full control of the company itself. A variety of this is development for reuse by a subcontractor, which in principle is no different from the internal form. Characteristics of development for internal reuse are that components

- Are owned centrally in the company
- Are independent of individual products
- Are parts of products
- Are included in deliveries for specific products or projects
- May form the basis for specific objects
- Are not changed in individual projects

Examples

Components may be everything from small modules linked into a product to large platforms, on which entire products are built. A small module may be a routine for calculating interest or the interval between two points in time. A typical example of a component is a data server on a mainframe. This is often used in large administrative systems, such as Web applications. Another example is a platform, which may be a standard apparatus composed of hardware and software, from which new products are developed as small modules that are added to the platform.

Components may also be templates, such as for requirement specifications, where generic requirements are included and just need finalization, perhaps by filling out specific numbers. In the flight industry, generic performance requirements are specified and filled out with actual numbers in each project.

Central Ownership of Components

Components may be created in various ways—as the result of a conscious management decision or in a specific project during the development work. Either way, the responsibility and the ownership should be placed centrally in the company, outside the projects where they're used. The collection of components should be regarded as an independent project, on an equal footing with other products, with all this entails in support functions (project management, quality assurance, configuration management).

This is not to say that the development and maintenance of components may not be "farmed out" to specific projects. This will often happen, since the expertise will be present in projects and not always centrally. These cases require extra time in the project plan. A company may have several component projects at the same time, as long as these projects are kept separate from each other and from main projects.

Configuration Management Considerations

Components, which may be either individual configuration items or deliveries, must be placed under configuration management just like other objects, along with related material. This must start at an early stage in their development, and must be performed even more conscientiously than in ordinary projects, if possible.

Ideally, the usage of components should be broader and less cliquish than for objects developed in an isolated project. Components are often developed in a context different from the ones in which they're later used, so it's important to have access to the full background and reasons for their presentation and functionality.

Identification

Components must be identified like all other configuration items, including a version designation. The unique identification should indicate that an item is a component and should avoid conflicts with identification of other items. Metadata can and should be expanded to include more information for each component, such as a description of its purpose and interface. Placement under configuration management should imply a component's approval, but it might be a good idea to include some sort of documentation of the test status—maybe even a test certification—in the metadata.

Storage

Components must be stored centrally, never with configuration items from other projects. Components of the module or platform type will always be part of a product delivery. Such a component cannot and must not appear as an individual configuration item in projects other than the one to develop and maintain it. This type of component may be part of deliveries at a lower level (a subsystem), which is part of deliveries at higher levels (a software system), which is part of an apparatus. One component will often be part of the total system in several places, as illustrated in Figure 21–2.

Projects that use these components must references them in their metadata. Component identifications will be used as the "consists of" element in metadata for deliveries. The components will subsequently be released for usage in connection with the deliveries.

To provide for this, the configuration management system for components must have special facilities to release components when they're needed. This could be in form of a subscription arrangement, so that projects fill out a release request for a component once and can then extract it when necessary.

Components of the template type may be individual configuration items or deliveries. References to them in metadata will be in the "derived from" data element. Such components will be released once as the basis for production of an independent configuration item. It's a little harder to prevent changes to the reuse part of such items, but it's possible with locked text or the like. For all types of components, it's advisable to register to whom they're released for usage. This might be made more manageable by collecting components in (object) libraries, which are then deliveries whose releases are registered.

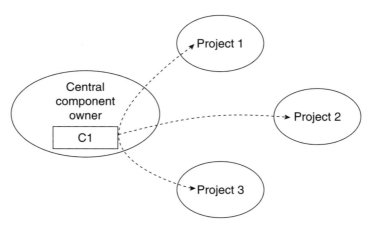

Figure 21–2 *Usage of Reuse Components in Projects*

Change Control

Components must never be changed outside the jurisdiction in which they're developed and maintained. The central owner always decides if a component is to be changed, and how. It may be a good idea to have a representative from the component project on one or more configuration control boards for projects where components are used. These boards must ensure that event registrations can be made to components if necessary. It's the responsibility of these boards to direct event registrations to the component project and follow up on them across the project interfaces. A project cannot raise a change request for a component, since changes in components are outside the jurisdiction of other projects.

This principle is illustrated in Figure 21–3, where a problem in Project 2 causes an event registration to be created and sent to the relevant configuration control board (not shown on drawing). The board finds that C1 is causing the problem and sends an event registration to the central component owner. The configuration control board at the central component owner would decide, in consultation with representatives from the three projects, whether a change request should be issued for C1 or if the registration is to be solved another way, such as by creating a component C2.

The configuration control board(s) for the central project where the components are owned will often have many stakeholders, who should be given a say in the handling of event registrations. The registration of who has which components may be used to determine who might be notified of a given event registration and/or implemented changes.

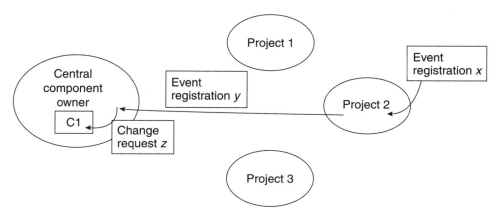

Figure 21–3 *Event Registration Involving a Component*

Projects using a component should always be informed when a new version is issued, but the project itself must decide if the new version should be used, because this might have unwanted effects in other parts of a product. New versions of components must never just be released without an explicit release request. This is where the requirement for full and unique identification in subscription arrangements shows its value.

Status Reporting

Status reporting is as important in component projects as in other projects. As with external components, it may be a good idea to provide a special status report in the form of a catalogue for available components, with extended information (purpose, prerequisites). Status reports may also include information about who has which components.

21.5 QUALITY SYSTEM, INCLUDING PROCESS MANAGEMENT

In this section, *quality system* refers to the collection of process descriptions used throughout a company. Process descriptions are descriptions of procedures or ways of working, methods, conventions, and templates for what is being done. In this context, what is being made are products with more or less software included. Typically, an independent organization unit, such as a quality management function or methods department, carries the responsibility for managing the company's quality system (processes).

Configuration Management Considerations

The contents of a quality system—all the process descriptions—should be placed under configuration management. The requirements in ISO 9000 include control of changes to the quality system—configuration management of the quality system is required. It may be important to know the history of the quality system, not least the reasons for decisions on the presentation of procedures and templates.

In some cases (e.g., for safety-critical systems), process descriptions used during the production of a product may have to be placed under configuration management with the rest of the items for and in the product. If so, the interface between the general configuration management for the process descriptions and the specific one connected to such a project must be clearly defined. This resembles internal component development.

Responsibility

The entity responsible for configuration management of the quality system must be clearly defined. Typically it will be the unit carrying general responsibility for processes performing this part of process management activities.

Identification

The principles for identification of documents apply to items in the quality system. Since these objects are to be used company-wide and may be included in deliveries for a specific project, their unique identification must be selected to avoid conflicts.

Storage

The quality system should be stored in it own isolated configuration management library. Release for usage may be the quality system in hard copy or accessible via an intranet or some other way. Electronic access should not allow uncontrolled changes to the contents.

Change Control

A quality system requires fast reaction to event registrations by users (employees). Employees should have an easy way to create event registrations for the quality system, and the configuration control board should provide an answer within a few hours. This does not have to be in the form of an implemented change but should at least provide information about the expected life of the event. All involved should receive frequent information during the life cycle of an event registration, and users of the quality system should be informed when changes are implemented. This should be presented in a manner that can not be easily overlooked, such as via an e-mail or verbally at an information meeting.

Status Reporting

The visibility and the accessibility of the quality system are important factors in its success. Status reports for the quality system must be available to all users of the process descriptions. It might be made possible for employees to search directly in metadata.

Part V

Improving Configuration Management

The task of improving configuration management may seem overwhelming. What to do? Where to go? How to get there? The maturity models for (software) development may help. Although this is not a book about process improvement, this part will deal with some general aspects of that subject from a configuration management point of view.

Capability Levels

One of the maturity models used today, CMMI, defines six capability levels, as shown in Figure V–1. Using CCMI or BOOTSTRAP, for example, a company can obtain an appraisal of the capability of its configuration management process. Even without a formal assessment, the definitions of capability levels and configuration management may be a guideline for implementing or improving those activities.

A project reaches capability level 1 when configuration management is performed to a degree that satisfies the goals for that capability level. To reach capability level 1, therefore, you have to start performing some configuration management. A project reaches capability level 2 when configuration management is planned and the products produced under it are themselves under configuration management to a sufficient degree.

To reach capability level 3, a company must have defined a standard process and supporting assets for performing configuration management. At capability level 4, the

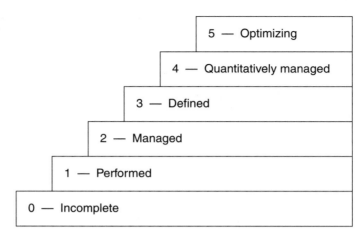

Figure V–1   CMMI Capability Levels

defined processes must be controlled using statistical and other quantitative techniques. At capability level 5, the company must continually optimize configuration management based on an understanding of the common causes of process variation.

At any capability level, you have to gauge the configuration management according to numerous conditions and constraints as discussed above.

Chapter 22

Getting Started on Configuration Management— up to Capability Level 1

Configuration management can be introduced and improved in many ways. No one way is "the" way—each company must find its own way. This chapter provides some inspiration and advice to companies facing the task of starting on configuration management from scratch.

22.1 HOW TO GET STARTED FROM NOTHING

Getting started on anything completely from scratch isn't easy but, on the other hand, it's hardly ever necessary. Even if a company has the feeling that no configuration management is being performed, that's rarely the case. Employees may have knowledge and practical experience of configuration management from previous jobs or from their education. It's also worth remembering that a company wanting to start some configuration management is not an island. The world at large can provide a lot of help and inspiration.

Getting the Right People

People drive changes and improvements. The success or failure of an enterprise like introducing configuration management in a company may depend on the people allocated to it. The person driving the initiative must be a fiery soul or "true believer." Without a burning desire to see configuration management at work in the company, the person in charge is prone to give up long before achieving success.

Such a person may well be found within the company. The original initiative may, in fact, come from a person with this passion. Build on that, especially if the person is someone with a good relationship to peers and superiors.

Collecting Best Practices Internally

All companies have dedicated, enthusiastic people who want to do as good a job as possible. When introducing configuration management for the first time, try to create a map of the knowledge on the subject within the company. Authorized assessments following one or the other maturity model are one way to do this, but lighter self-assessment methods may also be used. This could include interviews with employees working on ongoing projects or various types of questionnaires, such as on the company intranet.

It's well worth the effort to analyze information gained like this and collect existing information about practices and knowledge. Starting configuration management based on existing practices will significantly enhance its chances of success.

Looking at the Outside World

The maturity models offer a lot of inspiration. It may not always be easy to understand how to implement the requirements, but an assessment, including a detailed improvement plan, can be a stepping stone. Literature and conference attendance are also valuable sources of inspiration. A local interest group on configuration management can provide opportunities to participate in meetings and workshops. Training courses are also a source of information and inspiration.

Validate outside information and inspiration carefully against existing knowledge and practices. Do not overrule internal resources without a strong case for doing so.

Focus

To get configuration management off the ground, place as much focus on employees' understanding and capability for configuration management as on the company's need for control. This should not create a conflict with the company's interests, as the company ultimately depends on the employees' ability to carry out configuration management plans.

Look Ahead

When introducing configuration management, use a stepwise approach. Start with a few steps, then introduce more and more advanced aspects. This includes picking low-hanging fruit. Set up goals that are obtainable within a short time—say, two to three months at the most—and celebrate when the goals are reached. Even a step-wise approach should include at least some idea of where the long-term goal is. This will facilitate decisions being made along the way—such as selecting tools, which can grow as demands placed on them increase.

22.2 FIRST STEPS TOWARD CONFIGURATION MANAGEMENT

These goals, based loosely on the goals for configuration management defined in CMMI (see Chapter 2), are generally sequential, so some may not be doable before previous ones. Fulfilling these goals will bring the company to capability level 1 for configuration management.

> SG 1 Establish Baselines
>> SP 1.1–1 Identify Configuration Items
>> SP 1.2–1 Establish a Configuration Management System
>> SP 1.3–1 Create or Release Baselines
> SG 2 Track and Control Changes
>> SP 2.1–1 Track Changes
>> SP 2.2–1 Control Changes
> SG 3 Establish Integrity
>> SP 3.1–1 Establish Configuration Management Records
> SP 3.2–1 Perform Configuration Audits

Establish Baselines

The primary goal is to obtain control over source code and corresponding objects:

- Define what types of objects to place under configuration management.
  - Individual objects, such as source code modules
  - Deliveries like subsystems, partial deliveries to the customer, and entire systems
- Define a convention for unique identification of the objects to be placed under configuration management and *accept no other forms of identification.*

- Identify what has already been produced.
- Define authorization for all objects, document it, and *stick to it*.
- Place objects already produced under configuration management in storage in a controlled library, with the corresponding information.
- Define deliveries of what has been produced and place them under configuration management.
  - Name them.
  - Specify in detail what they are composed of.
  - Approve them.
  - Create proxy items if necessary.
  - Place them in storage in a controlled library, with the corresponding information.

Track and Control Changes

Formal change control must be established for code now under configuration management:

- Produce a template for event registrations.
- Establish at least one configuration control board. Remember that a CCB *does not have to consist of more than the author or producer of an object and maybe some peers.*
- Make sure event registrations are filled in for all events observed for the configuration items.
- Make sure all event registrations are treated by the configuration control board.
- Make sure everyone who has registered an event receives feedback on decisions.
- *Do not* implement changes based on any other input than a change request from the configuration control board.
- Store all event registrations and change requests.
- Make sure the configuration control board approves all implemented changes.
- Identify all new, changed configuration items and store them in the controlled library with the corresponding information.
- Define new, changed deliveries containing the new, changed individual configuration items.

Minimum Documentation

What must, as an absolute minimum, be described for the configuration management is therefore

- Responsible people
- The types of objects to be placed in configuration management
- Naming conventions
- Templates for event registrations and change requests
- Guidelines for filling these in
- Composition of the configuration control board
- A process for treating events from creation to closure

What must, as an absolute minimum, be produced during configuration management is therefore

- Lists of configuration items, including deliveries, with all available information for each item
- Completed event registrations and change requests

Establish Integrity

It's necessary

- To document what must be done and how to do it
- To make sure everybody involved has access to this documentation

It's unnecessary to produce comprehensive configuration management plans, including all configuration management aspects, for a system as described above. The documentation could be in the form of simple e-mails or informal memoranda. The important point is that the documentation should be stored and then changed and reissued when something emerges as not useful or expedient. The more formal planning and control of configuration management leads to capability level 2.

A configuration management system as described here is a good beginning, but in most cases, a project or company won't benefit fully at this level. Keep in mind, however, that the scope and degree of formality must never exceed what is profitable for the company.

22.3 EXPERIENCES IN IMPLEMENTING CONFIGURATION MANAGEMENT

This section provides some testimonials from companies that have experimented with introducing configuration management. At the time this book was written, not many controlled experiments existed on configuration management process improvement. However, the European Software Institute's SISSI (*The Business Benefits of Software Best Practice, Case Studies*) project has produced a number of short reports. Of these, five had configuration management as their subject. The contents and conclusions are presented in the following paragraphs.

The European Software Institute's Web site (see bibliography for the URL) contains European best practices for many processes within software development. See also *Introducing ClearCase as a Process Improvement Experiment,* a Norwegian survey of the profitability of introducing configuration management.

Overall Conclusion

The conclusions of these reports indicate some trends:

- Introducing configuration management is a great advantage.
- Management support is essential.
- Pilot tests of configuration management processes are important before rolling them out on a larger scale.
- Introducing configuration management is difficult.

Datamat Ingegneria dei Sistemi

Case Study: 10564

Project title: Introduction of Configuration Management

Description: Gaining a competitive edge. By introducing configuration management into the development process of their financial application products, Datamat Ingegneria dei Sistemi S.p.A. vastly decreased the time-to-market and the number of errors in their software products. The overall effect was to decrease development costs so that Datamat could gain a competitive edge.

Lessons Learned:

- **Top-level management support is essential.** Introducing formal processes where there used to be none can often generate opposition. Before seeing the benefits of introducing configuration management, it is first necessary to introduce what may seem like useless bureaucracy for a time. Top-level management support is necessary in order to make some team members believe in the importance of the task.

- **Choose a significant project.** In order to see the pay-offs from implementation of configuration management, it is advisable to choose a project with at least a moderate degree of complexity where the development team is big enough to benefit from a formal system of collaboration.

- **Take a realistic view of working practices.** It is easy to get carried away with the possibilities of a sophisticated software process model, risking failure due to its unworkable complexity. Datamat learned that it is better to start with a basic number of object states and roles, and then elaborate on that basis later if necessary.

- **Buy a configurable product.** The wrong configuration management tool can become a straitjacket, forcing your developers to follow a process model designed on the basis of "one size fits all." It is better to invest in a tool with more sophistication than you need (in terms of customizability) rather than less.

S.I.A. S.p.A.

Case Study: 21244

Project title: Applying GQM to Assess CM Practice for Better Interbank Services

Description: An effective and valuable measurement system is now working. SIA has succeeded in the implementation of the MIDAS project aimed at improving the reliability and availability of interbank services of the National Inter-bank Network of Italy, by establishing an effective Configuration Management (CM) process and defining a suitable measurement program based on the Goal-Question-Metrics (GQM) technique. This has led to higher visibility and ownership of the software maintenance process, supported by precise weekly anomaly reports.

Lessons Learned: Among the most interesting lessons learned in the running of the SPI project, the following can be outlined:

Technological point of view

♦ Establishing a CM process is not a trivial process. Therefore it has to be accurately managed; in particular modelling the production process is very critical, especially for companies—like SIA—that were at level 1 of CMM.

♦ A considerable amount of time and effort must be dedicated to the selection and customization of CM tools, because there are a great number of complex tools available and rarely do the features provided perfectly fit company needs.

Business point of view

♦ Management support is constantly required in order to convince the reluctant ones, mainly when the people responsible for introducing CM are not in a leading position.

♦ Constant support after the initial training must be given for CM tools and practices; otherwise people could revert to the old way of working.

♦ Incremental deployment of the tool was a winning factor. In this way, only relatively small amounts of software at a time were moved into the CM environment, and only a few people at a time had to be assisted in their initial impact with the new procedures.

Istiservice, S.p.a.

Case Study: 21269

Project title: Configuration and Change Management to Rising Quality of Service

Description: The change management process is now centralized and controlled. The implementation of this PIE [Process Improvement Experiment], focused on the Software Change and the Configuration Management system (SO.C.CO.MA), has led to establishing a centralized Change Management Process that really works and allows the management of environments with a combination of internally and externally developed software. Furthermore the introduction of quantitative measures about the new process represents the starting point toward a management by metrics.

Lessons Learned: The following lessons learned can be stated, among the most significant ones are:

♦ The approach can be taken to other processes (e.g., development, testing), by defining a set of proper metrics, establishing a similar collection of procedures, and defining quantitative goals to achieve.

- If the project were to be repeated, before starting the experiment, the indicators to be taken into account should be more clearly identified.

- A continuous sensibilization action shall be promoted through specific actions in order to minimize the most frequent risks, such as loss of interest, perception of the project as bureaucratic overhead, and so forth.

- The new process cannot be considered established; therefore a project review is mostly advisable at the effective start of the application phase.

Event A/S

Case Study: 21379

Project title: Introduction of Configuration Management in Very Small Organizations

Description: Improved customer relations. Through the introduction of configuration management three small Norwegian companies—Event AS, TSC AS, and Aktuar Systemer AS—were able to increase customer confidence in their products, as well as decrease the time taken to find and rectify errors.

Lessons Learned: There were many lessons learned during this experiment. The main lessons were

- The process of implementing CM routines is a very complex and time-consuming process. It is an iterative process that requires continuous refinement.

- CM routines need to be tested in a controlled, but real-life environment before implementing them on a large scale in the whole organization.

- The identification of appropriate data to quantify possible improvements in the software development process was difficult. Existing information should be used as a basis for defining metrics.

- An operative CM system has a concrete impact on customer relations. TSC has experienced positive feedback from customers inquiring about their CM routines.

- Document every stage of the process followed during implementation and ensure that clear procedural documents are produced. This will establish a practical way of operating the system within the company.

- Make sure that all personnel using the system are fully trained before using the system. This will ensure that once the system goes into operation, all personnel are comfortable with it and know how to operate it. This will ease acceptance of the system.

Sysdeco A/S

Case Study: 21568

Project title: Introduction of a Common Configuration Management Framework

Description: 36% reduction in errors. Through the introduction of a common configuration management system within their development department, Sysdeco GIS A/S vastly decreased the number of errors in their software products prior to release, as well as reducing the time-to-market. The overall effect of this exercise was to raise the awareness of the true cost of correcting errors, as well as to reduce product development costs.

Lessons Learned: There were many lessons learned during this experiment. The main lessons were

- To implement a configuration management system takes a long time. For the implementation to succeed, it should not be rushed. SGIS's initial estimate for the implementation was that it would take two months. In fact, it took twelve months.
- Do not underestimate the cost of implementing and maintaining a configuration management system.
- Do not underestimate the number of licences required (i.e., for the configuration management software). Plan on one license per developer.
- Ensure that the hardware on which the system is to operate is powerful enough. Err on the side of excess capacity rather than not have enough, as this will influence the performance of the system.
- Document every stage of the process followed during implementation and ensure that clear procedural documents are produced. This will establish a practical way of operating the system within the company.

Quotation from the report: "Implementing configuration management (CM) software is only part of the whole story. The major components of the whole exercise are to implement supporting CM procedures, to get CM accepted as an integral part of a company's culture, and to establish the correct measures."

Chapter 23

Planning Configuration Management— up to Capability Level 2

According to CMMI, an organization may reach capability level 2 in configuration management when configuration management for all projects is institutionalized as a managed process. Two key characteristics of a managed process are that it is planned and that products produced are themselves placed under configuration management.

Even if CMMI or other maturity models didn't promote planning, a plan is a starting point for good configuration management. It deepens the understanding of the task and provides the basis for performing configuration management. It's much cheaper to think everything through on paper rather than while trying to perform it. All configuration management activities must be described in the plan. This chapter offers suggestions for the contents of such a plan, which doesn't need to be an independent document—it may be included as a chapter in the overall project plan.

Just as with project planning, it's advisable to have a detailed configuration management plan only for the foreseeable future—typically for the next activity in the project's life cycle. Later activities should be planned at a higher level and details provided in a later version of the plan—typically, just before the project enters the later activity.

23.1 GENERAL PLANNING ADVICE

If you fail to plan, you plan to fail! When planning configuration management, keep the following in mind:

- Define the purpose, success criteria, and level of ambition.

◆ Document the plan. Not written = not there.

◆ Use the plan—no write-only information.

Start with a clear definition of the purpose, success criteria, and level of ambition. Clear goals and unambiguous success criteria will ensure that the configuration management will be useful, show results, and not grow beyond a reasonable limit. For defining the purpose, it may be helpful to use the mnemonic saying that every purpose should be S-M-A-R-T: specific, measurable, agreed, relevant, and time-specific.

The Plan Itself

Plan for the time to plan configuration management. Always produce a configuration management plan—if not more, then at least a chapter or section in the overall project plan. Make sure the plan is short, clear, and operational. Short, clear plans will be read and understood, are useful in everyday work, and may be kept up-to-date. Write only what is absolutely relevant. A rule of thumb is that a plan of more than ten pages indicates that something needs to be cut or moved to an appendix. Also include what has consciously been left out when writing the plan, in terms of objects or information.

The author of the plan may assume that the reader is familiar with the contents and purpose of the project and avoid repeating information from other documents. If the company provides general procedures or the like for some or all configuration management activities, refer to them rather than repeating them. Make sure all stakeholders, not least the employees on the project team, are familiar with the plan and willing to adhere to it.

Connection to the Project

It should be easy to see and understand the connections between configuration management activities and other activities in the project. It may be a good idea to integrate configuration management activities in the general time schedule for the project, typically produced in a project management tool and constituting part of the overall project plan. Alternatively, the plan may include a separate time schedule for configuration management, possibly as an appendix.

Plan configuration management from the start of the project but plan the details only for the period immediately ahead, such as the first activity. Avoid drowning, which makes it difficult to keep the plan up-to-date; fill in details as they become known. Make it clear what has consciously been left out, such as later activities.

Template

A template is a great help in getting over the first moments of staring at a blank sheet of paper. Many companies have templates for plans, maybe even for configuration management plans. Use those! Don't forget to provide feedback to the relevant function on how a template works and submit ideas and suggestions based on use of the template.

23.2 TABLE OF CONTENTS FOR A CONFIGURATION MANAGEMENT PLAN

A configuration management plan must be produced according to the context where it will be used. The plan should adhere to the rules for unique identification of documents. Even if the plan is not in itself to be placed under configuration management, provide all the metadata for a configuration item for the plan: name, version, status, date, author, and so on.

An example of a table of contents for a configuration management plan is provided below. It may be expedient to structure a plan differently from what is shown here. The important thing is to consider all sections and choose those that are relevant.

23.3 CONFIGURATION MANAGEMENT PLAN: INTRODUCTION

The introduction is one of the areas where a documentation standard exists in most companies. This chapter may be divided into the following sections:

1. Purpose
2. Scope
3. Vocabulary
4. References

Purpose

A short explanation of the purpose should be given, along with an indication of the audience for the plan.

Scope

Indicate the scope of the plan with regard to

- Project activities the plan covers and to what degree of detail
- Project activities the plan does not cover, and why
- The organizational unit for which the plan is valid
- Types of objects for which the plan is valid
- Types of objects the plan does not cover, and why
- Configuration management activities the plan covers
- Configuration management activities the plan does not cover, and why

Vocabulary and Reference Lists

The introduction may also contain a vocabulary related to configuration management and one or more reference list(s). (If lengthy, they can go in an appendix, with a reference in the introduction.) Other lists, such as typographical conventions, may be included as appropriate, and some may find a list of previous versions of the plan useful.

23.4 CONFIGURATION MANAGEMENT PLAN: MANAGEMENT AND RELATIONS TO THE ENVIRONMENT

This chapter describes the roles, organization, and allocation of responsibilities. It also describes the interface to users and marketing or customers, depending on whether a bespoke general product is being developed or a system for a customer. A special kind of interface may be to subcontractors or suppliers. This may be included in a separate chapter, depending on its importance. This chapter may be divided into the following sections:

1. Organization
2. Responsibilities
3. Interface Control
4. Subcontractor Management
5. Relevant Standards

Organization

This section specifies the overall organization of configuration management and how this fits into the rest of the project organization. It describes in general terms the roles to be filled.

Responsibilities

This section must define clearly and unambiguously

◆ Who is responsible for performing which configuration management activities—identification, placement in storage, change control, and registration and reporting of available information?

◆ What responsibility each of the organizational roles has in connection with approval of objects in general, especially deliveries, such as when does the project manager have the final word and when does the person responsible for quality assurance?

◆ What is the responsibility of users, customers, and marketing in connection with approvals?

The "who" in the first bullet may be in the form of roles and detailed descriptions of the responsibilities of the people filling the roles. It may be a good idea to structure this information in a RASIC chart, as shown in Figure 23–1. A detailed allocation of resources may be deferred to chapter 4 of the plan.

Outline the people responsible for deciding when an object is to be placed under configuration management. This section should include a reference to a quality assurance plan or the project plan that defines approval criteria for objects of various types. This is to ensure that objects are not placed under configuration management too early and that those that should be, are.

	Role					
	Project Manager	**CM Responsible**	**CM Librarian**	**Tool Responsible**	**Subsystem CCB**	**Full System CCB**
Task 1	R	S	I			
Task 2	I	R	I	C		
Task 3	I	R			A	C

R: Responsible; A: Approval; S: Support; I: Inform; C: Consult

Figure 23–1 *RASIC Chart Example*

Interface Control

Define how interfaces to external objects (software, hardware) are handled with regard to configuration management. The plan should especially identify:

- Who (which organizational unit) carries the responsibility for the systems and subsystems the system in question has interfaces to.
- Which people to contact in the external organizational units concerning collective management and coordination of interfaces.
- Who in the project/organization carries the responsibility for managing which interfaces.

Subcontractor Management

Subcontractors also make changes and new versions, and it's often necessary to consider that these may be released during the project's life cycle. To avoid problems, it's a good idea to define how new versions are to be tested for approval, who does it, and how deliveries from the subcontractor(s) are introduced into the project in a controlled way. In some cases, the contract will include requirements on this subject.

Relevant Standards

This section describes guidelines and policies to which the project adheres. Some companies have general configuration management guidelines and procedures. These are described with references, as well as details on how and why they have been tailored to the project.

23.5 CONFIGURATION MANAGEMENT PLAN: ACTIVITIES

This chapter describes, in fairly high-level terms, how to identify items and place them in storage, along with how to perform change control and status reporting. This chapter typically contains the following sections:

1. Identification
2. Storage
3. Change Control
4. Status Reporting

This chapter may contain references to an appendix with detailed descriptions of tools, techniques, and methods.

Identification

This section plans and describes naming conventions for configuration items and the rest of the configuration management data (metadata). Detailed techniques are found in an appendix or may be included here, if they don't take up too much space. For all deliveries of systems and subsystems, this section describes

- The name of the delivery
- The contents: which software, what tools, and possibly which documentation, event registration, and so on, are connected to it. Where applicable, distinguish between new developments and reused software.
- The external interfaces of the systems, if any
- Necessary reviews and approvals
- Effort needed from each role to establish the delivery
- Tracing to the project plan or design documentation for the delivery, as applicable

Note that most of the abovementioned topics are part of the metadata for a delivery. When planning, some of this information is typically unknown, such as module names. In this case, describe how and when this information will be provided. A description of how the information is stored may also be included, but this may also be placed in the section on status reporting.

Storage

This section describes how the controlled library is built and deployed, possibly along with other libraries (even if they're not strictly part of configuration management as such). Detailed procedures can go in an appendix about tools, techniques, and methods. To give an example, a company may use Visual Source Safe for storage of code, while corresponding documentation is stored in a fixed directory structure and the relationships between documents and code are described in a database. Here, the controlled library consists of a combination of three tools. This section should therefore include a short, stepwise description of how items are correctly placed in storage and extracted, using the three tools in a suitable sequence.

This section may describe how information is collected, but this information may also be placed in the section about status reporting. To ensure that necessary information is available while avoiding an overflow of data, consider how long to keep information. Some may be obsolete after a certain point, while others must be kept for a long time—even if just one customer is still using the system.

Finally, this section may describe how to perform backup of the libraries and other information. This is not, strictly speaking, a configuration management activity, but it's in the interest of configuration management to ensure that backups are made, are kept in a safe place (e.g., a fireproof box), and can be restored correctly.

Change Control

This section must define who has authority to request changes to a configuration item—who are members of the configuration control boards for the various object types. A board may consist of just the author or producer of an object and possibly some peers. Also plan and document a board's delegation of authority.

Determine how event registrations and change requests for various types of objects are to be handled: are fixed forms needed or are free-text e-mails sufficient? When these procedures are established, ensure that events and changes can be handled fast enough, so configuration management is not perceived as an unnecessary bottleneck in stressed situations.

Changes in external interfaces for the system are typically handled and approved differently from internal changes. The procedure for this is also defined in this section. An area often overlooked is changes in support software and tools, such as new versions of compilers, linkers, and libraries. It's a good idea to think about how to handle such changes, including how to introduce new versions in a controlled manner.

Status Reporting

This section defines how status information about configuration items is collected, treated, and reported on. Status information is partly extractable from the metadata for configuration items and partly included in information related to item approvals, release requests, event registrations, and change requests.

An important part of status reporting is defining periodic reports—contents, frequency, and recipients. Remember to consider status reporting requirements from customers and users. The handling of ad hoc or dynamic queries may also be defined: is it possible for certain roles to write queries directly in the database, and/or how are queries to be formulated and handed to the librarian? Status reporting considerations help decide which data should be registered and how long to keep it.

23.6 CONFIGURATION MANAGEMENT PLAN: SCHEDULE

This chapter describes tasks to be performed and the overall milestones and phases, or activities, for configuration management. Graphs and diagrams illustrating the schedule should be included, possibly in an appendix. This chapter may be divided into the following sections:

1. Tasks
2. Phases and Milestones
3. Diagrams and Charts

Tasks

Detailed tasks in connection with the activities are described here. Don't forget "invisible" work—work the staff has to perform but that isn't covered in the plan and the schedule. Also determine and plan required training. The tasks are closely connected to the roles to be fulfilled. As far as possible, document which people will be filling which roles. Also state interfaces or connections to the overall project plan, especially where people fill more than one role. Plan the resource needs so that it's clear who is to work when.

Phases and Milestones

Configuration management has, like a development project, a number of milestones:

- The configuration management system is ready for use for the next activity.
- Establishment of the configuration control board(s).
- Deliveries of subsystem and systems, possibly connected to project milestones.
- Product release.

Internal deliveries, such as software for testing hardware prototypes (or vice versa), should be treated like deliveries of subsystems. This applies to both care taken in testing and control and resources allocated to establish and release the delivery. A classical blunder is to underestimate the work connected with the release of an internal delivery or to believe that it's not so important if an internal delivery isn't perfect. Numerous examples show the hours wasted in trying to find an error in a system where both the software and the hardware turned out to be unstable. The milestone should be listed, as well as which phases require which roles and resources. This should preferably include a reference to the overall project plan, to show the connection with the activities and the milestones.

Diagrams and Charts

It's a good idea to support the planning descriptions with diagrams and charts. Most project management tools provide the facilities, and such tools may also be used for scheduling configuration management activities. Follow up on the schedules: mark clearly on diagrams and charts where the project is and what the rest of the project lifetime looks like.

23.7 CONFIGURATION MANAGEMENT PLAN: TOOLS, TECHNIQUES, AND METHODS

Depending on the capability level of the company, this chapter may be the easiest or the hardest part of the plan to write. If no help is available from a central place, such as an organization-wide quality system, the chapter will be hard to write, possibly long, and may take a long time. In this case, it should become an appendix, as it will probably also be the part of the plan that will change the most during the project. If general processes exist, simple references and a few descriptions may be sufficient. The information may even be included in chapter 3 of the configuration management plan. Don't underestimate the importance of this information and the work involved in providing it.

Tools

Tools may be dedicated configuration management tools, directory structures, databases, forms, and so on, deployed to facilitate and automate configuration management activities. The same tool or a number of tools may cover the configuration management activities, while different tools are often used for different types of configuration items. For example, many companies have a dedicated configuration management (read: version control) tool for source code, while other item types and information are handled on paper or e-mail, in ordinary databases, agreed directory structures, and the like. This section also describes which "homemade" tools are used: independently, in connection with other tools, or to connect other tools.

Techniques and Methods

Techniques and methods are descriptions of work and specific ways of doing things. These descriptions may be multidimensional— separate descriptions for configuration item types and degrees of formality for each type. This section should also include templates for forms to be used and reports.

Chapter 24

Processes for Configuration Management— up to Capability Level 3

Capability level 3, as defined by CMMI, is where the configuration management process is institutionalized as a defined process. A defined process is a managed process tailored from the organization's standard processes. Deviations beyond those allowed by the tailoring guidelines are documented, justified, reviewed, and approved.

This chapter provides a general introduction to the concept of processes and process models and a more specific list of possible procedures for configuration management, including two examples. A process model must always be tailored to the relevant company—preferably by combining the knowledge and working habits within the company with theory and best practices in the field. Process models may vary considerably from company to company—in layout, presentation media, degree of formality, coverage. The examples here should be used as inspiration.

24.1 PROCESSES IN GENERAL

When a company has gained some experience in and understanding of configuration management, it can begin collecting, documenting, and improving relevant process descriptions.

Connection with Maturity Models

Capability level 3 for configuration management in CMMI or BOOTSTRAP is reached when a company has defined its processes for configuration management so all projects can use the processes. The description must contain guidelines for how projects may tailor the processes to their needs. The process descriptions apply to the entire company or a well-defined part, such as a department. Based on their experiences with the process descriptions, users must provide feedback to the person responsible for maintaining the processes.

Definitions

The words "process," "procedure,"and so on are often used at random. The following definitions (a free interpretation of the dictionary definitions and the common understanding and use of the words) are used here:

A *process* describes how an input is used to create the expected output. A process is the descriptions of techniques, methods, procedures, conventions, and templates to be deployed within a specific area. All these words ("technique," "method," and "procedure") cover the same concept: the way to do something.

A *procedure* is a description of a number of actions to be performed in a sequence. A *convention* is guidelines for how to construct (or understand) something. A *template* is a description of the usual look or layout of something, sometimes including guidelines to make a copy of the item. A process must always have, at the very least, input, procedure, and output. The procedure may refer to other procedures, conventions, and/or templates.

A Process Is Like a Recipe

An analogy is sometimes made between a process description and a recipe. That analogy is not far off. A recipe includes a list of ingredients (input), workflow, and a description—maybe even a picture—of the expected result. A recipe may also include information about skills required to follow the instructions, suggestions for tools to use, expected time to produce the result, and expected calorie count. A recipe may be scalable—it's just a matter of multiplying the ingredients by the correct factor. Or it may not be scalable, say if you are cooking for a large number of people. It may be customized if some ingredient has to be substituted.

An identification process may be needed within the scope of configuration management. Figure 24–1 shows a simplified version.

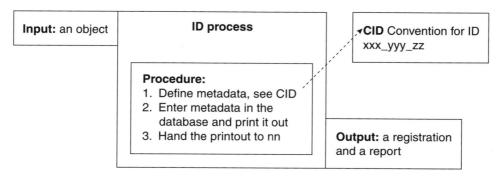

Figure 24–1 *Simple Identification Process*

Process Model

A high-quality configuration management system is characterized by all necessary processes being described, integrated, and automated to the highest possible degree, providing a complete workflow solution. It may be a good idea to produce a process model for all processes, to illustrate how they interact. This will provide an overview and a way to verify that all are used, all have input created in another process, and all have output used in at least one other process. A process model may also describe how responsibilities are assigned, providing an overview of who does what.

Process models may be produced to almost any level of abstraction. Start with the highest abstraction level and work your way down to the details, which have different intended audiences. The highest abstraction level may be for the CEO to get an overall understanding of the area, and the lowest level may be for an employee to perform a specific task. To stay in the recipe analogy, a process model may be an overall description of how to produce a three-course meal, set the table, and serve the guests. It may include references to the recipes and other descriptions used by the staff, such as the dessert cook or the waiter.

Don't underestimate the work involved in producing process models and process descriptions. It takes a long time, and it often requires a number of iterations to get it right. Don't be too ambitious to start with. It's better for descriptions to be a bit coarse rather than too fine. The latter will discourage both the people writing them and the people using them. Furthermore, as the world is never satisfied nor stable, the descriptions will have to be flexible and changeable over time. This brings the company on toward capability levels 4 and 5.

24.2 CONFIGURATION MANAGEMENT PROCESSES—OVERVIEW

This section contains lists of the processes needed for each configuration management activity. The lists here are "flat," whereas in a live project, the processes may be multidimensional: variations may exist, depending on the nature of the project and the configuration management. All the contents of the processes—procedures, conventions, and templates—are listed separately here, but they may well be combined.

Identification requires

- Procedure(s) for registration of metadata, including procedure(s) for tracing
- Procedure(s) for inheritance of metadata
- Convention(s) for unique identification
- Convention(s) for authorization, including restrictions on distribution, if any
- Convention(s) for identification of components in a delivery

Storage requires

- Procedure(s) for placement in storage and the related updating of metadata
- Procedure(s) for release for usage
- Procedure(s) for release to production
- Template(s) for item approval
- Template(s) for release request

Change control requires

- Description of the change control process structure
- Procedures in life cycles for events and changes
- Convention(s) for forming different types of configuration control boards
- Definition of the responsibility for each type of configuration control board
- Template(s) for event registration
- Template(s) for change request

Status reporting requires

- Procedure(s) for producing status reports

◆ Procedure(s) for ad hoc extracting of information

◆ Templates for status reports the configuration management system should be able to produce

Special Requirements for Configuration Management Processes

The fact that configuration management is performed during the entire lifetime of a product, for a number of different types of items, and under various circumstances imposes certain requirements on process descriptions. On one hand, they must be integrated with process descriptions for all other processes for which configuration management is performed. These may be coding, test, project management, and quality assurance, to mention a few. Special product requirements may also have to be taken into consideration, as well as special conditions that apply to a project. This could be integrated product development, multivariants, or product-line development of items for reuse.

On the other hand, variants of some process descriptions may be necessary, depending on the types of configuration items and/or degree of formalism required. Types of configuration items may be source code or plans, to mention just two. More comprehensive lists of both types can be found elsewhere in this book.

24.3 CONFIGURATION MANAGEMENT PROCESS— MODEL EXAMPLES

Appendixes A and B are examples of configuration management process models. Appendix A is a tiny extract of a quality system holding all the processes in an anonymous company, included to show how processes may be presented. The quality system is written in Lotus Notes and is available on the company's intranet. The extract is what is relevant for configuration management for source code and related items. The descriptions are therefore parts of a larger whole and include references to parts not shown. The degree of formalism is low, similar to the one in Chapter 5—Examples.

This example shows one process area. Each process area in the quality system is divided into a number of processes, which are again divided into activities. The process flows are illustrated in flowcharts, using the conventions shown in Figure 24–2. As the figure shows, each activity may have an associated procedure description and templates.

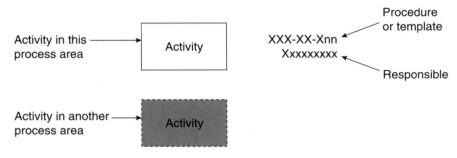

Figure 24–2 *Flowchart Conventions*

Appendix B is part of a user guide to a tracing tool at a small company. It is included for two purposes: to show how processes may be presented and as a practical example of how tracing is handled. The procedures shown are part of a quality system that contains more procedures. The quality system is written in the IMAP format and is available in hard copy and on the company intranet. The latter allows hypertext references to other procedures, templates, and so on.

Chapter 25

Continuous Improvement of Configuration Management— up to Capability Level 4 and 5

At capability level 4, configuration management process is institutionalized as a quantitatively managed process. This is a defined process that is controlled using statistical and other quantitative techniques. Product quality, service quality, process performance, and other business objectives are understood in statistical terms and are controlled throughout the life cycle.

At capability level 5, process is institutionalized as an optimizing configuration management process. An optimizing process is a quantitatively managed process that is improved based on an understanding of the common causes of process variation inherent in it. An optimizing process focuses on continually improving process performance through both incremental and innovative improvements. Such a process may be attained when a company has consolidated its process descriptions into company-wide descriptions.

25.1 GENERAL SOFTWARE PROCESS IMPROVEMENT ADVICE

In principle, improving configuration management is no different from improving any other process area of development. Especially when a company is getting toward capability levels 4 and 5, improvement will be more and more similar for different disciplines. However, this section provides a brief introduction to approaching higher capability levels and undertaking controlled improvement projects.

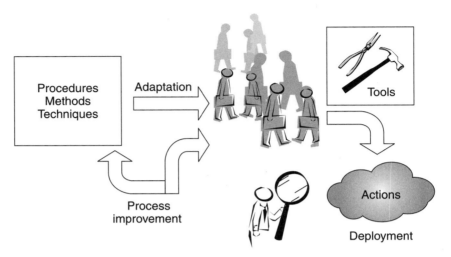

Figure 25–1 *Process Deployment and Improvement*

Processes in Use

Figure 25–1 shows an example of a company's deployment and improvement of processes. Processes, in the format of procedures, methods, and techniques, are defined, disseminated, and adapted by employees. The processes may be supported by tools. Employees act according to the processes using any tools available. The person responsible for process management surveys the deployment using measurement and analysis. Processes may, as a result, be improved (changed), or their adaptation may be improved. And so on . . .

Dissemination and Adaptation

Getting processes deployed is usually the most difficult part of process improvement. A number of factors influence the success of an improvement project. Factors that have shown a positive influence on the success of improvement projects are, among others,

- ◆ Management performed a comprehensive follow-up on improvement activities.
- ◆ People assigned to improvement activities were released from other duties.
- ◆ The improvement team included developers.
- ◆ The improvement project had clear, accepted, and agreed upon goals.

Factors that have shown a negative influence on the success of an improvement project are, among others,

- Extended politicization in the company
- Fights over areas of competence
- Bad experiences from earlier improvement attempts
- The notion that improvement activities stood in the way of "proper" development

Companies at Capability Levels 4 and 5

Investigation of companies at capability levels 4 and 5, according to CMM v.1.1, indicates certain common characteristics:

- They understand why they are acting as they are.
- They know what to do when problems occur.
- They do not overreact, but concentrate on finding the root causes.
- They secure their processes against human errors.
- They change blaming to challenge; i.e., they avoid using fear as a motivating factor.
- They balance authority and ownership with control.
- They measure and predict how far they are from reaching their goals.

25.2 METRICS FOR CONTROLLING CONFIGURATION MANAGEMENT PERFORMANCE

In *Principles of Software Engineering Management*, Tom Gilb says that everything can be made measurable in a way that is better than not measuring at all. One of the principles for good planning is to define specific and measurable goals for activities. But it's not enough for goals to be measurable: metrics must be defined, and measurements collected and used. This section provides a brief discussion of metric-related issues and gives examples of metrics related to configuration management.

Table 25–1 defines several terms related to measurement and metrics. To give an example, the metric for the size of a book is "the number of pages"; the measuring method is "look at the page number on the last numbered page"; the plan is "the reader when she starts on the book"; and the measurement for this metric for *Alice in Wonderland* in a certain edition is "54."

Table 25–1 *Metric and Measurement Terms*

Term	Meaning
Metric	The definition of what you want to measure
Measuring method	The description of how you are going to measure—how you are going to collect the measurements for the metrics
Measurement plan	The description of the metrics, measuring methods, who is going to measure, and when, and how the measurements will be analyzed and used
Measurement	The values collected for the metrics

Metrics in General

Metrics are the definitions of what you want to measure, both directly and by calculation. You can collect or produce a number of data types, as shown in Table 25–2. Data may be objective, with no personal evaluation involved. These are often enumeration, and tools may be used to collect the measurements. Conversely, data may be subjective, involving an element of evaluation. This entails some uncertainty, but the data is often cheap to collect, and its usefulness should not be underestimated. Metrics may well be simple. Nothing is wrong with a metric for which the measurement is a verbal answer of yes or no. This could be, for example, whether a convention is used or not.

Table 25–2 *Data Types*

Data Type	Description
Raw data	Collected data (e.g., time sheets or event registrations)
Direct measuring	A single feature extracted from the raw data (e.g., the number of events and the collection time interval)
Indirect measuring	Calculated features from direct measuring (e.g., event frequency = events/collection time)

It's important to agree on certain aspects when defining metrics, as shown in Table 25–3.

Table 25–3 *Aspects of Metrics*

Aspect	Description
Definitions	Examples: lines of code (new, changed, removed, comments, blank) and importance (1–5 or 5–1)
Units	Example: hours or seconds
Consistency	For suites of metrics that in total are to provide one answer

When defining metrics it's important to understand the various scales that may be used and what you can do with metrics in various scales. The most-used scales are listed in Table 25–4. Whatever you do, don't mix apples with oranges, unless you want to make fruit salad.

Table 25–4 *Scale Definitions*

Scale	Characteristics	Statistics	Examples
Nominal	◆ Undefined order ◆ = ◆ No arithmetic	◆ No average, median, or variance	◆ Classifications, like language (Pascal, C, C++) ◆ Problem type
Ordinal	◆ Defined order ◆ =, >, < (monotone) ◆ No arithmetic	◆ Median, but no average and no variance	◆ Ordered data set, such as capability levels ◆ Scales (low, middle, high)
Interval	◆ =, >, < ◆ Addition, subtraction	◆ Average and variance	◆ Dates and time ◆ Degrees Celsius or Fahrenheit
Ratio	◆ All arithmetic may be used ◆ Includes 0	◆ Average and percent deviation	◆ Time intervals ◆ Degrees Kelvin ◆ Length, height, cost
Absolute	◆ Count		◆ Number ◆ Probability

Measuring Methods

The measuring method is the description of how you are going to measure. Measuring is assigning a value to a metric. Table 25–5 shows a number of qualities to consider when defining measuring methods, which should be as simple as possible.

Table 25–5 *Requirements for Metrics*

Measurements Should Be	Meaning
Repeatable	Example: same measuring time and same instrument
Precise	Valid scale and known source
Comparable	Example: over time and/or between sources
Economical	Affordable to collect and analyze compared to their value

Measurement Plan

A measurement plan defines metrics and measuring methods. It describes who is going to measure, and when, and how the measurements will be analyzed and used. The measurement plan is individual from company to company.

When planning, ensure that the defined metrics answer questions to which you want answers. Don't measure for the sake of measuring. Also, collecting the measurements should be as simple as possible. Ideally, all measurements should be producible from already registered information, so that collection doesn't entail extra work. Maybe available data just needs to be used in a new way.

Not only should measurements be used; the usage should be visible for those who provide them. So only measure what will be used immediately and will provide quick and precise feedback. The plan must also create confidence. Measurements from process usage must never be used to punish or reward individuals. Remember: unwise measuring may induce a lot of strange behavior in people.

Examples

A number of techniques describe the process of selecting and defining metrics for configuration management, such as Goal—Question—Metrics (GQM) or Goal Driven Software Measurement. Following is a list with suggestions for metrics that may be used to analyze how configuration management is performed. The list focuses on configuration management processes, not other processes and not the product. It is by no means exhaustive but may serve as inspiration. Metrics may be

- The number of registrations of identified items made, maybe by item type
- The time interval in which the registrations have taken place
- The time used for registration, maybe also by configuration item type
- Events in connection with registrations, maybe by type and/or configuration item type
- The event rate for registrations, such as number of erroneous registrations per hundred
- The average time for registration, maybe by configuration item type

  Identical metrics may be defined for

- Placement in storage
- Extract for use
- Extract for production
- The handling of event registrations
- The handling of change requests
- The completion of milestones defined in the configuration management plan

Metrics may be defined including cost, such as the cost of the activities. Measurements may show new aspects of things you thought you knew everything about.

25.3 ANALYZING METRICS FOR CONTROL AND IMPROVEMENT

There is no reason to collect measurements if nobody is going to analyze them or act according to the results. Measurements must be collected over time, in order to calculate, say, the balance point and variation. This permits control of processes and their improvement. This section provides a brief introduction to the statistics used in process control and process improvement.

Process control finds reasons for variations from the norm. Control over processes is gained by constantly analyzing new measurements in relation to expected values, to identify unexpected behavior. This may be revealed by a measurement that lies outside the normal variation, either positive or negative. An example might be handling time for an event that is suddenly faster than normal. Is this because the configuration control board didn't do its work properly, is it an event that it has handled many times before, or is it some other reason?

Process improvement changes reasons for the normal. This may be done by identifying what normal is—where the balance point is and what the variation is—then ask oneself questions such as

- Why is the balance point where it is?
- How can the balance point be moved?
- Why does the variation have the size it has?
- How can the variation be decreased?

A balance point may be the average time it takes for an event registration of a certain type to be handled. It may be worthwhile to find out if the handling process has bottlenecks that might be eliminated to decrease average handling time.

Statistics

All configuration management work is a series of processes, which can be followed over time. Statistics is the science of patterns; it also handles "chances" or "coincidences." You could say that statistics make the invisible visible or that they help understand the past, control the present, and forecast the future.

However, you can prove almost anything with statistics if you want to, or if you're not careful. The following example illustrates the point. (The numbers are made up, but the orders of magnitude are correct.)

In Denmark, we have 30 accidents each year on three-lane roads and 200 accidents a year on two-lane roads. Which type of road is more dangerous?

There are, however, 30 kilometers of three-lane roads and 1,000 kilometers of two-lane roads. Which type of road is more dangerous?

But the three-lane roads are used by 3,000 cars a year and the two-lane roads by 10,000 cars a year. Which type of road is more dangerous?

Balance Point

There are three usual ways of finding the balance point in a group of measurements:

- Mean: the arithmetic mean
- Median: the value that splits the group into two subgroups of equal size
- Mode: the most frequent value

In the group of measurements 3, 5, 4, 7, and 5, the following can be calculated measurements:

Mean: 4.8

Median: 5

Mode: 5

The mean is affected by outliers—values far away from the others. If the numbers represent children's ages, all the children can't be above average, but half of them will always be on or above the median.

Variation—What Is Normal

Anything in nature has smaller or larger variations. The normal has wide limits, as the saying goes—but how wide? Depending on the type of measurements to analyze and control, the two most used calculations are

- Range: the difference between the smallest and largest values
- Standard deviation: a measure of the variation around the balance point

These values may be used to calculate so-called control limits for measurements under analysis.

Control Charts

Control charts are graphical ways of looking at measurements, to detect if something goes wrong with the process for which the measurements are being collected. A control chart is useful for

- Focusing on process variation over time
- Showing special events that may require intervention
- Helping improve processes, to make them more consistent and predictable
- Providing a common ground for working with processes

There are many different types of control charts, depending on the series of measurements to analyze. Examples include

- Average and Range
- Average and Standard Deviation

- Fraction Defective
- Number of Defects

Figure 25–2 shows an average and range control chart, with the average, control limits, and value points over time. The two value points by the arrows are outside the lower control limit, and their causes should be investigated.

Examples of indicators that would show the process out of control might include

- A point outside either the lower or upper control limit
- A number of consecutive points on the same side of average
- A number of consecutive changes of direction

Control charts provide a lot of information in an easily understandable way with a manageable amount of work, especially if statistical or other tools are used.

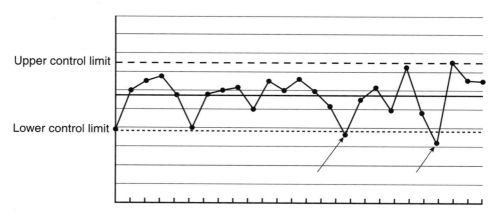

Figure 25–2 *Average and Range Control Chart*

Chapter 26

Tool Support for Configuration Management

It's possible to perform configuration management without tool support. Tool support doesn't improve process capability—it won't buy a higher level of capability and a more profitable way of performing activities. Tools must support the capability a company has already achieved, contributing to the most effective performance of procedures.

You could also say that a tool is 10% of the solution, the rest being the design of procedures to be automated. However, the 10% should not be underestimated. The right tool(s) can provide a far more effective and reliable configuration management system. The tool industry for configuration management has evolved enormously in the last 10–15 years. Over a hundred tools are available, of which some are old and some are relatively new, some are freeware available from the Internet and some cost a small fortune.

This book does not contain a list and an evaluation of tools, among other reasons because the information quickly becomes obsolete. Instead, refer to Ovum, an internationally recognized analysis and consultancy company. Ovum performs assessments of tools, including configuration management tools, and issues reports on the results. This chapter discusses various aspects of configuration management tools and their selection. Web addresses for Ovum and tool developers mentioned below can be found in the bibliography.

26.1 CLASSES OF TOOLS FOR CONFIGURATION MANAGEMENT

The purpose of using tools for configuration management is to automate as much as possible of the noncreative, tedious activities. Every configuration management tool automates some of activities to a certain degree. Few tools automate everything. Many people are involved in configuration management; therefore, there are many points of view about tools.

When you discuss tools, it's helpful to classify them. One way consists of three classes: individual support, project-related support, and full, company-wide process support. These are illustrated in Figure 26–1. Arrows indicate the relationships between classes. This means that the classes may be seen as following each other in terms of complexity and maturity.

Individual Support

Examples of individual support tools are those for version control, build handling, and change control. These are the most primitive forms of configuration management tools.

Version control tools handle storage of individual configuration items, primarily source code, in a space-saving manner, by means of the so-called delta technique, storing only the differences from the previous version. Most if not all of these tools will re-create any given version of an item. Some are able to handle files in non-ASCII

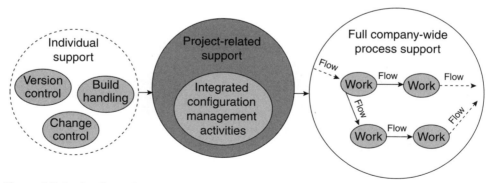

Figure 26–1 *Configuration Management Tool Classes*

format—such as documents written in Word, executable files, and various types of graphic files—but many of them can't, which a buyer needs to be aware of.

Build handling tools may, in their simplest form, be scripts that control compilation and linking of individual items to form deliveries. More advanced tools may be able to handle parallel processing, to speed up builds of large systems. One of the newest build tools is Cruise Control, originally from Thoughtworks. This tool, which is open source and uses an agile approach, extracts the latest checked-in set every 15 minutes, runs regression tests, and e-mails everyone whose code failed a test.

Change control tools include simple ways to control event registrations and change requests. Most of these tools don't integrate easily with other tools, so reporting on the relationships between event registrations, change requests, and configuration items is difficult.

Despite the above descriptions, individual-support tools are by far the most used in the industry today. Examples are PVCS from Intersolv, Visual SourceSafe from Microsoft, and Cruise Control from Source Forge.

Project-Related Support

These tools support many of the needs of development teams and integrators. Most of the tools can handle development in a distributed environment and can create, merge, change, and release deliveries and individual configuration items. The tools often include some workspace handling—they're able to handle controlled libraries apart from working libraries, such as by allowing users to copy part of or an entire system to their own workspace to support their development.

In fact, some will say that workspace management is one of the key features of modern automated configuration management systems. These tools should integrate as smoothly as possible in an existing development environment and include as many configuration management activities as possible. Examples of tools from this class are ClearCase from Rational and StarTeam from Starbase.

Full, Company-Wide Process Support

Also called total-process-oriented tools, these tools support an integrated process approach to configuration management. Their advantage is that they can support and automate total process models—they support workflow, roles, and responsibility in an integrated configuration management system consisting of the handling of many types of items, metadata, and event life cycles. Examples of tools from this class are Harvest from Computer Associates and WorkManager from CoCreate/Hewlett-Packard.

Who Should Use Which Tool?

Tools from the various classes fulfill different needs. One cannot say, for example, that a full, company-wide process-support tool is "better" than a version control tool. Each class contains good, useful tools. In general terms, you could say that

- ◆ Individual support tools fit smaller companies or development groups, with a small number of releases and no variants, where complicated configuration management activities are few and can be handled manually.

- ◆ Project-related support tools fit medium to larger companies that have a need for handling variants and parallel development but not for formal development (e.g., certification or security approval).

- ◆ Full, company-wide process-support tools fit larger companies that have a need for handling variants and parallel development and that work with structured process improvement in configuration management and related areas. Such tools may also be suitable for companies that develop composite systems, that need to perform configuration management for hardware, software, and other types of items.

Selecting the most suitable configuration management tool or tools is easier if the first decision is the class in which the tool is found.

26.2 ORGANIZATIONAL CONSIDERATIONS

Acquiring and implementing a tool requires organizational considerations—it's not something you just rush in and do. Conscious decisions about what to do and how to do it must be made first. Some of the aspects to consider are (in alphabetical order) business goals, buy it or do it yourself, environmental constraints, existing products, financing, organizational scope, ownership, planning for the future, and willingness to change.

Business Goals

The point to consider here is how a new tool will fit into the company's overall goals, such as for general process improvement or achieving a certain level of capability or a specific certification. This may have an impact on the type of tool to choose.

Buy It or Do It Yourself

Either way has advantages and disadvantages. Table 26–1 shows some considerations worth taking into account. The list is by no means exhaustive. Developing a tool internally must be undertaken like any other development project—at least as seriously as a project undertaken for an external customer.

Table 26–1 *Buy It or Do-It-Yourself Considerations*

Buy	Do-It-Yourself
Some customization must always be foreseen, either to the tool or to the company processes (or, more likely, both).	The tool can be made exactly as the company wants it (provided it knows what it wants).
The price is usually easy to calculate.	The final cost may be difficult to estimate.
Usually the payment must be made within a relatively short time.	The development and hence the "payment" can be done at the company's own pace.
Do what you do best—that's what suppliers do.	Maybe you're best suited to develop your own tool.

Environmental Constraints

The "environment" in this context is a broad concept. Constraints may exist in terms of platforms available, such as UNIX, Windows, or a mixture of platforms. Network constraints may have to be reckoned with. Other constraints may be project plans, which must be kept but may not include the work occasioned by introducing a new tool.

Legacy from the Past

A decision must be made on whether existing configuration items are to be handled as usual or by the new tool. The former may cause inconvenience in daily work, while the latter entails an extra expenditure for migration.

Financing

Who is going to pay for a new tool, and what are the financial limits? Aspects to consider are, among other things, the number and type of licenses to buy and the cost of maintenance (both immediate, as for customization and training, and long-term, for support and upgrades). Reckon both the direct expenses (money crossing the counter) and indirect (working hours spent by the staff).

Organizational Scope

This factor is perhaps the most important. How much of the organization will use the new tool?

- Everybody—requiring a company-wide solution?
- At the project level, so a solution covering the needs for an individual project is sufficient?

This decision may have far-reaching consequences, with regard to both direct costs and working hours. Examine the different classes of configuration management tools in relation to organizational needs.

Ownership

Make clear at an early stage who carries overall responsibility and who is the overall driver (not necessarily the same person) in introducing a configuration management tool. It's a good idea to get at least one representative from management to support the introduction. Ownership and financing are usually tied together.

Planning for the Future

It may be worthwhile to look ahead when choosing a configuration management tool. If possible, have an idea of the "final" goal for configuration management in the company, so that the tool will accommodate growth. Converting in three years, when the "new" tool becomes too small, will be just as painful as converting a legacy system to the new tool. You run the risk being able to move only the latest version, losing the product history—one of the more important aspects of configuration management.

Willingness to Change

Introducing a new tool will inevitably change demands on the way people work, which will produce reactions. These reactions are partly related to the amount of influence people have on decisions leading to the changes. It's important to consider the general willingness for change among those affected. The bibliography contains a few examples of literature on this subject.

26.3 SELECTING A CONFIGURATION MANAGEMENT TOOL

Defining requirements for a configuration management tool is the first step toward introducing it successfully. Such a selection process is, in principle, no different than for any other tool. It may include the following steps:

- Forming an evaluation group
- Describing an evaluation method
- Producing a prioritized list of requirements for the tool
- Studying all sources of information on configuration management tools
- Selecting a number of candidates
- Selecting two finalists
- Performing detailed evaluations of the finalists
- Nominating the winner

Some of these steps are described below.

Evaluation Group

The evaluation group should be put together as broadly as possible, with representatives from all potential users of the tool. This may be project managers, analysts, designers, developers, and people responsible for tools. These representatives can contribute their view of the evaluation method and their requirements.

Evaluation Method

The evaluation group must agree on how evaluation is to be carried out and what will be decisive to selection. An evaluation method includes describing both the scale to be used for fulfilling the requirements (e.g., fully, almost, partly, not—or a scale from

0% to 100%) and the selection criteria (e.g., all priority 1 requirements fulfilled at least 80% and at least half of priority 2 requirements fulfilled 100%). It's a good idea to define different evaluation methods for different selection phases, such as most restrictive in selection of the winner.

Requirements

Like any other software product, a configuration management tool must fulfill a number of requirements. These may be functional as well as non-functional requirements, such as usability and requirements regarding the supplier. All requirements should be taken into consideration in the evaluation, not just the functional requirements and the price.

Detailed Evaluation

The two final candidates should undergo a detailed evaluation that includes at least a demonstration and preferably a trial period, to test the tools in as realistic an environment as possible.

Nomination of the Winner

. . . and they lived happily ever after!

Unfortunately, this is not necessarily the case. After selecting the tool, the real work begins. Now the tool is to be used, usage must be sustained, and the tool must be maintained.

26.4 REQUIREMENTS FOR CONFIGURATION MANAGEMENT TOOLS

Acquiring and implementing a tool can be a large investment. It's of course necessary to determine if a tool fulfills a company's general requirements for configuration management. Therefore, it's necessary to be aware of these requirements, preferably in relation to a classification of needs and available tools. Some of the aspects that should also be considered are (in alphabetical order) integration with other tools, performance, scalability, usability, and Web access.

Integration with Other Tools

Investigate how a configuration management tool the company is considering will integrate with tools already in use. Some configuration management tools offer integration with publishing tools, such as FrameMaker. This may be important if configuration management involves documents with composite items, such as drawings and diagrams, or Web pages with many embedded components. Some configuration management tools (such as 4GL tools) may be integrated with complex development environments.

If the development tools in use do not fulfill the requirements for configuration management, they should be compatible with configuration management tool(s) to be used. Investigate how such integration may be accomplished and the effort required, with regard to both supplier(s) and the company itself.

Performance

The many aspects of performance have a greater impact on everyday life than most people think. This may involve the time needed for

- Placement in storage
- Extract for use, for both individual configuration items and large deliveries
- Consolidation and synchronization of data
- Production of status reports, both simple and complex

Performance aspects should be evaluated under realistic circumstances—both locally and over distances, if that is the need—and in an environment with a normal load, not just in an isolated test environment.

Scalability

Investigate whether a tool can handle the requisite volumes. As an example, the volume of information (or contents) of a Web system may be enormous, especially if the system contains many pages that change rapidly and/or are quickly replaced by new pages, or where it's necessary to re-create an entire Web system for a specific day for commercial or legal reasons. Volume may also be a question of a large number of users of the configuration management tool and/or a large number of platforms involved, possibly over great distances. A configuration management tool should be able to grow with the company, at least for the foreseeable future.

Usability

Usability is a measurement for how easy a configuration management tool is to get to know and to use. It encompasses aspects like intuitive human interface, help facilities and user documentation, correspondence with existing work processes (both manual and computer-assisted), and customization facility. A usability assessment should be part of the evaluation of prospective configuration management tools.

Web Access

Tools used to support development of Web systems should have a Web interface, to permit using the same environment for all parts of the development. Some tools have Web interfaces, while others are targeted specifically for the development of Web systems (e.g., Web Integrity from MKS, Web Synergy from Continuus, and StarTeam from Starbase). Test a tool thoroughly to see if it fulfills Web needs—sales material can come on strong.

26.5 REQUIREMENTS FOR THE TOOL SUPPLIER

Acquiring and implementing a tool is not just a large investment here and now; it also has far-reaching consequences, both economic and organizational. When choosing a tool, you don't choose only a tool. Just as you get the in-laws thrown in when choosing a spouse, you get the supplier thrown in when selecting a tool. Therefore, it's important to also look at the supplier during the selection process. Some of the aspects to consider are (in alphabetical order) the supplier's acquaintances, employees, financial status, focus, use of the tool, reputation, and support facilities.

Acquaintances

In today's IT world, no supplier can live in isolation. Tools run on platforms and work together. It's important to look at which other companies a supplier cooperates with in areas such as distribution, marketing, and technology.

Employees

The supplier's employees are the ones the company will deal with in implementing and maintaining a tool. This may include management, sales, technical consultants (for installation and customization), trainers, support/helpdesk, and development. If possible, look at the employees and their backgrounds and education. Listen to the tone and try to feel the atmosphere in the supplier's company, among the employees and their attitude toward a third party and toward the company itself. Are they friendly and helpful or pressed and too busy to bother?

Financial Status

A look at a potential supplier's financial status may be worthwhile. Is the supplier a sound company that will stay in business for the foreseeable future? Or will it fall flat on its face in the lightest breeze, jeopardizing the long-term maintenance of the tool?

Focus

A supplier's focus on its product lines can be both an advantage and a disadvantage. Investigate whether the tool is the supplier's main product or is placed in a far corner. A main product will be maintained, but it may be difficult to get it to cooperate with other tools. The company must decide what is most important. A number of smaller companies developing configuration management tools are being bought by other companies producing larger development environments, who don't necessarily have expertise in configuration management tools.

Tool Use

Some companies live by the slogan "Use what we sell—sell what we use." It's a good idea to find out if the supplier uses its own tool and, if so, how. Presumably, a supplier must keep its own products under configuration management. It should therefore not be too difficult to get some information about this regarding the tool. This could be done by asking the supplier for

- A short description of internal use of the tool
- Relevant status reports, such as a list of the contents of a delivery
- A description of the event registration procedure
- A description of the handling of event registrations

Reputation

Every evaluation of a tool should include inquiries about references to other companies that use the tool in comparable situations. The supplier may be able to explain, at least in broad terms, how others are using the tool. This will provide two other useful items of information:

◆ Does the supplier posses information it's fair to believe it has (in this case, an extra check on how the configuration management is working)?

◆ Does the supplier give out types of information that the company itself would not want to see distributed to third parties?

Talk to some of the references, to determine whether the supplier's information reflects the facts and how the other companies regard the tool and the supplier. It may also be a good idea to ask about other companies' plans for the future, especially if use of the tool will expand, either horizontally in the company and/or vertically to cover more for each product.

Support Facilities

Investigate support conditions, such as price in relation to the number of hours delivered or number of calls allowed, as well as possible upgrade guarantees. Geographical location of support facilities may also be important.

26.6 CUSTOMIZING CONFIGURATION MANAGEMENT TOOLS

A configuration management system consists of one or more tools and a set of process descriptions. The trick is to get the tool(s) to work together as smoothly as possible and to get it or them to support the described processes. In principle, there are three grades of customization (with many variations):

◆ The tools are tailored completely to the processes—they are developed as bespoke software for or by the company.

◆ The tools are customized to suit each other and the processes as well as possible.

◆ The tools are used as is—the processes are changed to the tools.

One Tool or More

It's an advantage to have as few tools as possible, because getting tools to work together smoothly always presents difficulties. Therefore, a tool should cover as many requirements as possible.

Changing Tools or Processes

Tools should support the processes the company has defined. But if they don't, it's easier to change the processes rather than the tool. This provides the best processes in the long term and may help keep maintenance costs down for the tool .

From Class to Class

It may be tempting to buy a tool of a certain class and then try to expand it to a higher class by the means of "homemade" scripts, as described earlier. In some cases this may be successful, but in most cases you run the risk of getting an unstable tool that doesn't quite fulfill the requirements anyway. It may also be difficult to maintain such tools, especially if the supplier often releases new versions—which will also have to be customized. This kind of customization should be considered carefully and preferably avoided.

Appendix A

Configuration Management Process Model: A Software Code Example

In this example, an object's unique identification is indicated by <CI name>. ("CI" stands for "configuration item.") The name alone is depicted as <Module>. The example includes only a few procedure descriptions and templates referenced in the flow diagrams.

AAC	**Document:**	**SDT-CM-A02** Configuration Management
	Department:	Software Development and Test
	Doc. Type:	Process Area
	Item type:	Source code and related items
	Status:	Accepted

Written by: NN   **Date:**   8-31-2001

Change History

This is the first accepted version.

Purpose

Ensure that configuration management is performed in a structured way.

Scope

This process area description is valid for source code and related items developed in the Software Development and Test Department.

Responsibility

Ms. Anni Capella holds the overall responsibility for configuration management.

Input

Source code files and related files.

Procedure

This process area is divided into four main processes:

- Creation
- Release
- Change control
- Status reporting

Each process is shown with its activities below.

Creation During creation, source code or a related item is identified and placed in storage in the controlled library.	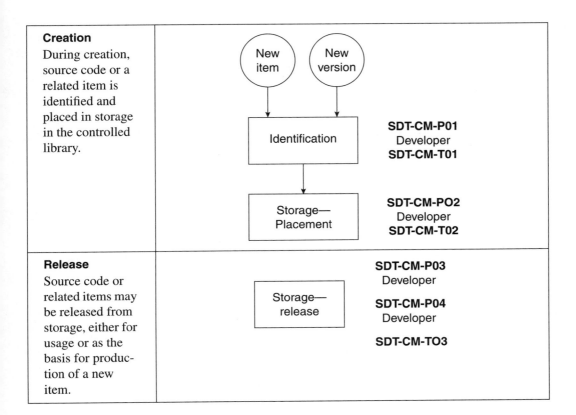
Release Source code or related items may be released from storage, either for usage or as the basis for production of a new item.	

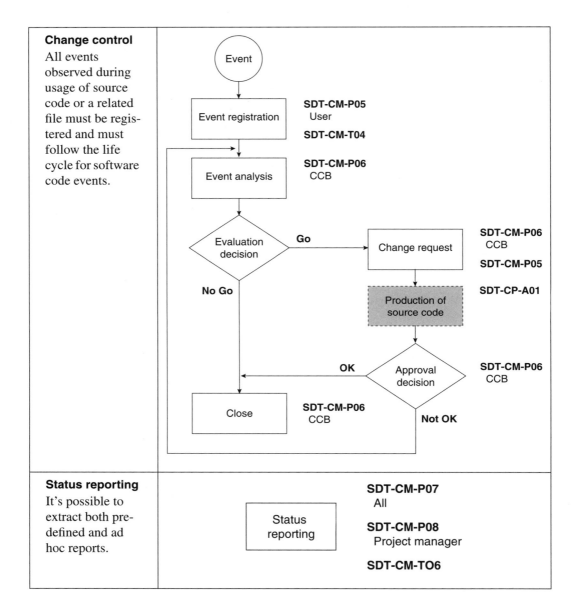

Change control
All events observed during usage of source code or a related file must be registered and must follow the life cycle for software code events.

Event

Event registration — **SDT-CM-P05** User / **SDT-CM-T04**

Event analysis — **SDT-CM-P06** CCB

Evaluation decision — Go → Change request — **SDT-CM-P06** CCB / **SDT-CM-P05**

Production of source code — **SDT-CP-A01**

Approval decision — OK / Not OK — **SDT-CM-P06** CCB

No Go

Close — **SDT-CM-P06** CCB

Status reporting
It's possible to extract both pre-defined and ad hoc reports.

Status reporting — **SDT-CM-P07** All / **SDT-CM-P08** Project manager / **SDT-CM-TO6**

Output

Source code files and corresponding files in controlled storage, associated metadata, and report facilities.

References

SDT-CM-P01 Unique Identification

SDT-CM-P02 Placement in Storage

SDT-CM-P03 Release for Usage

SDT-CM-P04 Release for Production

SDT-CM-P05 Event Registration

SDT-CM-P06 Event and Change Request Life Cycles

SDT-CM-P07 Extraction of Predefined Report

SDT-CM-P08 Extraction of Ad Hoc Report

SDT-CM-T01 Source Code Header

SDT-CM-T02 Source Code Approval Form

SDT-CM-T03 Source Code Release Request

SDT-CM-T04 Event Registration

SDT-CM-T05 Change Request

SDT-CM-T06 Predefined Status Reports

Reference to other process area:

SDT-CP-A01 Code Production

AAC	**Document:**	**SDT-CM-P02** Placement in Storage
	Department:	Software Development and Test
	Doc. Type:	Procedure
	Item type:	Source code and related items
	Status:	Accepted

Written by: NN   **Date:**   9-05-2001

Change History

Correction of scope since the version dated 8-31-2001.

Purpose

Ensure that all source code files and related items are stored in the controlled library when they are supposed to be under configuration management.

Scope

This procedure is used when source code files and related files are approved according to **ATP-QA-P03** and therefore to be placed under configuration management. This means that the source module is in a state where it can compile and at least one operation is working such that modules using it may benefit from the implemented functionality.

Responsibility

The developer of the file to be placed in storage is responsible for this being done correctly.

Input

A source code module and related file(s) (objects) to become configuration items.

An approval form, **SDT-CM-T02**, correctly filled in for the module.

Procedure

The command to use to place an object in storage is

Format: `propose [-h|-u|-b] <CI name>`

This command saves the configuration item with status "proposed" and copies and creates derived files according to the type of configuration item (`-h` for header file; `-u` for unit, `-b` for build).

After successful storage, the approval form, **SDT-CM-T02**, must be handed to the project manager.

Explanation:

First of all, .hxx and .h files are to be shared. This is made possible by issuing the command `propose -h <Module>.hxx`. This command will prompt for a comment and save the new version of `<Module>.hxx` in the controlled area, where it receives the status "proposed." It will then retrieve the `<Module>.hxx` in a read-only version into the appropriate subdirectory in the development area and recompile whatever needs to be recompiled in this area as a consequence of the new .hxx file.

This must be done before the `<Module>.cxx` may be proposed, which is done by issuing the command `propose <Module>.cxx`. This command will check that the `<Module>.o` file was actually created with the latest available .h and .hxx files. If not, the proposal is rejected and the developer must ensure that the module is still in a "useful" state. If everything is OK, the command will prompt for a comment and

1. Save the new version of `<Module>.cxx` in the controlled (AtFS) area, where it receives the status "proposed."
2. Retrieve the `<Module>.cxx` in a read-only version into the appropriate subdirectory in the development area.
3. Place the `<Module>.o` in the appropriate subdirectory in the development area.
4. Re-create the library.
5. Place the `<Module>_dep.txt` in the appropriate subdirectory in the development area, but not under version control in the controlled area, as it's a derived file.

This is illustrated below, where `<Module>` = `U1`.

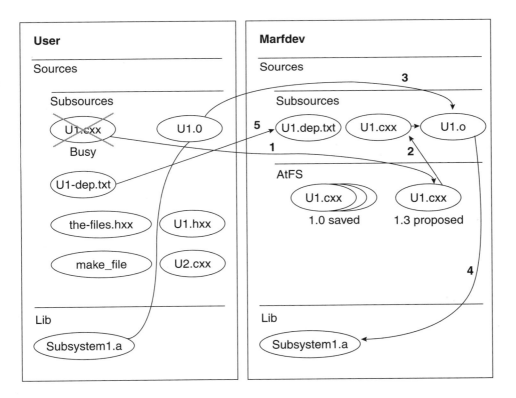

Output

A configuration item in controlled storage with the status "proposed."

References

SDT-CM-T02 Source Code Approval Form

Reference to other process area:

ATP-QA-P03 Approval of Source Code

AAC	**Document:**	**SDT-CM-P04** Release for Production
	Department:	Software Development and Test
	Doc. Type:	Procedure
	Item type:	Source code and related items
	Status:	Accepted

Written by: NN   **Date:** 8-31-2001

Change History

This is the first accepted version.

Purpose

Ensure that a source code file and related items are extracted correctly when they are going to be used as the basis for production of a new version of the same file family.

Scope

This procedure is used when source code files or related files are the basis.

Responsibility

The developer of the file is responsible for the release of a file as a basis for production.

Input

A change request for the module, stating what needs to be changed

Procedure

The commands to use to extract objects from storage as basis for production are

Format: `user-update`

This command copies all files from the central marfdev area to the developer's area. This is done to get the production started.

Format: `make -f Makefile.<CI name> depend`   This command creates the `<CI name>_dep.txt` file, containing the names of all files on which `<CI name>` depends directly for compilation. This file must be available during development and test, as all other commands may use the information in it.

Format: `retrv -lock <CI name>`   This command retrieves a writable version of `<CI name>` from the marfdev area to the developer's area and locks the configuration item for other developers.

Format: `get-deps [-u|-b] [-nocheck] <CI name>`

This command copies files on which the CI depends from the marfdev area to the developer's area, for either a unit CI (`-u`) or a build CI (`-b`). If the `-nocheck` option is not given, all dependent configuration items will be checked for proper status.

Explanation:

When the developer starts work on `<Module>`, he/she must retrieve a working copy of `<Module>.cxx` from the AtFS repository to his/her own area. This is done by issuing the command `retrv -lock <Module>.cxx` to place a writable copy of the `<Module>.cxx` in the user's area, where it has the status "busy." This is illustrated below, where `<Module>` = `U1`.

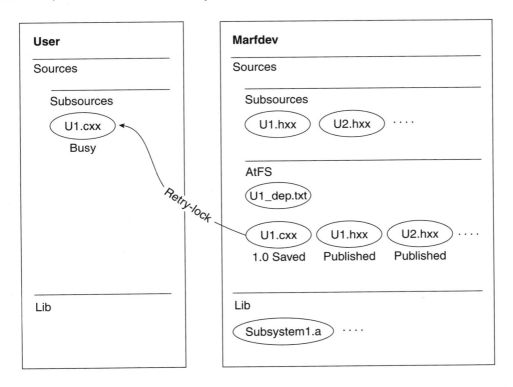

The same may be done for `<Module>.hxx` if the developer needs to work on that file as well. The developer then needs to get all the files necessary for compilation and linking of `<Module>`. This is done by issuing the command `get-deps -nocheck <Module>.cxx` to copy the newest version of all .h and .hxx files on which `<Module>.cxx` directly depends to the developer's area (using the `-dep.txt` file) and to copy all object libraries to the users' area.

This command may be used anytime during development to ensure that work is done with the newest available version of the dependency files. Note that files retrieved by `get-deps` may not be changed by the developer—a changed version cannot be stored. This is illustrated below.

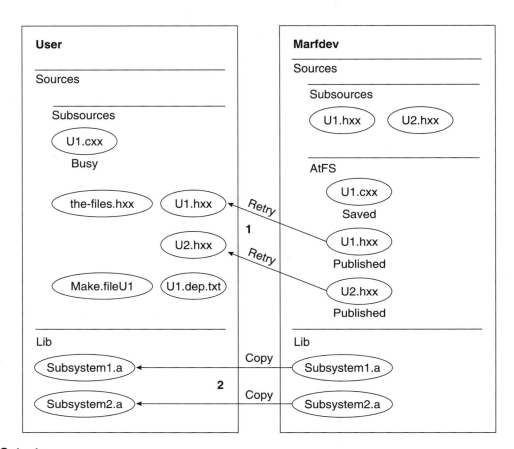

Output

A set of files to be used as the basis for development of the new version of `<Module>.cxx`

References

None.

AAC	**Document:**	**SDT-CM-P05** Event Registration
	Department:	Software Development and Test
	Doc. Type:	Procedure
	Item type:	Source code and related items
	Status:	Accepted

Written by: NN   **Date:**   8-31-2001

Change History

This is the first accepted version.

Purpose

Ensure that events are registered correctly.

Scope

This procedure is used when an event is identified for a source code file or a related file.

Responsibility

Everybody who identifies an event in a source code file or a related file is responsible for correctly registering the event.

Input

An identified event and all possible documentation to support the description of the event

Procedure

In Word, create a new file, based on the event registration template **SDT-CM-T04**.

Fill in the event registration.

Mail the event registration and any supporting documentation to CCB@marfdev.com.

Output

An event registration. A receipt will be mailed.

References

SDT-CM-T04 Event Registration

AAC	**Document:**	**SDT-CM-T01** Source Code Header
	Department:	Software Development and Test
	Doc. Type:	Template
	Item type:	Source code and related items
	Status:	Accepted

Written by: NN   **Date:**   8-31-2001

Change History

This is the first accepted version.

Content

```
#ifndef FILENAME_H
/***************************************************************
file: $Source$       $Revision$
Responsible $Author$      checked in at $Date$

Log:
$Log$
***************************************************************/
#endif
```

Example 1:   **Before first placement in storage**

```
#ifndef MOTOR_H
/***************************************************************
file: $Source$       $Revision$
Responsible $Author$      checked in at $Date$
Log:
$Log$
***************************************************************/
typedef double speed;
typedef double position;
typedef double time;

speed ac(time t);
position where(speed s, position p, time t);

#endif
```

Example 2:   **After a change request**

```
#ifndef MOTOR_H
/****************************************************************
file: $Source: /home/cj/amj/motor.h,v $      $Revision: 1.2 $
Responsible $Author: cj $     checked in at $Date: 2002/02/06
22:54:39 $

Log:
$Log: motor.h,v $
Revision 1.2  2002/02/06 22:54:39  cj
add dif function(request 33)

Revision 1.1  2002/02/06 22:52:02  cj
Initial revision


****************************************************************/
typedef double speed;
typedef double position;
typedef double time;

speed ac(time t);
position where(speed s, position p, time t);
time dif(position p1, position p2, speed s);
#
```

Appendix B

Configuration Management Process Model: A Tracing Example

In this example, underlining indicates hyperlinks, such as IT Support. Most of the referenced links are not included here. The Tracy tool is written in Access, and the normal ways of navigating and operating in Access are available, along with pushbuttons for specific actions. This example includes only a few procedures.

Using Tracy—the Tracing Tool

Overview

Purpose

This chapter provides guidelines for using Tracy.

Contents

This document contains the following sections:

Tracy—System Overview

Purpose

The purpose of this description is to introduce you to the system and its elements. It also describes how the elements are used and how they are tied together.

The System

The system works with two types of documents—the requirement specification and the test specification. The system enables registration of information about the requirement specification and the test specification for an application, and the connections between them—the traces. The way to use the system is as follows:

Step	Action
1	Create a new requirement specification document. It will have the status "Working."
2	Enter the detailed requirements into the new document—either with identification only or with the entire requirement information.
3	When all requirements are entered to the extent known and the document is approved, change the status of the document to "Frozen."
4	When you start writing test cases, you create a new test specification document with "Working" status.
5	As you go along writing test cases, enter them into the document or identify them, if they are already written in full elsewhere.
6	When all test cases are entered to the extent known and the test specification document is approved, change the status of the document to "Frozen."
7	Select the documents to trace between.
8	Now you can create the detailed trace between requirements and test cases. Connecting the requirements to the test cases is a "forward trace." Connecting the test cases to the requirements is a "backward trace."
9	If it's necessary to add new requirements or test cases or change the ones already registered, create a new copy of the relevant document with a new version number and status "Working." The new or changed requirements or test cases will automatically receive the new version number from the document.
10	If you later create new versions of either document involved in a trace, you can have the existing traces copied over, and then you'll have to change them (via the Establish Detailed Tracings option) according to the changes to the involved documents.

The Requirement Element

The requirement element is used to register requirements for the system. The requirement element contains the following information:

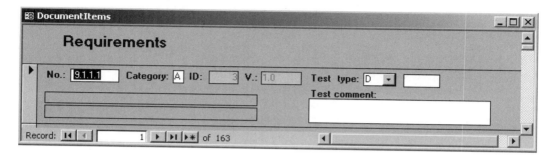

Field	Description
No.	A sequential number giving the position of the requirement in the document. This number is used when presenting the requirements on screens and reports. This field is mandatory.
Category	A letter identifying the priority of the requirement. This field is mandatory.
ID	A unique number assigned by the system when the item is created. The user cannot edit this number.
V.	The version number of the requirement. The system sets this to the version number of the document to which the requirement belongs when the requirement is created or changed.
Test type	A letter identifying the type of requirement. The values can be selected from the drop-down list. This field is mandatory.
[Upper gray box on left]	The full text of the requirement. This field is optional.
[Lower gray box on left]	Any comments relevant to the requirement. This field is optional.
Test comment	Any comments concerning the testing of the requirement. This field is optional.

The Test Case Element

The test case element is used to register test cases for the system. The test case element contains the following information:

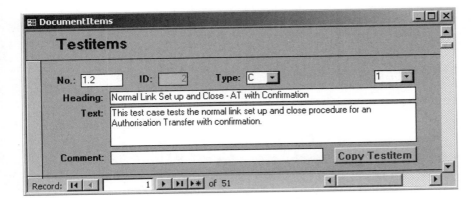

Field	Description
No.	A sequential number giving the position of the test case in the document. This number is used when presenting the test cases on screens and reports. This field is mandatory.
ID	A unique number assigned by the system when the item is created. The user cannot edit this number.
Type	A letter indicating whether this is a test case or a test case group. The latter serve as section headings and cannot be traced. This field is mandatory.
Heading	The heading of the test case or group. This field is mandatory.
Text	The full text of the test case or group. This field is mandatory.
Comment	Any comments relevant for the test case. This field is optional.

The Forward Trace

The forward trace is used to register traces from the requirements to the test cases. The element contains the following information:

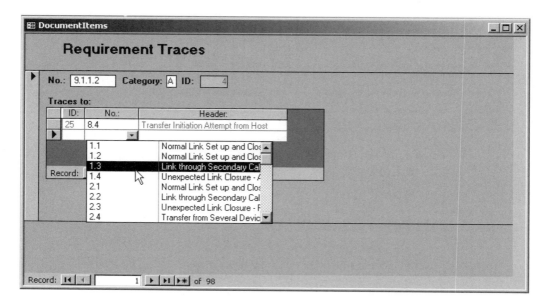

Field	Description	
No.	The number of the requirement to trace from.	
Category	The category of the requirement.	
ID	The unique identification of the requirement.	
Traces to	No.	The user-assigned number of the test case.

The ID and header of the test case are shown for information, when a test case to trace to is selected using the drop-down list of traceable test cases.

The Backward Trace

The backward trace is used to register traces from the test cases to the requirements. It's the same traces as above, just shown and edited the other way around. The element contains the following information:

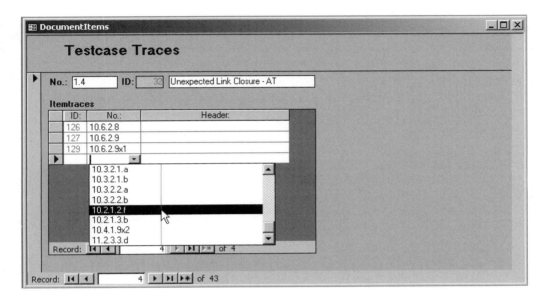

The ID and header of the requirement are shown for information when a requirement to trace to is selected using the drop-down list of requirements.

Getting Started

Purpose
The purpose of this procedure is to start Tracy—the Tracing Tool.

Responsible
Everybody who has been granted access to Tracy may start the tool. For access rules, see <u>Roles</u>.

Input and Prerequisites
None, apart from access rights.

Getting Started
Activate the Tracy icon on the desktop. If you don't have the Tracy icon, contact <u>IT support</u>.

Procedure
There are no steps in this procedure. Tracy—the Tracing Tool may be used from this starting point as described in
<u>Creating a New Document</u>
<u>Edit Contents of Document</u>
(etc.)

Result
The Tracy main window appears:

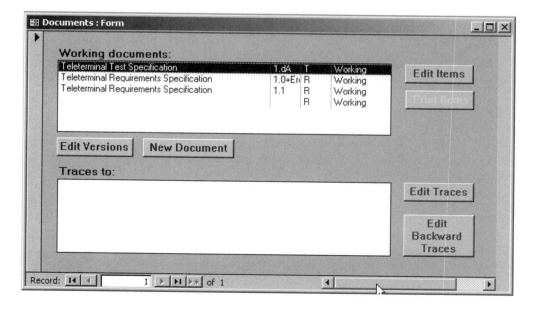

Tracing Documents

Purpose

The purpose of this procedure is to create a connection between two documents, so detailed tracing can be created later.

Responsible

The owner of the document is responsible for maintaining the items. Everybody with access rights to Tracy may view the items.

Input and Prerequisites

The documents to trace must exist in Tracy.

Getting Started

On the Tracy main window, choose a document from the list of working documents and activate <Edit Versions>. See <u>Using Tracy—the Tracing Tool</u> if you don't know how to reach the main window.

Procedure

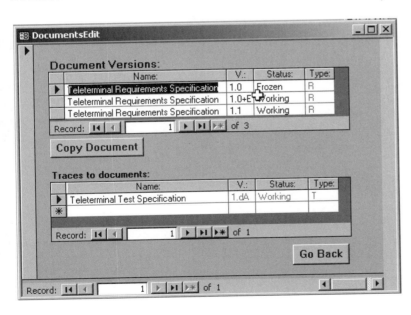

A pop-up window will appear on top of the Tracy main window. This pop-up window is modal—it's not possible to work outside it. It contains a list of all documents in the system.

The steps in this procedure are:

Step	Action
1	Highlight the document you want to use in the "Document Versions" list.
2	Click on the line with "*" in the "Traces to documents" list and select from the drop-down list the document you want to trace to the document selected above it.
3	Click the <Go Back> button.

Result

A connection between the two documents is created.

Appendix C

Agile SCM

by Stephen P. Berczuk and Brad Appleton

Software Configuration Management (SCM) is crucial to the success of agile projects. A team without effective SCM practices gets slowed down by the extra work each developer must perform when there is no easy way of synching up with his or her teammates. A well-designed and light SCM process actually speeds up the project.

This appendix is divided into two sections. In the first section, we identify key strategies, or *patterns*, that should allow the agile team to stay safe with an ultralight selection of SCM practices.[1] In the second section, we describe how the SCM terms in this book map to the practices of the common agile project.

The key to understanding the agile mappings is to recall that agile projects rely on good, two-way dialogue with the user; delivery of running, tested code every two to twelve weeks; and frequent, early feedback on the quality of both the requirements and the design. With this three-layered safety net in place the following mappings become effective.

---

1. Adapted, with permission, from Stephen P. Berczuk and Brad Appleton. 2003. *Software Configuration Management Patterns: Effective Teamwork, Practical Integration*. Boston: Addison-Wesley.

Keeping Agile Projects Safe

There are many aspects of SCM that are relevant to the agile project —the difficult part is knowing when to apply them. We want agility, not chaos. Some practices work together to build an effective development environment with the right amount of SCM practice.

Your agile project should use a simple branching structure. Branches of development for a configuration item's source-code library files are commonly called *codelines*. One or two codelines are usually sufficient for agile projects that don't require multiple parallel releases or variants.

The key concepts for organizing the evolution of your code are: a *Mainline*, an *Active Development Line*, and a *Release Line*. A *Mainline* is the single, central codeline that controlled library artifacts are checked in to. Having a single integration point makes it easy to re-create the latest state of the SCM-controlled items. An *Active Development Line* is a codeline that is set up with a *Codeline Policy* that permits ongoing work to be checked in without overly rigorous precheck-in validation. A *Release Line* is a codeline for system states that are available to customers for fixing system problems in preparation for your regular release cycle. A *Release Line* has a more restrictive *Codeline Policy* that ensures stability.

Having a *Release Line* simplifies the SCM rules and allows you to be a little less strict on the check-in policies for the *Active Development Line*. With these two separate codelines in place, the developers can make their hourly or daily changes into the *Active Development Line*, and the customer-release process can use the more carefully controlled *Release Line*.

Here is what a typical agile developer's day looks like in terms of the SCM strategies or patterns they use:

Each developer works in a *Private Workspace* that contains the code that the developer is working on, populated from a *Repository*—a single point of access for everything that a developer needs to build his or her project. The developer gets external components from a *Third Party Codeline*. If he or she does not want to build the entire system from scratch, the developer can populate some of their workspace from an *Integration Build*, which is a snapshot of the codeline.

The developer, progressing through the day, will check changes into the *Active Development Line* so that they are visible to the rest of the team, as well as available for the integration build. Because the codeline isn't required to be bullet-proof, the developer does not need to run exhaustive tests before checking changes in. But he or she should create a *Private System Build*, which is just like the *Integration Build*, and run a *Smoke Test* on the result to make sure that the check-in will not cause any problems. Since this cycle repeats with every developer, the current state of the system is available in the *Integration Build*.

The codeline may have mistakes in it, but they should be few and minor. The team relies on the *Smoke Test* to catch show-stopper defects and on *Unit Tests* to ensure that changes don't change any interface behavior for the module that the developer is testing. After the *Integration Build*, the *Regression Tests*, as well as the full suite of *Unit Tests*, are run to catch integration issues. It is a trade-off, but it's a reasonable one, since the only way to ensure a pure codeline would be to have a developer lock the entire codeline, run a full suite of tests, check in the changes, and then unlock the codeline. This approach would severely limit progress, and for agile projects you realize more value from changes in functionality early on. Once the project reaches a certain milestone, the code can be branched onto a *Release Line*, where a more restrictive *Codeline Policy* may be in effect.

Mapping Terms for the Agile Project

With those strategies in place, we can examine the main concepts in this book that need to be mapped for an agile project:

- Change Control
- Identification and Storage
- Change Authorization
- Integration and Build Management
- Status Reporting

Change Control

Change control starts on Day One of an agile project! In two-way dialog with the user, customer or executive sponsors, the agile team elicits requirements in the form of feature requests and user scenarios. These requests may be for brand-new functionality, or for changes or additions to already implemented functionality. Developers estimate each requested chunk of functionality, and the customer then gives priorities for the features to work on over the next iteration.

Agile iterations are typically short (two to twelve weeks), so there aren't usually many features to track for a given iteration. Requirements are managed by keeping track of the list of features for the current iteration, and a current backlog of requested but not yet implemented features. At the end of an iteration, the current backlog of requests, along with any new requests, are once again prioritized by the customer so that the developer can decide which set of features will be worked on during the next iteration.

This frequent reprioritization and selection process is the most common agile equivalent of a change control board (CCB). The customer drives the priorities and need for change while development accommodates those needs as much as possible in each iteration, focusing almost exclusively on the features for the current iteration.

In some cases, the features or change requests are written to the change-control system. In more informal projects, particularly Extreme Programming projects, requests are documented on a four-inch by six-inch white index card or two-foot by four-foot flipchart taped to the wall, whose text is updated throughout the iteration period, so that everyone who reads it sees the original request and the modifications that have been made to it.

Identification and Storage

Identification of configuration items is typically done with text and source code repositories using commercial and open-source version control tools such as CVS, Visual Source-Safe, Perforce, BitKeeper, and simple out-of-the-box installations of higher-end tools like ClearCase. Items are checked-out of and checked-in to controlled library storage (the *Repository* or "code base") to and from a dynamic storage library called the developer's *Private Workspace*.

A brief textual description is typically created to convey the overall source-code directory structure of the code base. Build scripts such as Makefiles or ANT recipes, along with the instructions necessary to successfully build the system with minimal recompilation, describe physical build-dependencies. Any special configuration files, or external tools, libraries, or databases required to build, install, or upgrade the software are often checked-in directly to the *Repository*, or else separately archived and versioned with noted dependencies of the corresponding compatible version(s) of the code base.

Releases and significant build milestones are identified in the code base using the "tag" or "label" facilities of the version control tool. The label makes it possible to reproducibly identify every revision of every file in the *Repository* that participated in the build or release.

The metadata maintained by the version control *Repository*, combined with the physical code structure description, and build and dependency information is typically sufficient identification for the agile project.

Change Authorization

The developer on the agile project is authorized to change the source code in two cases:

1. To implement an agreed-upon feature for the current iteration.
2. To improve the simplicity (readability and maintainability) of the source code.

Agile development teams work hard—as a matter of principle and through peer pressure—to develop only what the customer has requested for the current iteration, and to keep the design simple. They also are working in short iterations, and so they have less time in which to gold-plate their design. These factors together have the effect that very few gratuitous features get put into the code, which reduce the worries surrounding development change control.

Agile teams are typically authorized to make small *refactoring* changes at any time without prior management approval, provided that the code complies with team-defined coding conventions and continues to pass all the same tests as before. (*Refactoring* is revising the code structure without changing its functionality.)

Development change control is often informal. The source-code control system marks the changes, and may perform change notification automatically upon check-in or check-out. Changes are announced by e-mail between developers, or word-of-mouth when teams sit together. This works because of the small amount of gold-plating, the short iterations, the close contact between developers and good testing habits.

Integration and Build Management

Agile teams work in short and frequent small releases, and even more frequent integration and building. Developers run *Unit Tests* and perform *Private System Builds*, and *Smoke Tests* before committing changes from their *Private Workspace* to the *Active Development Line*. *Integration Builds* must pass *Regression Tests* and may be rebuilt from scratch (to ensure build reproducibility) before being required to pass functional acceptance tests.

XP preaches continuous integration, in which changes are integrated many times a day or even several times each hour. Since the changes are very small and comprise the smallest possible set of consistent files for a testable chunk of functionality, the time to integrate and incrementally rebuild the system is very small.

Non-XP agile teams tend to build and integrate every day or two, often running a daily or nightly build that checks for build failures and immediately reports the results. If a build breaks, fixing the build becomes development's top priority. Since all developers are typically required to do a *Private System Build* of their changes before check-in and ensure the code passes their unit and regression tests, broken builds tend to be infrequent due to such disciplined testing on such small sets of changes.

Status Reporting

A report of physical contents usually includes version label names and a manifest (or packing list) of all the files in the released build. In addition, a file name and revision ID is often maintained in each source-file. This enables (with help from the version control tool) reporting of a bill-of-materials (BOM) listing all the source-file names and revision numbers that were used to build the target executables and libraries.

A report of functional content usually includes all the features/requests that were implemented for an iteration. Each developed feature is typically associated with one or more tests that verify its proper implementation (for development) and functionality (for customer acceptance). Once again, simplicity is preferred in tracking tests to features: each functional test is associated with a named feature in a spreadsheet or simple tracking database, or on index cards (perhaps even on the back-side of corresponding story-card). Sometimes the functional test is expressed exclusively in the source code (and comments) that exercises functionality under test. Tests are automated to the greatest extent possible and stored as a regression test-suite that is run after every build. Testing results/status are usually reported with each delivered version of the software.

Some agile teams use a spreadsheet to track feature-lists and backlogs, or a simple database to track the requests. Some teams use simple out-of-the-box request/defect tracking systems or open source systems, the most popular of which at this time are Bugzilla, GNATs, and Jitterbug. In either case, the tracking system (or mechanism) can easily be used to sort and report requests by date, priority, estimate, and target iteration/release. These systems enable the agile team to report the status of implemented, and to-be-implemented, functional requests for any iteration.

Glossary

Audit Checking that a configuration item released for usage meets demands—that it fulfills specifications and, when released, is complete according to configuration management information. In this book, this is regarded as a quality assurance activity.

Baseline This expression is not used in this book, except in direct quotes from standards or maturity models.

Binaries Files whose contents are translated (compiled) into binary presentations, with strings of only two symbols (0 and 1).

Check-in Placement of a configuration item in storage in the controlled library.

Check-out Release of a configuration item from storage in the controlled library to production.

Company This term is used in many places where the term "organizational unit" would be equally or more appropriate. It's used to avoid writing "company/ organization unit" or the like.

Configuration Control Board (CCB) or **Configuration Change Board** A group of people responsible for assessing, and approving or rejecting, proposed changes to configuration items and responsible for the performance of approved changes.

Configuration item Any intermediate work product, product component, or product placed under configuration management.

Configuration management system All the procedure descriptions, templates, and tools that collectively support configuration management performed in a given context.

Dynamic library A repository used during production. It is not regarded as belonging to the configuration management process area.

Event   Something that happens or is noticed, especially when it is important.

Library   A repository for a collection of items.

Life-cycle-dependent process   A process in operation for a limited period during the product's lifetime, such as design or unit test. Such a process may be repeated throughout the product's lifetime in an iterative development model.

Life-cycle-independent process   A process that must be in effect throughout a product's lifetime, such as project management or configuration management.

Master library   A controlled repository for storing configuration items. Also called a configuration management library.

Metadata   Information about configuration items. For instance, a document placed under configuration management is a configuration item, while the name and number of the document are metadata for the item.

Procedure   A number of activities following one another in a given order, producing a certain output on the basis of a certain input.

Process   Describes how an input is used to create an expected output. The work within a process may be divided and described in a number of process descriptions.

Process description   A description of the techniques, methods, conventions, and procedures employed in connection with a certain activity.

Product   Something produced. It may be for internal use, such as a design sketch, or for delivery, such as an entire software system.

Release or **Baseline**   A collection of configuration items that together form one configuration item. The collection is formed to be deliverable and useful as an entity.

Static library   A repository for items in use. It is not regarded as belonging to the configuration management process area.

Support process   Processes used in all other processes at various points in a software project's life cycle. Support processes in themselves make no sense; they make sense only with other processes. For instance, naming is a support process; naming only makes sense if another process has created a product to name.

Bibliography

BOOKS

Beyond Version Control, Pure Atria, 1996.

BOOTSTRAP V3.2 Report Template, DELTA and BOOTSTRAP Institute, 2000.

CMMI for Systems Engineering/Software Engineering, version 1.02, (CMMI-SE/SW, V1.02), Continuous Representation, CMU/SEI-2000-TR-029, ESC-TR-2000-094, CMMI Product Development Team, November 2000.

CMMI for Systems Engineering/Software Engineering, version 1.02, (CMMI-SE/SW, V1.02), Staged Representation, CMU/SEI-2000-TR-028, ESC-TR-2000-093, CMMI Product Development Team, November 2000.

Configuration Management, The Changing Image, Marion V. Kelly, McGraw-Hill, 1996.

GAMP Guide, Validation of Automated Systems in Pharmaceutical Manufacture, version 3.0, March 1998, GAMP Forum. Available from ISPE European Branch Office, Stille Veerkade 27, 2512 BE The Hague, The Netherlands, +31 (0)70-3645678.

Guide to Software Configuration Management, ESA PSS-05-09 issue 1, November 1992. Available from BSSC/ESTEC Sekretariat, Att.: Mr. A. Scheffer, ESTEC, Postbox 299, NL-2200 AG Noordwijk, The Netherlands.

Håndbog i Struktureret Programudvikling, Stephen Biering-Sørensen et al., Teknisk Forlag A/S, 1988. (in Danish).

IEEE Std 1042-1987, *IEEE Guide to Software Configuration Management (ANSI),* www.ieee.org.

IEEE Std 610.12-1990, *IEEE Standard Glossary of Software Engineering Terminology,* www.ieee.org.

IEEE Std 828-1990, *IEEE Standard for Software Configuration Management Plans,* www.ieee.org.

Improving Software Organizations, Lars Mathiassen, Jan Pries-Heje, and Ojelanki Ngwenyama, Addison-Wesley, 2001.

Introducing ClearCase as a Process Improvement Experiment, Jens-Otto Larsen, Helge M. Roald, proceedings of the SCM-8 Symposium, Brussels, Belgium, July 1998, Springer Lecture Notes in Computer Science, no. 1439.

ISO 9000-3:1997 Quality Management and Quality Assurance Standards—Part 3: Guidelines for the Application of ISO 9001:1994 to the Development, Supply, Installation and Maintenance of Computer Software, www.iso.ch.

ISO 9001:1994 Quality Systems—Model for Quality Assurance in Design, Development, Production, Installation and Servicing, www.iso.ch.

ISO 9001:2000 Quality Management Systems—Requirements, www.iso.ch.

ISO/IEC 9126-1:2001 Software Engineering—Product Quality—Part 1: Quality Model, www.iso.ch.

ISO/IEC TR 15504-2:1998 Information Technology—Software Process Assessment—Part 2: A Reference Model for Processes and Process Capability, www.iso.ch.

Iterative Software Development—A Practical View, Morten Korsaa et al., DF-16, Datateknisk Forum (Denmark) 2001.

Measuring the Software Process: Statistical Process Control for Software Process Improvement, William A. Florac and Anita D. Carleton, Addison-Wesley, 1999.

Meeting the Challenge of Multi-Platform Development, Atria Software, Inc. 1996.

The Memory Jogger II: A Pocket Guide of Tools for Continuous Improvement & Effective Planning, Michael Brassard & Diane Ritter, GOAL/QPC, 1994.

The 1999 Survey of High Maturity Organizations, Paulk, M. C. February 2000. CMU/SEI-2000-SR-002.

The Prevention of Errors through Experience-Driven Test Efforts, Otto Vinter et al., DELTA Rapportserie D259, 1996.

Principles of Software Engineering Management, Tom Gilb, Addison-Wesley, 1988.

Rapid Application Development, J. Martin, Maxwell Macmillan International Edition, 1991.

Software Configuration Management, Ole Andersen et al., DELTA, Kursusmateriale, 1991–1992 (in Danish).

Software Configuration Management Patterns: Effective Teamwork, Practical Integration, Brad Appleton and Stephen Berczuk, Addison-Wesley, 2002.

Survey of Existing and In-Work Software Engineering Standards and Specifications, Business Planning Group of IEEE Software Engineering Standards Committee, December 23, 1996, version 1.2, draft.

Testing Web-Based Applications, G. Bazzana and E. Fagnoni, tutorial given at EuroSTAR 2000.

Understanding Variation: The Key to Managing Chaos, D.J. Wheeler, SPC Press, 2000.

ARTICLES

"Achieving the Best Possible Configuration Management Solution," Susan A. Dart, Dart Technology Strategies, Inc., 1996. www.stsc.hill.af.mil/crosstalk/1996/sep/achievin.asp.

"Adopting an Automated Configuration Management Solution," Susan A. Dart. www.continuus.com/developers/developersACEE.html.

"Adopting SCM Technology," Julie Kingsbury, Software Technology Support Center. www.stsc.hill.af.mil/crosstalk/1996/mar/adopting.asp.

"Building a CM Database: Nine Years at Boeing," Susan Grosjean. www.stsc.hill.af.mil/crosstalk/2000/jan/grosjean.asp.

"CCB—an Acronym for Chocolate Chip Brownies?" A Tutorial on Control Boards, Reed Sorensen, Software Technology Support Center. www.stsc.hill.af.mil/crosstalk/1999/mar/sorensen.asp.

"Configuration Management, Coming of Age in the Year 2000," Clive Burrows, Ovum, Ltd., 1999. www.stsc.hill.af.mil/crosstalk/1999/mar/burrows.asp.

"Configuration Management during Unit and Integration Test of a Large OO System," Anne Mette Jonassen, Conference Papers, EuroSTAR '94. The complete articles may be requested at amj@delta.dk.

"Configuration Management (CM) Plans: The Beginning to Your CM Solution," Susan Dart, Nadine Bounds, SEI, 2001. www.sei.cmu.edu/legacy/scm/abstracts/abscm_plans.html.

"Demystifying Software Configuration Management," A.J. Marshall, PROSOFT. www.stsc.hill.af.mil/crosstalk/1995/may/demystif.asp.

"A Distributed Source Code Control System," Claus Tøndering, ERFA group contribution, 6 May 1999.

"Join the Team," Alan Radding. www.informationweek.com/755/55adtea.htm.

"The New Methodology," Martin Fowler. www.martinfowler.com/articles/newMethodology.html.

"Not ALL TOOLS Are Created EQUAL," Susan Dart. www.adtmag.com/pub/oct96/fe1002.htm.

"Notes from the Front Lines: How to Test Anything and Everything on a Web Site," Ted Fuller, Proceedings of QW2000, www.soft.com/QualWeek/QW2K/Papers/2W1.html.

"The Past, Present, and Future of Configuration Management," Susan A. Dart, July 1992, Technical Report CMU/SEI-92-TR-8, ESC-TR-92-8.

"Process-Based Configuration Management: The Way to Go to Avoid Costly Product Recalls," Tani Haque, SQL Software. www.stsc.hill.af.mil/crosstalk/1997/apr/configuration.asp.

"QA & Softwaregenbrug [Software Reuse]," Peter Hübel, ERFA group contribution 16.08.2000.

"Stop-Gap Configuration Management," Ted Gill, Puget Sound Naval Shipyard. www.stsc.hill.af.mil/crosstalk/1998/feb/stopgapcm.asp.

"Testing Beyond Your IQ," Fabián Scarano, Contribution to EuroSTAR 2001.

"What Is Configuration Management?" Jack Daley et al., CMstat. www.pdmic.com/cmic/introtoCM.shtml.

"What Is Configuration Management?" G. W. Allan, 1997. www.dis.port.ac.uk/~allangw/papers/pub97a.htm.

WEB SITES

ACME Project, http://acme.bradapp.net

AdCoMs Project, http://adcoms.finmeccanica.it/theproj.html

Agile development, www.agileManifesto.org

Belbin team roles, www.belbin.com

BOOTSTRAP Institute, www.bootstrap-institute.com

ClearCase tool, www.rational.com/products/clearcase/index.jsp

CM and related books, www.cmiiug.com/Books.htm

CMII user group, www.cmiiug.com

CMM version 1.1, www.sei.cmu.edu/cmm/obtain.cmm.html

CMM version 2.0, www.sei.cmu.edu/cmm/draft-c/c26scm.html

CMMI, www.sei.cmu.edu/cmmi/products/models.html, www.sei.cmu.edu/cmmi/general/genl.html

CM Today Yellow Pages, www.cmtoday.com/yp/configuration_management.html

Cruise Control tool, http://cruisecontrol.sourceforge.net

DaSC Project, www.sel.iit.nrc.ca/projects/scm

European Software Institute, www.esi.es

European Software Institute, SISSI Reports, www.esi.es/VASIE

Harvest tool, ca.com/products/ccc_harvest.htm

Institute of Configuration Management, www.icmhq.com

International Workshop on Software Configuration Management, www.ics.uci.edu/~andre/scm10

ISO, www.iso.ch

Memory Jogger, www.goalqpc.com/products/pockguidlist.html

Ovum, www.ovum.com

Product Line Practice Initiative, www.sei.cmu.edu/plp

PVCS tool, www.merant.com/pvcs/ technology_center/elipse.html

RASIC charts, www.te-assoc.com/Pitex/RasicChart.html

Software Engineering Institute, www.sei.cmu.edu/sei-home.html, http://seir.sei.cmu.edu

SPICE, www.sqi.gu.edu.au/spice, www.spiceworld.hm

Standards, http://computer.org/standards/sesc/survey0.htm

StarTeam tool, www.starbase.com/products/starteam

Visual SourceSafe tool, www.microsoft.com/catalog/display.asp?subid=22&site=606

Web Integrity, www.mks.com

Web Synergy, www.websynergy.co.za

WorkManager tool, www.hp.com/technicalsolutions/pdd/cpc/apps.html

Index

The Agile Software Development Series

Surviving Object-Oriented Projects
Foreword by Rebecca Wirfs-Brock
Alistair Cockburn

0201498340

Writing Effective Use Cases
Alistair Cockburn

0201702258

Improving Software Organizations
From Principles to Practice
Foreword by Bill Curtis
Lars Mathiassen
Jan Pries-Heje
Ojelanki Ngwenyama

0201758202

Agile Software Development
Alistair Cockburn

0201699699

Agile Software Development Ecosystems
Foreword by Tom DeMarco
Jim Highsmith

0201760436

Patterns for Effective Use Cases
Foreword by Craig Larman
Steve Adolph
Paul Bramble
With Contributions by Alistair Cockburn and Andy Pols

0201721848

informIT

Register
Your Book

at www.awprofessional.com/register

You may be eligible to receive:

- Advance notice of forthcoming editions of the book
- Related book recommendations
- Chapter excerpts and supplements of forthcoming titles
- Information about special contests and promotions throughout the year
- Notices and reminders about author appearances, tradeshows, and online chats with special guests

Contact us

If you are interested in writing a book or reviewing manuscripts prior to publication, please write to us at:

Editorial Department
Addison-Wesley Professional
75 Arlington Street, Suite 300
Boston, MA 02116 USA
Email: AWPro@aw.com

Addison-Wesley

Visit us on the Web: http://www.awprofessional.com